# STEVE GAINES

HFYF
Publishing

Hope For Your Future Publishing
Gardendale, Alabama

*Morning Manna*
Seventh Printing
Copyright © 2003 by
Dr. Steve Gaines

ISBN: 0-935515-50-X

Published by:
*HOPE FOR YOUR FUTURE, INC.*
P.O. Box 1210
Memphis, Tennessee 38088-1210

Produced by:
*EVANGEL PUBLICATIONS*
Huntsville, Alabama

Scripture quotations are from the New American Standard Version
of the Bible.

Printed in the United States of America.

~~~~~~~~~~~~~~~~~~~~~~~~~~~~~~~~~~~~

*What others are saying about:*

# Morning Manna

"Steve Gaines sets the table in the wilderness of the soul and feeds us with bread from heaven. MORNING MANNA is just what the Holy Spirit ordered. These powerful and practical devotions will move your heart, stir your soul, and change your life."

**Dr. Jerry Falwell**
Founder and Chancellor
Liberty University
Lynchburg, Virginia

"Steve Gaines is a man with a message! This message is one not created by others for him nor delegated to him from an institution; however, it is a message placed into his life by a mighty God who has been with him through suffering as well as victory. In MORNING MANNA you will learn about Steve's God and how this God wants to work in your life — Read it daily!"

**Dr. Ronnie Floyd**
Pastor, First Baptist Church
Springdale, Arkansas

"A good book of daily devotionals can only be written by an author who has a vital walk with God, an unusual knowledge of the Bible, and an ability to make profound truths understandable. Steve Gaines' commitment to the Word of God, his keen insight into the Scriptures and the depth of his spiritual life are what make MORNING MANNA such an outstanding devotional work. It will appeal to both one's head and one's heart. A devotional for each day of the year, these readings will stimulate one intellectually and inspire one spiritually. What a way to start a day!"

**Dr. Roy Fish**
Professor of Evangelism
Southwestern Baptist Theological Seminary
Fort Worth, Texas

"Steve Gaines, one of the most gifted and articulate preachers in America, has led First Baptist Church of Gardendale, Alabama to become a real miracle story of evangelism and church growth. Now this greatly anointed pastor has penned a devotional book, MORNING MANNA, that will bless and inspire all who use it. Not only will it give fervor, joy and encouragement to the reader, but it is also a wonderful gift idea to share with a treasured friend."

**Dr. Junior Hill, Evangelist**
Hartselle, Alabama

"Like the Israelites rising early for precious manna, so God's people need morning refreshment. Dr. Steve Gaines, who for many years has practiced the almost lost art of genuinely walking with the Lord in the cool of the day, takes us into the Holy of Holies of his own walk to share the MORNING MANNA which he, himself, has ingested — and it is much too rich to pass. Join him at this table in the wilderness of life."

**Dr. Paige Patterson, President**
Southwestern Baptist Theological Seminary
Fort Worth, Texas

"Manna in the morning! Essential for Israel in the wilderness experience. Essential for Christians as we face our daily wilderness experiences. Dr. Steve Gaines gives us good biblical direction from the Bread of Life for the day. From his heart to our hearts from God's heart. Read these daily devotionals with profit and blessing."

**Dr. Jerry Vines, Pastor**
First Baptist Church
Jacksonville, Florida

"Powerful truths from God's Word applied to our daily lives, these devotionals give us strength for today and hope for tomorrow. Read them expectantly."

**Dr. Fred Wolfe**
Barnabas Ministries
Brandon, Mississippi

~~~~~~~~~~~~~~~~~~~~~~~~~~~~~~~~~~~~~~~~~

# Preface

In the summer of 2000, my family and I were vacationing in Southern California. While there, I began having double vision and my left eye closed. When we returned to Birmingham, a neurologist informed me that I had a disease called Myasthenia Gravis, which means "Grave Weakness." I also had a tumor in my Thymus Gland that was facilitating the advancement of the disease, and it had to be removed immediately. It was located just under the sternum, requiring the same surgical procedure as heart by-pass surgery.

To say that I was in shock is an understatement. I had enjoyed robust health all my life. I had played football at a small college in Tennessee, and had worked rigorously since I was thirteen. Now my body was weak — very weak! I was in the wilderness.

But just as the people of Israel discovered that Jehovah was faithful, and that His lovingkindnesses and compassions were new every morning, I also learned afresh that God loves me, provides for me, ministers to me, and feeds me with precious Manna. I am recovering now. My long-term prognosis is good. I should be symptom-free and medicine-free within a few years. God has been, and continues to be wonderful.

These devotionals were written during the weariest, most difficult days of my life. As the song says, "Life is hard, but God is good." Some of these devotionals are synopses of sermons I have preached over the years. Others are simple thoughts I have entertained and enjoyed as I reviewed and meditated upon various Scripture Memory verses. There is at least one devotional based on a text from every book of the Bible. The reader will find almost as many entries written from Old Testament texts as from the New Testament. This book has been demanding, but it has also been a labor of love.

I want to thank my sweet wife, Donna, for being so kind and loving, especially through my illness. She has done things for me that I never thought anyone would have to do. She has also read every one of these entries and offered valuable advice. I look forward to growing old with her. She is the greatest Christian I have ever met.

I also want to thank my sweet children, Grant, Lindsey, Allison, and Bethany, more affectionately known as Bubby, Diddy, Alli, and BetBet. With all due respect to everyone else, I have the best kids on the planet!

Thanks to David Jett and the staff at G.F.B.C. for "carrying the load." Our good friends, Bill and Dayna Street, helped us immeasurably in the editing of this work. Thanks guys! Wears Valley, The Peddler, and The Log Cabin Pancake House were great! Thanks to my good friend, Junior Hill, for encouraging me to put my thoughts in print. Special thanks to "the Prince of Preachers" of our day, Dr. Adrian Rogers, the man I respect most as both a pastor and a man of God, for writing the Foreword. Sam Wolfe, at Evangel Publications in Huntsville, Alabama, has been a wonderful publisher. Most of all, I want to thank my precious, heavenly Father who has fed me faithfully every day from His table of abundance since I received His gift of salvation through His sweet Son, Jesus, in 1976. It has been a blessing!

A great missionary once said, "I'm just a beggar, telling other beggars where to find bread." That is exactly how I feel as I share this work with you. I am on the way to heaven offering hope to others on the journey.

May these devotionals bless your heart, feed your soul, and nourish your thoughts. Jesus has set a table for two. He invites you to dine with Him (Revelation 3:20). Pull away, weary pilgrim. Hunger no longer. His Morning Manna awaits you. "O taste and see that the Lord is good" (Psalm 34:8). As they say at the Mexican restaurant, "Enjoy!"

III John 2,
Steve Gaines
Memphis, Tennessee

~~~~~~~~~~~~~~~~~~~~~~~~~~~~~~~~~~~~~~~~~~

# Dedication

To my dear wife, Donna,

Who faithfully rises each morning

To gather and partake of the Master's Manna.

Sweetheart, you are more like Jesus

Than anyone I know.

I love you.

~~~~~~~~~~~~~~~~~~~~~~~~~~~~~~~~~~~~~~~~~~

*"He humbled you and let you be hungry, and fed you with manna which you did not know, nor did your fathers know, that He might make you understand that man does not live by bread alone, but man lives by everything that proceeds out of the mouth of the LORD."*

(Deuteronomy 8:3)

## A Prayer For The New Year

**1 Chronicles 4:10** — _"Now Jabez called on the God of Israel saying, 'Oh that You would bless me indeed and enlarge my border, and that Your hand might be with me, and that You would keep me from harm that it may not pain me!' And God granted him what he requested."_

A New Year. A fresh start. January is synonymous with a new beginning. We can _look_ at the past and even _learn_ from it, but we must not _live_ in it! Rather, we must _leave_ it behind and reach forward to the New Year that lies ahead. As we do, may I suggest that we pray the bold prayer of a man named Jabez on a regular basis?

Jabez lived in Old Testament times. His name meant, "pain." There was something about his birth that was so difficult, his mother shackled him with this horrible name. Nevertheless, Jabez refused to allow his name to determine his life. He prayed a big prayer to a big God and, in time, experienced big results. What did he ask for?

First Jabez prayed for _increased abundance_. He prayed for God to bless him "indeed." He wanted what God wanted — the very best for His life. Jabez continued by praying for _expanded influence_. He asked God to enlarge his borders so he could impact more people for God's glory. He then asked God for _spiritual anointing_. He wanted God's hand to empower him at all times. Jabez concluded by asking for _supernatural protection_. He knew that unless God defended him, he would keep watch in vain.

Does Jabez's prayer sound selfish to you? It should not. Indeed, God granted his requests! And what God did for Jabez, He will do for you — if you will pray! What could this year hold in store if you prayed this way every day? Heaven only knows. May this be the most blessed year you have ever experienced as you spend time with the heavenly Father in prayer. The heavens will open and God will do more than you can ask or think.

## DEATH IS DEFEATED

**1 Corinthians 15:54-55** — *"But when this perishable will have put on the imperishable, and this mortal will have put on immortality, then will come about the saying that is written, 'Death is swallowed up in victory. O death, where is your victory? O death, where is your sting?'"*

The cold wind blew across the rolling hills beneath the blue Tennessee sky. I stood with my mother at my father's grave. As I looked at the double dates chiseled in granite, "January 2, 1924 — June 11, 2000," I realized that dad was really gone.

As I thought about his body that rested beneath the earth, my mind raced back to happier days of throwing a football with him in the back yard, hitting a single in little league baseball as he looked on, and sitting back-to-back in the cornfields as we hunted doves. I could hear him singing "The Old Rugged Cross" at church, and see him laugh when I caught that big crappie. I could feel the seats of his big railroad truck as we drove and listened to the St. Louis Cardinals play baseball. I could see him sitting at the dinner table wearing his white, tank top T-shirt, with that simple smile on his face. When I finally regained focus, there again was that stone with his name and those dates.

Then it dawned on me — that stone does *not* have the final say! Why? Because dad *was* and *is* a Christian. He knew Jesus before he died, therefore he knows Jesus now. I thought of the words: "O death, where is your victory? O death, where is your sting?" The One who is the Resurrection and the Life has defeated death forever!

What began as a chilling experience turned into a thrilling one. As I drove away, I knew that Jesus really had defeated death and removed its sting. Dad's body will rest there until the Rapture, but then no grave will hold his body down! Take that death! In your face grave! Jesus, the Prince of Life, has conquered you forever! You are defeated!

## WE CANNOT STOP SPEAKING

**Acts 4:20** — _"For we cannot stop speaking about what we have seen and heard."_

John was from Romania. Under the communists, he had been persecuted and even tortured before the authorities banished him from their country. He was expelled because he refused to stop preaching about Jesus. He was allowed to go to his home with his wife and children, pack a suitcase apiece, and board a jet for America. They left all behind — family, house, possessions, and friends — all for the sake of the Gospel.

Centuries earlier, Peter and John stood before the Jewish high court. They too were told by the authorities to stop preaching about Jesus. But Peter and John boldly announced that they _could_ not, therefore, they _would_ not stop speaking about the Lord. They had _seen_ too much to stop speaking. They had seen Jesus heal the sick, raise the dead, cast out demons, calm the storm-tossed sea, and feed the five thousand. They were among the first of the disciples to see Jesus after His resurrection. They had also _heard_ too much to stop speaking about Him. They were present when Jesus preached the Sermon on the Mount (Matthew 5-7). They had learned lessons from His parables. They were the first recipients of His Great Commission (Matthew 28:18-20). How could they deny Him by not sharing with others? It was incomprehensible. They had to speak!

Like these men, we must not allow a hostile world to silence us from speaking about Jesus. We have also _seen_ and _heard_ too much to be silent. Christ has changed us through salvation. He has answered our prayers. We _will_ not stop speaking about Jesus because we _cannot_ stop speaking! Until death silences your tongue, you should speak of His grace and glory to all who will listen. Share His Good News with someone today.

## THREE KEYS TO REVIVAL

**2 Chronicles 7:14** — *"And My people who are called by My name humble themselves and pray and seek My face and turn from their wicked ways, then I will hear from heaven, will forgive their sin and will heal their land."*

The Church needs revival. Traditionalism, formalism, fanaticism, legalism, and liberalism are strongholds that stifle God's power in our churches. We need a fresh movement of God. Too few are being saved and set free. The Lord has revealed three keys that can unlock the door to real revival. What are they and how do they operate?

**Humility.** "And My people who are called by My name *humble themselves.*" God demands that we walk humbly before Him (Micah 6:8). When pride walks in, God walks out. When we focus on ourselves, we miss Him. We must wait submissively before the Lord with a broken and contrite spirit. Humility always attracts His presence.

**Hunger.** "And *pray and seek My face.*" For revival to come, God's house must become a house of prayer. Prayer is not what we do *before* the real business; prayer *is* our real business! Our priority must not be the latest church growth technique, program, or method. Rather, we must desperately seek *Him!* He must become our sole focus.

**Holiness.** "And *turn from their wicked ways.*" We must repent and be cleansed by the Lord. When our sins are confessed and forsaken, He will pour out His grace and compassion (Proverbs 28:13). We will ascend His holy hill of revival when we have hearts and hands cleansed and purified by Him. He places His Spirit in *holy* vessels.

When you use these keys, God *may* sovereignly send revival. It is His gift to give as He sees fit. You can only prepare yourself. The keys are in your hand. Revival is in God's heart. May humility, hunger, and holiness be characteristic of your life today.

## A LASTING CITY

**Hebrews 13:14** — _"For here we do not have a lasting city, but we are seeking the city which is to come."_

I am on the road to heaven. I am a child of the King who redeemed me and made me a citizen of Glory. His Spirit lives within me. His blood covers my sin. His Word abides in my heart. I am a pilgrim passing through. I seek a city yet to come.

**The Problem.** "For here we do not have a lasting city." This world and its lusts are passing away. It is a modern Tower of Babel built for vainglory and destined for destruction. Man's sin has ravaged its original beauty. Its fair flowers have turned into thorns and thistles. It is not evolving toward perfection, but is deteriorating toward destruction. Man's life here is only a vapor. This world is anything but a lasting city.

**The Priority.** "But we are seeking." Christians are seekers. The Savior sought and found us with salvation. Now we seek Him and His heavenly kingdom. He is our life and His city is our desired haven of rest. We care not for Wall Street, Time Square, Tinsel Town, or the "odds" of Las Vegas. Our affections are set on things above.

**The Promise.** "The city which is to come." Jesus offers an eternal city infinitely fairer than this world. It knows nothing of sin, sickness, suffering, disease, or death. There, Jesus, the loving Lamb, reigns forever. We will soon ascend the bloodstained stairway to His throne and cast our crowns at His pierced feet. We will gaze upon His beauty and worship Him forever. What glory awaits us yonder in that city!

Are you seeking a lasting city? Renounce this fallen world. Enter at the Narrow Gate (Jesus) and walk the narrow way that leads to life. "Come then and join this holy band, and on to glory go; to dwell in that celestial land where joys immortal flow!"

## PRAYING IN JESUS' NAME

**John 14:13-14** — *"Whatever you ask in My name, that will I do, so that the Father may be glorified in the Son. If you ask Me anything in My name, I will do it."*

Soon after I became a Christian, a friend of mine and I began singing and sharing God's Word in various places. We decided that we needed a sound system, so we went to a bank and asked for a loan of two thousand dollars. The loan officer asked us what we planned to use as "collateral" to assure the payment of the loan. Neither of us owned anything. All we could do was promise to pay the loan promptly. As you might have guessed, the bank would not loan us the money without more assurance than our word.

As I dejectedly walked out the door, the officer said something I have never forgotten. "Your parents have several accounts here. If they will guarantee the loan, we will give you the money." I went straight home, told my parents, and they agreed to co-sign the note. We got the money and our sound system, and I learned a valuable lesson. What I could not get from a bank in my name, I could get based on my parents' name.

Jesus taught us to pray to the Father in His name. Our works are insufficient spiritual collateral with God. I am to pray to the Father in Jesus' name because He paid the price for me by shedding His blood and dying for my sins. When I pray based on who Christ is and what He has done, God listens and answers. It is in Jesus' name, in His authority, that I can experience answers to my prayers.

"In Jesus' name" is the only spiritual collateral that heaven will honor. Those simple words should not be a phrase you merely tack on to the end of your prayers. They are absolutely essential! The Father desires to bless you and supply your every need. He is waiting for you to pray and allow His Son to co-sign your requests "in Jesus' name."

## THE GREATEST COMMANDMENT

**Mark 12:30** — _"And you shall love the Lord your God with all your heart, and with all your soul, and with all your mind, and with all your strength."_

One day a scribe asked Jesus to point out the greatest of all the commandments in the Bible. Jesus' immediate reply was based on Scripture and therefore perfect. He said, in essence, that the greatest commandment is this: "Love God!" How are we to do that?

**Love God Emotionally.** "And you shall love the Lord your God with all your _heart,_ and with all your _soul._" The words "heart" and "soul" show that we are to love God with our emotions. God is a Person, not an abstract entity. He desires to share emotional intimacy with us. This can occur without yielding to fanatical emotionalism.

**Love God Intellectually.** "And you shall love the Lord your God...with all your _mind._" Loving God also involves our thoughts. Jesus desires to renew our minds (Romans 12:2), and take our thoughts captive to His obedience (2 Corinthians 10:5). We are to think on the best things (Philippians 4:8) as He teaches us with His wisdom.

**Love God Practically.** "And you shall love the Lord your God...with all your _strength._" We are to love God with practical obedience. Love is something we do! If we love God, we will prove it by keeping His commandments (John 14:15). We will display love for Him through our Christ-like behavior (1 John 3:18). Faith without works is dead (James 2:17). We prove our love for God through obedient actions.

The greatest of all commandments is to love God. Intimate communion with Him is more important than any religious ritual in which you may participate. Do you truly love God? Have you embraced His amazing love for you? Obey God's greatest commandment today. Love Him with all of your heart, soul, mind, and strength.

## CHRIST'S WORD IN YOU

**Colossians 3:16** — *"Let the word of Christ richly dwell within you, with all wisdom teaching and admonishing one another with psalms and hymns and spiritual songs, singing with thankfulness in your hearts to God."*

As I read a sermon by C. H. Spurgeon, I marveled at the many Bible references it contained. For almost forty years in the 1800s, he preached to over six thousand people in London every Sunday. Like Apollos, he was "mighty in the Scriptures" (Acts 18:24). The sacred text richly dwelt within him. God used him to reach masses of poor people for Christ. Communism later lamented its inability to infiltrate England with its devilish doctrines because Spurgeon had already saturated the common people with the Gospel!

God desires for us to allow His Word to richly dwell within us. How can we do that? First, we can *read* God's Word. Each day we can read it slowly, out loud, and expectantly to absorb its truths. We can also *hear* God's Word proclaimed by Spirit-filled preachers and teachers, as well as sung by musicians ("psalms and hymns and spiritual songs"). We can *study* God's Word, "examining the Scriptures daily" (Acts 17:11) to discover their meaning. We should *memorize* God's Word, storing it in our hearts as the valuable treasure it is (Proverbs 7:1). Like Mary, we too can *meditate* on God's Word, pondering it again and again in our hearts until its meaning is clear. We should also *obey* God's Word, doing what it says as well as hearing it. Finally, we should *share* God's Word, "teaching and admonishing" Christians and non-Christians alike.

The Bible is heavenly manna for our hungry souls and living water for our dry hearts. It is milk and meat through which we can taste and see that the Lord is good. Open your Bible. Sit down for a spiritual feast. Let His Word dwell richly within you today!

## CONSIDER YOUR WAYS

**Haggai 1:3-5** — *"Then the word of the LORD came by Haggai the prophet, saying, 'Is it time for you yourselves to dwell in your paneled houses while this house lies desolate?' Now therefore, thus says the LORD of hosts, 'Consider your ways!'"*

The phone in my office at church rang. On the other end of the line was a church member who greeted me with these words: "Pastor, my husband and I just bought two new rocking chairs and we want to donate our old ones to the church for the nursery. Of course, we'd also like a tax deduction for them." I was young, and probably a little too forthright in my reply. Nevertheless, I answered, "No ma'am, we will not be able to give you a tax deduction because we do not want the chairs. God deserves your best. If you want to give us the new chairs, fine, but God does not need your second-hand furniture."

Haggai the prophet lived during the time when the people of God were returning to Jerusalem from their exile as prisoners in Babylon. Upon their return, the Lord had commanded them to rebuild the Temple in Jerusalem. Instead, the people had rebuilt their homes, while neglecting the house of God for fifteen years. They kept saying, "It is not time to build the Temple." Haggai confronted them and said, "Is it time for you to live in nice, paneled houses while God's house lies in shambles? Consider your ways!"

God does not want your second-hand gifts or service. He deserves your very best. Today too many people have money to pay for their homes, cars, and other possessions, but they refuse to support their local church with tithes and offerings. Ask yourself whether or not the building in which you worship looks as nice as your own home. If not, why? Make sure that you give God your best in all that you do. He gave His best to you when He sent Jesus to this earth. Remember that, and consider your ways!

## SOMETHING TO BRAG ABOUT

**Jeremiah 9:23-24** — *"Thus says the LORD, 'Let not a wise man boast of his wisdom, and let not the mighty man boast of his might, let not a rich man boast of his riches; but let him who boasts boast of this, that he understands and knows Me, that I am the LORD who exercises lovingkindness, justice and righteousness on earth; for I delight in these things,' declares the LORD."*

Proud, arrogant boasting is distasteful and improper. Nevertheless, despite how obnoxious, rude, and offensive it is, bragging is still prevalent in our day, even among Christians. Our text tells us what a child of God should and should not brag about.

**We Should Not Boast of Wisdom.** A wise man should not boast of his wisdom. There are many intelligent people who possess magnificent comprehension and abilities of reason. Yet they should never boast before God. His ways and thoughts are higher than man's. The smartest person is a mental moron compared to our omniscient God.

**We Should Not Boast of Strength.** A strong man should not boast of his might. Today's athletes are bigger, faster, and stronger than ever before. Nevertheless, no human being should brag before God regarding his might. Any display of human strength is pitifully feeble compared to the strength of Almighty God.

**We Should Not Boast of Riches.** A wealthy man should not boast of his riches. Millionaires may control the world's wealth, but it gives them a false sense of security and power. Money does not represent true riches. God's blessings make a person rich (Proverbs 10:22). We are rich because we are blessed, not blessed because we are rich.

Those who know God personally and intimately through Jesus Christ, are the wisest, strongest, and richest people on earth. Jesus is heaven's supreme glory, and the only One worth bragging about. Pride yourself in Him alone, today and forever.

## LEAVE FOR GALILEE

**Matthew 28:10** — *"Then Jesus said to them, 'Do not be afraid; go and take word to My brethren to leave for Galilee, and there they will see Me.'"*

When Jesus came to earth, He was placed by God in a remote area on the eastern shores of the Mediterranean Sea. Our Lord grew up in the country, reared by a common family in a rural town in Galilee called Nazareth. Most of His miracles took place near the Sea of Galilee, a place surrounded by rolling hills and picturesque landscapes. It should not surprise us that even in His resurrected state, Jesus preferred to leave behind the busy hustle and bustle of Jerusalem to meet His disciples in His favorite place of retreat — Galilee. It was in that peaceful setting that He gave them the Great Commission (Matthew 28:18-20). Jesus understood the value of retreating to be alone with God.

Today we lead frenzied, stress-filled, hectic lives. We have shackled ourselves with cell phones, fax machines, beepers, palm pilots, e-mails, the Internet, and other annoying gadgets. Frantic and fatigued, we rush to-and-fro trying to cram more onto our to-do lists. We only have time for "fast food." Too many of us can identify with the country song that says, "I'm in a hurry to get things done. I rush and rush until life's no fun. All I really have to do is live and die, but I'm in a hurry and I don't know why!"

Maybe you should follow Jesus' example and "leave for Galilee." Perhaps it is past time to step aside from the rat race to an isolated place of rest and worship. When is the last time you sat alone, read your Bible, prayed, and quietly worshiped God? Jesus is calling you to lie down in green pastures beside still waters so He can restore your soul.

God placed Adam and Eve in a garden, not an airport. Be still and know Him. Commune intimately with Jesus. You will find that "Galilee" is still a place of miracles.

## KEEP UP YOUR COURAGE

**Acts 27:25** — *"Therefore, keep up your courage, men, for I believe God that it will turn out exactly as I have been told."*

As I sat down with over one hundred pastors, I realized that I did not know any of them personally. Most of us sat quietly and alone. As I talked with some and observed others, I became aware of the fact that most all of them were lonely and discouraged. Indeed, Satan loves to discourage God's people. It is one of the most devastating weapons he uses against us. Jesus wants us to walk in faith and "keep up (our) courage."

The Apostle Paul was on his way to Rome as a prisoner to face trial before Caesar. As he crossed the Mediterranean Sea, the ship on which he sailed was caught in a terrible storm that lasted for many days. As the tempest continued to rage, those on board lost all hope of being saved. Suddenly, an angel appeared to Paul at night and promised the Apostle that he would make it safely to Rome to bear witness for Jesus. The angel also promised him that all those aboard the ship would be saved as well. Paul announced this news to the discouraged men, quoting the words of our text. Everything happened just as the Lord promised. God encouraged Paul, he encouraged others, lives were spared, and many souls were saved as a result of the Lord's timely intervention.

Are you discouraged today? Have the storms in your life caused you to abandon hope for a better tomorrow? If so, stop looking at the storm and start looking to the One who can save you from it — Jesus! He will help you walk by faith and not by sight. The devil will try to frighten and discourage you (literally, "steal your courage"). But you can submit to God and resist Satan! Focus on Jesus and the promises of His precious Word. He *can* and *will* come through for you. Do not fear, Christian. Keep up your courage!

## BLESSED ASSURANCE

**1 John 5:13** — _"These things I have written to you who believe in the name of the Son of God, so that you may know that you have eternal life."_

Life has its uncertainties. Today, people are consulting New Age psychics and every kooky means imaginable trying to forecast their futures. While no person knows what tomorrow may bring, we _can_ know for sure that we are on our way to heaven.

**The Author of Salvation.** The only source of salvation is Jesus, "the Son of God." His name means, "Jehovah is salvation." He came to seek and save the lost (Luke 19:10). He is the only hope of salvation for the entire world (Acts 4:12). Jesus is the only way a person can know God and enter heaven (John 14:6). He is the sole mediator between God and all mankind (1 Timothy 2:5). He is the exclusive provider of salvation.

**The Acceptance of Salvation.** After a person comes to Jesus, he must "believe in (His) name." Belief is more than mere head-knowledge. Even the demons believe the facts about Jesus' life, death, and resurrection (James 2:19). Nevertheless, they will go to hell. A person must believe that Jesus died for his sins, was raised from the dead, and then _receive_ Him as Lord and Savior (John 1:12). At that moment, eternal life begins.

**The Assurance of Salvation.** After receiving Jesus, a person can be assured of salvation. Nothing can snatch him from God's hand (John 10:27-29), nothing can separate him from God's love (Romans 8:38-39), and nothing can break the seal of God's Spirit (Ephesians 1:13-14). God, who saves us, also keeps us and secures our salvation.

Though no one knows the future, we _can_ know that when we die we will go to heaven to live with Jesus forevermore. Do you have that blessed assurance? If so, share it with others. If not, ask the Lord to come into your heart to save and secure you today.

## FRESH OIL

**Psalm 92:10** — *"But you have exalted my horn like that of the wild ox; I have been anointed with fresh oil."*

My dad sighed as he checked the oil level in my Snapper mower. "This oil looks dirty, Son. When is the last time you changed it?" "I don't know, Dad," I replied, "last year?" "Last year?!? Son, you're about to burn up the engine!" Needless to say, I changed the oil then and there. I was a teenager making good money cutting grass, but I was about to lose my mower simply because I did not understand the need for fresh oil.

At the age of eighteen I became a Christian. I started out with boundless spiritual energy and seemingly unlimited zeal and power. But after a few months, I began to lose some of my fervor. I eventually joined a Bible study with some other college students, and they shared with me the importance of daily Bible-reading and prayer. They told me that a Christian must feed himself spiritually each day just as he does physically. They also taught me the importance of being filled regularly with the Holy Spirit (Luke 11:13; Ephesians 5:18). I learned the value of eating daily spiritual manna (God's Word) and being anointed with daily spiritual oil (the Holy Spirit). As I partook of those fresh, daily feedings and fillings, I was strengthened and began to mature more consistently.

Many Christians are "burned out" spiritually. They have not lost their salvation, but they have lost the joy of salvation. David said that the Lord had exalted his horn (i.e. strength) like that of a wild ox by filling him with "fresh oil." We need that as well!

Is your spiritual oil outdated and insufficient? If so, ask God to give His "fresh oil" to you. His Spirit will fill and empower you. Do not "burn up" your spiritual engine. Rather, maintain it by walking with Jesus *daily*. His oil is fresh. His supply is limitless.

## JEHOVAH-MEKADESH: THE LORD WHO SANCTIFIES

**Leviticus 20:8** — *"You shall keep My statutes and practice them; I am the LORD who sanctifies you."*

God is holy and pure. He is absolute light. Angels circle His throne day after day as the centuries pass, never ceasing to shout that He is, "Holy, holy, holy!" This God who is the essence of absolute holiness and perfection has sanctified and called out a people from this world to be His peculiar and pure possession. In our text God reminded Israel that He was the One who had sanctified and set them apart from all the other nations to be His. They belonged to Him, and they were to imitate Him in His holiness. They were consecrated from this world to worship Him, serve Him, witness for Him, and imitate His character. As long as Israel sought to be His holy people, God blessed them. When they tried to embrace and imitate the pagan world around them, He disciplined them. He demanded that they be holy, and He refused to take "No" for an answer.

Today we as Christians are set apart and sanctified by God. He has called us out from a life of darkness and sin to a holy life of light and obedience. We are not to love this world or the things of it (1 John 2:15). We are to be God's sanctified spiritual race, His royal priesthood, and His *holy* nation on this earth (1 Peter 2:9-10). We are to walk, talk, think, and act differently than the people of this world. God is still Jehovah-Mekadesh, "The LORD who sanctifies." He is holy, and He has sanctified us to be holy.

If Christ has saved you, He has set you apart to be one of His chosen vessels. You are to unashamedly bear His name while living in this unholy world. Ask the Lord to fill you today with His power and purity. Allow Him to make you delightfully different and pleasantly peculiar. He is the Lord who sanctifies you for His pleasure.

## FIRST LOVE

**Revelation 2:4** — *"But I have this against you, that you have left your first love."*

Why do we do what we do as Christians? For instance, why do we pray? Simply to receive more of God's blessings? Why do we serve? To be noticed by men? Why do we give? To be blessed financially? Motives are tricky things. It is hard to know them because our hearts are deceitful (Jeremiah 17:9). The only proper motive for serving Christ is a sincere love for Him. Laboring for Jesus without loving Jesus is sin.

The Church at Ephesus was a remarkable church with an outstanding history. Paul had founded it in a blaze of revival fire (Acts 19). Timothy and the Apostle John had served as its senior pastors. It was the mother church of all the other churches in its region. Jesus Himself commended it in many ways. It was an active church, filled with deeds. Its members toiled and served Christ to the point of fatigue. It persevered under persecution, and was doctrinally pure. It even exposed false apostles for the imposters they were. Yet, Jesus found a fatal flaw in that fellowship. They had left their first love for Him. The thrill and passion they once had for Jesus had waned into a mechanical, ritualistic habit of simply "going through the motions." The fire of revival was all but extinguished. The honeymoon was over, and the Groom was upset!

Does that sound like you or your church? Do you love Jesus today more than ever? Do you love Him with all your heart, soul, mind, and strength (Mark 12:30)? Is there a genuine passion for Jesus burning in your heart this moment? If not, why? What has taken His rightful place in your life? Whatever it is, realize that it is not worth it. Return to Jesus today. Repent and ask Him to be your "first love" forevermore.

## KNOWING OUR ADVERSARY

**1 Peter 5:8** — _"Be of sober spirit, be on the alert. Your adversary, the devil, prowls around like a roaring lion, seeking someone to devour."_

Every Christian has a spiritual opponent called "the devil." Though some deny his existence, his reality is irrefutable. Jesus not only taught about him, but actually confronted him (Luke 4). The devil is behind the evil in our world today. God originally created him as a powerful, high-ranking archangel. He possessed unparalleled perfection, beauty, and glory among the other angels. His superiority led to pride and rebellion, and He attempted to usurp God's authority. God cast him from heaven with the angels who followed him (Isaiah 14:12-17; Ezekiel 28:11-19). Those fallen angels are the evil spirits and demons mentioned in the Bible. Subservient to Satan, they still wreak havoc today.

The Bible refers to the devil as Satan (adversary) (Zechariah 3:1f), the evil one (1 John 5:19), the serpent (Genesis 3:1f), the great red dragon (Revelation 12:3-4, 9), the accuser of the brethren (Revelation 12:10-11), the tempter (Mark 1:12-13), Beelzebub, the ruler of the demons (Matthew 12:22-29), the ruler of this world (John 12:31), the god of this world (2 Corinthians 4:3-4), and the prince of the power of the air (Ephesians 2:2). He is also called the father of lies (John 8:44). His primary activity on earth is to blind the minds of lost people to keep them from receiving Christ as Savior (2 Corinthians 4:4). He also tempts Christians to sin to tarnish their witness for Christ (1 Thessalonians 3:5). He is a thief who steals, kills, and destroys people and relationships (John 10:10).

The devil is real, dangerous, and active today. You will experience victory over him only when you walk in the filling of the Holy Spirit and begin to appropriate Jesus' name, Jesus' blood, and God's Word. Your adversary is real, but Jesus has defeated him!

## Overcoming Our Adversary

**1 Peter 5:8** — *"Be of sober spirit, be on the alert. Your adversary, the devil, prowls around like a roaring lion, seeking someone to devour."*

The devil is dangerous but any child of God can defeat him. Jesus conquered Satan and gave us authority over him and all demonic forces. How can we overcome Satan?

**We Must Know Our Position.** Jesus is Lord over the spirit world. He sits sovereignly at the right hand of God the Father who is making all of His enemies, including the devil, a footstool for His feet (Psalm 110:1). As Christians, we are seated in the heavenlies with Christ (Ephesians 2:4-6). Since Satan is under Christ's feet, he is under ours as well. "In Christ" we have the authority to cast out demons (Mark 3:14-15), and to tread victoriously upon demonic "serpents and scorpions" (Luke 10:19).

**We Must Use Our Protection.** Christians must regularly put on the whole armor of God through prayer in order to defeat the devil (Ephesians 6:10-18). The girdle of truth, shoes of the Gospel of peace, breastplate of righteousness, helmet of salvation, shield of faith, and sword of the Spirit (Word of God) are spiritual weapons that empower us to tear down demonic strongholds and defeat the enemy (2 Corinthians 10:3-5).

**We Must Rely on God's Power.** Believers have power over the devil through the indwelling Holy Spirit (1 John 4:4), the name of Jesus (Acts 16:18), the blood of Jesus (Revelation 12:10-11), and the Word of God (Ephesians 6:17). If we appropriate and utilize these resources, we will see the demonic forces around us begin to fall.

Has the devil defeated you? As a Christian, you do not have to take his abuse any longer. Fight back! Unleash the authority of Christ in you. Appropriate your position, protection, and power in Jesus. The Lord will give you victory over the adversary today!

## THREE GLORIOUS NAMES

**Revelation 1:5** — *"And from Jesus Christ, the faithful witness, the firstborn of the dead, and the ruler of the kings of the earth. To Him who loves us and released us from our sins by His blood."*

The Apostle John was worshiping God one Sunday when suddenly in a vision he beheld Jesus, the resurrected, exalted Son of God. From that vision, John described Jesus with three vivid names that enhance our understanding of who He is.

**The Faithful Witness.** The word "witness" is the Greek word from which we derive our English word, "martyr." Jesus was "the faithful *martyr*." John had witnessed Jesus' crucifixion (John 19:26-27). He knew that Jesus had died for the sins of man. Christ died for us in order to release us "by His blood" from the power of sin.

**The Firstborn of the Dead.** Jesus' resurrection was unique. Others had been raised from the dead before Him, but all of them eventually died a second time. Jesus was the first to be resurrected never to experience death again! He said of Himself, "I was dead, and behold, I am alive *forevermore*" (Revelation 1:18).

**The Ruler of the Kings of the Earth.** Jesus is King of kings and Lord of lords. No earthly potentate has authority over Him. No one can thwart His plan. He turns the hearts of kings wherever He wishes like streams of water in His hands (Proverbs 21:1). He will consummate history and be worshiped by all in the end (Philippians 2:9-11).

Jesus is more than a religious teacher, a philosopher, or a social leader. He is the One who died for our sins, was raised from the dead, and is the King of all kings. He is worthy of our praise, our adoration, and our humble, contrite, absolute obedience. Bow before Him and exalt Him today as you view Him through these three glorious names.

## THE CALL OF THE GOSPEL

**Acts 3:19** — *"Therefore repent and return, so that your sins may be wiped away, in order that times of refreshing may come from the presence of the Lord."*

The world is filled with bad news. Earthquakes, famines, droughts, wars, murders, rapes, and other tragedies top the headlines in the media. The word "Gospel" means "good news." The greatest news we will ever hear is that Jesus came to die for our sins. He came to forgive us and grant us eternal life. That is the call of the Gospel.

**A Call to Repentance.** A crowd gathered after the healing of a lame man. Peter, whom God had used in the healing, told the crowd that Jesus had healed him. Even though they had encouraged Pilate to crucify Jesus, God would forgive their sins if they would repent. When we repent and turn to Him, we too are forgiven (Proverbs 28:13).

**A Call to Reconciliation.** After repentance, God removes the barrier of sin that stands between Him and us. Our sin separates us from God (Isaiah 59:1-2). God must wash and redeem us from the guilt of our sin through the blood of Jesus (1 Peter 1:18-19). When that barrier is gone, we are restored and reconciled to the living God.

**A Call to Refreshment.** After God reconciles us to Himself through Christ (2 Corinthians 5:19), He sends us "times of refreshing." In His presence there is fullness of joy (Psalm 16:11). His Spirit breathes life into our hearts. In His presence we eat the Bread of Heaven and drink the Living Water. There we are saved, sealed, and satisfied.

If you are searching for some good news, look no further than our text. He is calling you to repent, be reconciled, and be refreshed. It all happens when you say "Yes" to Jesus. Have you ever done that? If not, answer His call right now. If you have answered that call already, then share the Good News of Jesus with someone else today.

## A Sermon In The Sky

**Psalm 19:1** — *"The heavens are telling of the glory of God; and their expanse is declaring the work of His hands."*

My wife and I sat in the boat gazing in awe at the midnight sky above us. The lake that was nestled between the rolling Ozark Mountains of northern Arkansas reflected the light of the millions of stars above. We held hands beneath that celestial sanctuary. We worshiped the Lord as we acknowledged the majestic beauty displayed in the sky above us. There was a silent sermon in that sky. We heard its message loud and clear.

Foolish people say in their hearts that there is no God (Psalm 14:1f). They say it in their hearts because in their minds they know better. Everyone knows there is a God. The beauty of creation proves it. The Lord's "invisible attributes, His eternal power and divine nature, have been clearly seen" through the created order of the Universe (Romans 1:20). To smugly deny that such a Creator exists is foolish speech indeed (Romans 1:22). The majestic mountains cry out, "There is a God!" The vast oceans teeming with life proclaim, "The Creator made all of this!" The innocent face of a newborn baby shouts aloud, "I am not an accidental result of nature, nor am I the product of billions of years of random, biological mutation. Rather, I have been fearfully and wonderfully made by a holy God!" Creation is preaching even if no one is listening.

I have seen the sun rise over the hills of the Golan Heights as its rays reflected off the waters of the Sea of Galilee. I have ascended the slopes of the Colorado Rocky Mountains at nighttime and seen the same stars we saw in Arkansas. I have stared in rapture as the sun sank into the majestic plains of Texas. I have seen these, and many other sermons in the sky. Do not tell me there is no God. The sky is shouting, "He is!"

## THE FRUIT OF REPENTANCE

**Matthew 3:8** — *"Therefore bear fruit in keeping with repentance."*

A word that seems to have vanished from the modern Christian vocabulary is the little, yet powerful word, "repent." Few people, including preachers, mention repentance anymore, although it is a key concept in the Bible regarding salvation and holy living. To repent is to experience a change of heart and mind on the inside that results in a change of action on the outside. *Repentance* and *faith* are inseparable requirements in order for genuine salvation to take place (cf. Mark 1:14-15; Acts 20:20-21).

John the Baptist preached in the Judean wilderness just before Jesus' earthly ministry began. He was preparing the way for Jesus, the Jewish Messiah. Multitudes thronged to hear his prophetic voice. He baptized his listeners in the Jordan River as a symbol of their repentance toward God and their anticipation of the coming Christ. One day, some Jewish religious leaders (Pharisees and Sadducees) came to hear John. He immediately began to rebuke them, calling them a "brood of vipers." Then he spoke the words of our text concerning repentance. John told them in no uncertain terms that true repentance resulted in a changed life! Unless there was a change in their hypocritical actions, he would have no part in their immersion. He demanded the fruit of repentance.

If John's words seem too harsh for you, perhaps you do not understand God's demand for repentance. Many people today have made some sort of "decision for Christ," but not as many have repented. Jesus said that anyone who refuses to repent will perish (Luke 13:3, 5). You must repent for your sins to be wiped away (Acts 3:19). The fruit of repentance is a Christlike change. No Jesus, no change. No change, no Jesus.

## No Worthless Thing

**Psalm 101:2b-3** — _"I will walk within my house in the integrity of my heart. I will set no worthless thing before my eyes; I hate the work of those who fall away; it shall not fasten its grip on me."_

Christianity should begin at home. Someone has well said, "If you are not living for Jesus at home, don't try to export your Christianity outside to others." Indeed, Christ wants to transform our entire lives, starting with our family life. Our homes are to be havens of the Holy Spirit where Christ is honored, worshiped, and obeyed. Nothing in our house should dishonor the name of Jesus Christ. Everything that comes across our television sets, computers, and radios should be monitored to see if it pleases Him. If there is the slightest question regarding the suitability of anything in our home, we must remove it. Better to err on the side of caution and be safe than to invite disaster.

The Psalmist desired to live a godly life in his home. He wanted to walk as a man of "integrity" before God and his family members. He determined never to set any "worthless thing" before his eyes in his home. He was referring to an idol. He said that such an abominable thing would "not fasten its grip" on him. He wanted to be morally and spiritually pure, so he declared war on any vile and vulgar thing within his home.

Many Christians today need to do spiritual housecleaning. Is there any "worthless thing" in your house that could hinder your walk with Jesus? What about television programs, movies, magazines, the music you listen to, and what you see on the Internet? Anything in your home that is sinful will give Satan a foothold to wreak havoc in your family. Walk prayerfully through your house and surrender every part of it to Jesus. Reject every "worthless thing" so that your faith will be genuine "within (your) house."

## You Too, Be Ready

**Luke 12:40** — *"You too, be ready; for the Son of Man is coming at an hour that you do not expect."*

The rusty sign beside the highway read, "Jesus Is Coming Soon!" Years earlier, a believer had placed that sign as a witness to those who would pass by. Some probably looked at it and thought, "Yeah, right. I've heard that all my life. Sounds like a Christian scare tactic to me." As I continued to drive, it dawned on me that even though the sign had faded, its message was still true. At any moment God's trumpet could sound, the archangel could shout, and Christ could return to take His people away from this world.

We all live busy lives. We become so immersed in our daily activities that we do not live with the anticipation that Jesus could come back at any moment. Jesus told His disciples that they should watch for His return like servants who were waiting for their master to return from a feast. They were to "be dressed in readiness" (Luke 12:35), ever "on the alert" watching for His return (12:37). He promised to come back at an hour when people were not expecting Him. Thus, they were to live each day anticipating that at any moment He would appear. The early Christians lived every day watching for the imminent return of Jesus. Such anticipation added urgency to their prayers and evangelism that is seldom seen among Christians today. They believed that man's time and God's time were running out. They sought to live holy, productive lives because they were convinced that at any moment the Lord could appear from heaven!

Is that how you are living? Are you watching each day for Christ's return? If not, why? I have seriously considered repainting that old sign by the road. The paint may be old, but the message is still up to date. Jesus *is* coming soon. We need to be ready!

## THE RAPTURE GENERATION

**1 Thessalonians 4:16-17** — *"For the Lord Himself will descend from heaven with a shout, with the voice of the archangel and with the trumpet of God, and the dead in Christ will rise first. Then we who are alive and remain will be caught up together with them in the clouds to meet the Lord in the air, and so we shall always be with the Lord."*

Every Christian should be aware that there are six major end-time events mentioned in the Bible. The first is *The Rapture*. Our text describes this event when Jesus will return for His people to snatch us away from earth into heaven. The Rapture will inaugurate the second end-time event, *The "Great Tribulation"* (Matthew 24:21). For seven years, hell-like horrors will break loose on the earth (Revelation 6-19). At the end of that time of unprecedented suffering, the world will witness *The Return of Christ*. In this third end-time event, Jesus will return with His saints to defeat Antichrist at the Battle of Armageddon (Revelation 19:11-21). His return will usher in the fourth end-time event, *The Millennial Reign of Christ*, a thousand years of worldwide peace (Revelation 20:1-6). After that comes the fifth event, *The Final Judgment*. Satan and all unbelievers will be sentenced and cast into hell (Revelation 20:7-15). The final end-time event will be the destruction of the heavens and earth by fire, and the ushering in of a new heaven, a new earth, and *The New Jerusalem* (Revelation 21-22). In that celestial city, God's people will dwell forever with Jesus our King in a state of indescribable bliss.

We could be The Rapture Generation! The end of time draws closer with each passing day. These could be the "perilous times" which will immediately precede the Rapture (2 Timothy 3:1-5). At any moment, God's trumpet could sound and launch these six end-time events into motion. Are you ready? If not, make your preparations today.

## THE RAPTURE

**1 Thessalonians 4:16-17** — *"For the Lord Himself will descend from heaven with a shout, with the voice of the archangel and with the trumpet of God, and the dead in Christ will rise first. Then we who are alive and remain will be caught up together with them in the clouds to meet the Lord in the air, and so we shall always be with the Lord."*

A time is coming, and it could be today, when Jesus will take away His children from this earth. That event is called "The Rapture," (from Latin *rapio*, "to snatch away"). No one knows its exact time (Matthew 24:36), but prior to it, people will be going about their lives with a "business as usual" attitude (Luke 17:26-30). There will be a falling away from the true faith of Christianity and a turning toward false religions, Satanism, and the occult (1 Timothy 4:1-2). There will also be severe stress throughout society (2 Timothy 3:1-5). These characteristics vividly describe the times in which we now live.

The Rapture will occur before the Great Tribulation. God's people will suffer man's persecution, but not God's wrath. Those who teach that Christians must endure the horrors of the Tribulation do not believe that Christ could return at any moment. They are wrong! We are to live in light of Christ's imminent return (Matthew 24:40-44).

The Rapture will be *spectacular*. Jesus will appear, the archangel will shout, God's trumpet will sound, and the saints will be caught away. It will be *sudden*, in the twinkling of an eye (1 Corinthians 15:51-52). It will also be a time of *separation*. Christians will be taken up and non-Christians will be left behind (Luke 17:34-36).

Are you ready for the Rapture? Jesus alone can save you from "the wrath to come" (1 Thessalonians 1:10). Trust Him as Savior and serve Him faithfully. Consider the words of the old hymn: "Jesus is coming to earth again, what if it were today?"

## THE GREAT TRIBULATION

**Matthew 24:21** — _"For then there will be a great tribulation, such as has not occurred since the beginning of the world until now, nor ever will."_

There is coming a day when God will pour out His unbridled wrath upon this earth and its inhabitants. Jesus called that time the "Great Tribulation." It is a seven-year period of "hell on earth" that will begin immediately after Christ comes for His Church in the Rapture. Revelation 6-19 describes the events of this horrible time. Seven seals of judgment will be broken by Jesus to unleash the wrath of God on sin and sinners. War, famine, disease, and death in unprecedented proportions will be the worldwide norm. The future will no longer appeal to anyone. Man will prefer death instead of life.

After the seven seals, seven trumpets of judgment will sound forth. Among the plagues from these trumpet blasts will be a five-month period during which literal demons will torture mankind relentlessly. Following the trumpets, God will pour out seven bowls of judgment. Every mountain and island will disappear, and the oceans and fresh water will be turned into blood. Malignant sores will plague all people. Antichrist will rise to power and will rule the world, issuing a "mark" without which no one can purchase anything. He will demand to be worshiped and will blaspheme God. At the end of those seven years, Jesus will return with the Christians who were raptured, defeat Antichrist at the Battle of Armageddon, and be crowned King of kings and Lord of lords!

Gratefully, those of us who know Jesus Christ as Savior will escape this time of tribulation that the Bible also calls "the wrath to come" (1 Thessalonians 1:10). But millions of lost people will be left behind at the Rapture to face the horrors of the Great Tribulation! What about you? Will you go up in the Rapture or will you be left behind?

## THE SECOND COMING OF CHRIST

**Acts 1:11** — *"They also said, 'Men of Galilee, why do you stand looking into the sky? This Jesus, who has been taken up from you into heaven, will come in just the same way as you have watched Him go into heaven.'"*

The Apostle John was in his nineties when he was arrested for preaching the Gospel. He was sentenced to a labor camp on the small island of Patmos. While there, the aged preacher received a series of visions from God's Spirit that make up the last book of the Bible — Revelation. The highlight of that book is the Second Coming of Christ (Revelation 19:11-21). John saw what will happen when Christ returns to earth. In our text, the angels promised that Jesus would one day come back to this earth just as He left it. He ascended to heaven in the clouds with great glory. He will return the same way, escorted by angels and God's saints. Jesus left this earth, but He *will* come again!

Christ's return was predicted in the Old Testament (Zechariah 14:1-9), and in the New Testament (Philippians 2:9-11). Like His first coming (i.e. His birth), Christ's return will be a precise event. It will occur after the Great Tribulation (Matthew 24:29-30), and before the Millennial Reign of Christ (Revelation 19-20). Jesus will return literally, bodily, and visibly at His Second Coming. At the Rapture, only Christians will see Him, but at His Second Coming everyone will see Him (Revelation 1:7). His glory will be revealed, His heavenly army will be deployed, and His enemies (Antichrist and his allies) will be defeated (Revelation 19:17-21). Jesus will reign as Judge and King.

Jesus is coming again! This world will grow spiritually darker as the end of time draws near. After the Rapture and the Great Tribulation, Christ will return. God began history as we know it and will bring it to His desired end. History is indeed *"His*-story."

## THE MILLENNIAL REIGN OF CHRIST

**Revelation 20:4** — _"Then I saw thrones, and they sat on them, and judgment was given to them. And I saw the souls of those who had been beheaded because of their testimony of Jesus and because of the word of God, and those who had not worshiped the beast or his image, and had not received the mark on their forehead and on their hand; and they came to life and reigned with Christ for a thousand years."_

Peace in the Middle East. It is something that every American president seeks to facilitate and achieve. Yet, the Bible teaches that there will be no permanent peace in the Middle East, or in the rest of the world, until the Prince of Peace, Jesus Christ, returns to earth. At the end of the Great Tribulation, Jesus will return to establish Himself as sovereign King over all. He will not lead a democracy, but a theocracy. People will not get to "vote" or help decide how the earth will be governed. Rather, Jesus will be in charge. His capital will be Jerusalem. From there, God's Word will go forth and cover the earth as the waters of the sea. King David will reign under Jesus as His regent (Ezekiel 37:24-28). The twelve apostles will rule over the twelve tribes of Israel (Matthew 19:28). Our text says that other saints will also be resurrected to rule on earth.

The Millennial Reign of Christ will be a time of unprecedented peace. It will follow the least peaceful time on earth, the Great Tribulation. Animals that normally attack one another will live harmoniously. Children will play with animals that once were "wild." Wars will cease. Man will live in perpetual peace (Isaiah 2:1-4; 11:1-10).

You might ask why the Millennial Reign of Jesus is necessary in God's history of salvation. The Millennium will restore the paradise of Eden. It will also reverse the Great Tribulation. Christ will rule instead of Antichrist. It will be a foretaste of heaven. Will you be there? If Christ is your Savior, you _will_ one day see Him rule as King on earth!

## THE FINAL JUDGMENT

**Revelation 20:15** — *"And if anyone's name was not found written in the book of life, he was thrown into the lake of fire."*

Each of us will stand before Almighty God one day and give an account for the life we have lived on earth. Reincarnation is a myth. Purgatory is unbiblical. There is no second chance at life. All will die once. After that comes judgment (Hebrews 9:27).

At the end of the age, a series of judgments will take place. Christians who are alive at the Rapture will stand before Jesus at His judgment seat to have their works tested (2 Corinthians 5:10). Their works that are pleasing to God will result in eternal, heavenly rewards. The works that displease Him will be burned up (1 Corinthians 3:10-15). Later on, when Jesus returns in His Second Coming after the Great Tribulation, the Old Testament saints will be resurrected and judged to receive rewards (Daniel 12:1-3). At that same time, people saved during the Tribulation will be judged (Revelation 20:4-6). The survivors of the Tribulation who are not Christians will also be judged at Christ's return and sentenced to Hades (Matthew 25:31-46). At the end of Christ's Millennial Reign, Satan and the demons will be judged and sentenced to the lake of fire (Revelation 20:7-10). Finally, all lost people will be taken out of Hades and cast for eternity into the lake of fire with Satan (Revelation 20:11-15). That will be the Final Judgment. After that, the Lord will destroy the heavens and the earth and send down the New Jerusalem.

You *will* stand before God. Are you ready? Christian, your works will be judged. Will there be rewards, or will your works of disobedience be burned up? If you are lost, you will be cast into the lake of fire. God does not want that! Give your life to Christ. He will bless you in this life, and save you from the dreadfulness of the Final Judgment.

## THE NEW JERUSALEM

**Revelation 21:1-2** — _"Then I saw a new heaven and a new earth; for the first heaven and the first earth passed away, and there is no longer any sea. And I saw the holy city, new Jerusalem, coming down out of heaven from God, made ready as a bride adorned for her husband."_

There is coming a day when this world will be destroyed by divine fire (2 Peter 3:7-13). God will replace it with a new heaven and earth, and unveil the glorious city called "new Jerusalem." The redeemed of all the ages will abide with Him there forever.

The last two chapters of the Bible tell us about that wonderful place. It will be a _new_ city (21:1-2, 4-5). Unlike the cities of this earth, it will never deteriorate or require constant maintenance. Rather, it will be perfectly and perpetually adorned. It will also be a _holy_ city (21:2-3, 8). It will be like a pure and holy "bride." Sinners who reject Christ will not be there. It will be a _happy_ city (21:4). There will no longer be any sickness, sadness, or suffering. All will be joyful in Jesus' presence. It will also be a _blessed_ city (21:6-7; 22:1-3). Void of sin's curse, living water will flow there causing the tree of life to blossom with healing in its leaves. It will be a _beautiful_ city (21:9-21) with golden streets, jeweled walls, and gates of perfect pearls. It will be a _Christ-centered_ city (21:22-26). Jesus will shine in place of the sun, moon, and stars. Finally, it will be an _exclusive_ city (21:27; 22:10-17), entered only by those who know Jesus as Savior.

Will you be in the New Jerusalem? Will you see those golden streets? Will the light of Jesus shine on your face in that fair land? Will you drink from God's stream of living water? If so, rejoice and sing: "What a day that will be when my Jesus I shall see, when I look upon His face, the One who saved me by His grace; when He takes me by the hand and leads me to the Promised Land; what a day, glorious day, that will be!"

## OUR CREATING GOD

**Genesis 1:1** — *"In the beginning God created the heavens and the earth."*

"Prove that God exists!" The arrogant college professor smirked as he addressed the classroom filled with wide-eyed, naïve, intimidated freshmen. "Science has *proven* that the biblical account of creation is just a religious fable. We have *conclusive* evidence that man has evolved over millions and billions of years as a result of random mutations of various life forms. There was never a 'creation' and there is no God!" Is the professor correct? Is man really no more than an animal? Is this life all there is to life?

One must turn to the Book of the Ages, not a science book that will be out of date in a few months, to discover the facts about the origin of the Universe. The Bible says that when time as we know it began, God alone existed. He existed immutably as the infinite uncaused Cause. All-powerful, all-knowing, and eternal, He created everything from atoms to solar systems through the power of His spoken Word. He was and is the source of life. Man may manipulate pre-existing biological building blocks, but only God can create life out of absolutely nothing. That is the power of our creating God!

The unscientific theories of atheistic evolutionists are flawed with biased gaps and inconsistent hunches. They reject the idea of a Creator because that would require man's accountability to Him. The atheistic evolutionist is too self-centered for that!

There is a God, and we can know Him personally. The fact of creation demands a Creator. We are not an accidental, random mutation that evolved from a lower form of life over billions of years. God created us in His image, for His glory. He will recreate us through salvation in Jesus Christ. All praise and glory to the God of creation!

## GOD'S STEADFAST WORD

**Jeremiah 23:28-29** — _"'The prophet who has a dream may relate his dream, but let him who has My word speak My word in truth. What does straw have in common with grain?' declares the LORD. 'Is not My word like fire?' declares the LORD, 'and like a hammer which shatters a rock?'"_

The Bible is God's reliable Word. It should be the ultimate authority for every Christian. It consists exclusively of the thirty-nine books of the Old Testament and the twenty-seven books of the New Testament. People have tried to add to the Bible with false revelations, claiming special visions and dreams from God. God warns against such bogus spiritual guides by giving us three vivid descriptions of His steadfast Word.

**God's Word Is Grain.** The messages of false prophets are "straw" compared to the "grain" of Scripture. Today, some claim to have special "words" from God; perhaps an apparition in a field, or a message from a so-called prophet. These must be examined in the light of the Bible, and must _never_ be considered as being on the level of Scripture.

**God's Word Is Fire.** Jeremiah said that God's Word was "fire in his bones" that had to be spoken (20:9). As we share it today, Scripture still burns through the stubble of false ideas and blazes into people's lives with the power of salvation and deliverance.

**God's Word Is a Hammer.** God's Word is a spiritual hammer that shatters the false ideas of man. His Word will have the final say. It is the ultimate hammer of truth that can destroy the lies of the evil one and his false prophets on earth.

We do not need to lust for a vision, prophecy, or dream. We need to hunger for the written Word of God. In the Bible we will find the grain we need to feed our hungry souls, the fire we need to keep us ablaze for Jesus, and the hammer we need to shatter the false ideas of our pagan, confused society. Who needs a dream when we have the Bible?

## THE BANK OF YOUR SOUL

**Luke 6:45** — *"The good man out of the good treasure of his heart brings forth what is good; and the evil man out of the evil treasure brings forth what is evil; for his mouth speaks from that which fills his heart."*

Recently I went to a local automatic teller machine to get some cash. When I typed in the amount, the machine indicated that my account did not have sufficient funds to cover the request. Unknowingly, I had written a check the month before without subtracting it from my balance. The ATM was correct! I quickly made the necessary deposit. That was the first time I had ever been told that I had "insufficient funds."

Jesus said that we all have "treasure" stored up in our hearts/souls. Good people store up good treasure, and evil people store up evil treasure. Sadly, many Christians in our day are making spiritual withdrawals from the banks of their souls with "insufficient funds" in their accounts. They rarely make spiritual deposits by worshiping God, reading the Bible, praying, fellowshiping with other believers, and witnessing to non-Christians. They barely get by with insufficient power to walk victoriously with Christ in this life.

God wants each of us to have a full spiritual account. There is no shortage with Him. He has all that we desire and is ready to make deposits until our hearts overflow. He will supply all of our needs according to His riches in glory, with baskets of blessings left over. Our job is simply to make regular spiritual deposits into the banks of our souls.

Being overdrawn at the bank is annoying and painful. How is the balance in your spiritual bank doing? Do not wait until you need to make a spiritual withdrawal to discover that you have "insufficient funds." Begin to make regular deposits today. Your account was opened the moment you were saved. Make sure you manage it well.

## SONGS OF DELIVERANCE

**Psalm 32:7** — _"You are my hiding place; You preserve me from trouble; You surround me with songs of deliverance."_

Music is a powerful force. Studies show that the two primary influences on teenagers are the friends with whom they associate, and the music to which they listen. When as a teenager I became a Christian in 1976, God began to teach me about the power of music. For many years I avoided listening to secular music and listened exclusively to Christian songs. I bought albums by The Imperials, Bill and Gloria Gaither, and Andre' Crouch. I can still hear the speakers blasting out, "Jesus Is the Answer," "Because He Lives," and "My Tribute." I had surrounded myself with "songs of deliverance."

David was a musician who loved to play his harp and sing praise songs to God. When wicked King Saul was tormented by an evil spirit, David would play praise music until the demon departed (1 Samuel 16:23). In our text, David had just confessed a sin to the Lord and received forgiveness. He immediately bathed Himself in the Lord's presence by worshiping Him and surrounded himself with "songs of deliverance."

You and I should do the same. Christ-centered songs help focus our thoughts on the Lord. The devil will leave us because he is allergic to our praises to God! God's manifest presence will engulf us because He inhabits (lit. "enthrones Himself upon") the praises of His people (Psalm 22:3). He routs His enemies (2 Chronicles 20:22) and saves His people from distress when we worship and sing praises to Him (Acts 16:25-26).

Listen exclusively to Christian music for a week and see how it changes your life. The Lord will become your hiding place and preserve you from trouble as you become disciplined regarding music. Let Jesus surround you with songs of deliverance today.

## CHILD, BE STILL

**Psalm 46:10** — *"Cease striving and know that I am God; I will be exalted among the nations, I will be exalted in the earth."*

The lightning flashed and the thunder rolled across the heavens with a noise that literally vibrated the foundations of our home. In the middle of the night, the storm was making so much noise that I could hardly sleep. Suddenly, I sensed the presence of someone else in our bedroom. I looked and saw a small pair of eyes staring at me. "Daddy, I'm scared. Can I get in bed with you?" I lifted the covers as our daughter climbed into our "big bed." I said, "Relax, sweetheart. It's only rain and thunder. The Lord will protect us. Just be still and close your eyes." In a matter of moments she was fast asleep. The storm continued to rage, but she never heard it again. She was tucked in safely between dad and mom. Everything in her little world was at peace.

Relaxing can be hard for a frightened child, even a child of God. Regardless of our age, sometimes it is hard to be still, relax, and let go of the problems that we face. The storms of life often cause us to panic. In those times, God tells His children not to be afraid, but to "relax and let go" of all that bothers them. That is exactly what "cease striving" means. He wants us to be still and relax physically, emotionally, and spiritually. He is in control of our lives and will protect us from any circumstance that seeks to paralyze us with fear. We can be assured that His plan for us *will* prevail if we trust Him.

Is the thunder and lightning in your life causing you to panic? If so, come to your heavenly Father. Climb into His presence through prayer. Let Him wrap the protective covers of His love and grace around you. His tender voice will quiet your troubled heart. "My child, don't be afraid. There is no need to worry. Just relax, let go, and be still!"

## THE CALL OF DISCIPLESHIP

**Matthew 4:19-20** — _"And He said to them, 'Follow Me, and I will make you fishers of men.' Immediately they left their nets and followed Him."_

Great leaders attract followers. A leader influences others to go where he goes, do what he does, and share life's journey with him. Jesus is the greatest of all leaders. More people have followed Him than any other person in history. He calls His disciples to follow Him immediately and wholeheartedly. What does that mean?

**A Call to Follow Someone.** Jesus does not ask us to follow religious rules. Rather, He says, "Follow _Me._" He desires a personal relationship. "And He walks with me, and He talks with me, and He tells me I am His own!" In His presence we are transformed into His likeness. He holds our hand each step of the way as we follow.

**A Call to Become Something.** Jesus calls us to become "fishers of men." He leads us to share the Gospel of Christ with lost people. If you follow Him, He will teach you how to win non-Christians to faith in Him. Those who fish for men's souls are following Jesus closely. Those who do not are not. It is that simple.

**A Call to Leave Something.** The early disciples heard Jesus' call, left their fishing business immediately, and followed Him. Their decision was drastic and costly. Yet, that which they gave up at the Sea of Galilee was nothing compared to the blessings they would eventually experience. Likewise, whatever we leave in order to follow Jesus will be replaced with blessings far more fulfilling than we can imagine.

Jesus still calls people. If you have not said, "Yes," to His call, do so today. If you have answered His call, forget the old life and let Jesus teach you to fish for the souls of lost people. Heed His call today, and be His faithful, obedient disciple.

## A HEALTHY CHURCH

**Acts 9:31** — *"So the church throughout all Judea and Galilee and Samaria enjoyed peace, being built up; and going on in the fear of the Lord and in the comfort of the Holy Spirit, it continued to increase."*

I love the church. I love its foundation — Jesus Christ (1 Corinthians 3:11), its fellowship — those who have been born again (1 Peter 1:23), and its future — the Rapture and eternity with Jesus (1 Thessalonians 4:13-18). What constitutes a healthy church?

A healthy church is *peaceful* ("enjoyed peace"). It is void of fussing and fighting. The ministries operate in a kind, spiritual manner. The members love each other. Factious folks are not tolerated. A healthy church is also *edifying* ("being built up"). Members encourage one another. Jealousy and selfish ambition are absent. Each member views others as more important than himself. A healthy church is also *reverent* ("going on in the fear of the Lord"). The members fear and revere the Lord Jesus with an affectionate awe. He is their sole object of worship, and the only One they obey and exalt. A healthy church is also *anointed* ("in the comfort of the Holy Spirit"). The Spirit empowers the worship, preaching, praying, giving, ministries, planning, and personnel of the church. Finally, a healthy church is *growing* ("it continued to increase"). The natural by-product of good health is growth. The Lord adds to the church those who are being saved (Acts 2:47). A church that is not growing is spiritually sick and needs healing.

Local churches are not perfect because the pastor, staff, and members are mere sinners saved by grace. Nevertheless, the church at its worst is infinitely better than the world at its best. Christian, be involved in a local church. Jesus loves the church and gave Himself for it (Ephesians 5:25). If He still loves the church, we should too!

## GOD'S WILL FOR EVERYONE

**1 Thessalonians 5:16-18** — *"Rejoice always; pray without ceasing; in everything give thanks; for this is God's will for you in Christ Jesus."*

God has a specific plan for every Christian. His will is "good, acceptable, and perfect" (Romans 12:2). It is "good" in that it will bless us, "acceptable" in that we should willingly embrace it, and "perfect" because it comes from the heart and hand of our divine, heavenly Father. God also has a general will for *all* believers represented in His Scriptural commands. Three of those are mentioned in our text.

**Be Joyful at All Times.** "Rejoice always." Christians cannot lose their salvation, but they can lose the *joy* of salvation (Psalm 51:12). God refills us with His joy, an aspect of the fruit of His Spirit (Galatians 5:22-23). That joy strengthens us (Nehemiah 8:10). We should rejoice always despite our circumstances (Philippians 4:4).

**Be Prayerful at All Times.** "Pray without ceasing." We cannot become spiritual hermits, but, as The New Living Translation renders this phrase, we can "keep on praying." We are to live in a constant attitude of prayer (Colossians 4:2). Such intimate communication is what Jesus had in mind when He told us to abide in Him (John 15).

**Be Thankful at All Times.** "In everything give thanks." We are not to thank God *for* all things, but we are to thank Him *in* all things, knowing that He is able to work all that happens in our lives for good (Romans 8:28). He works miracles for those who praise Him even in the midst of tragedy and difficulty (Acts 16:25-26).

God desires for every Christian to be joyful, prayerful, and thankful at all times. Whoever knows God's will but refuses to do it is living in sin (James 4:17). Obey these simple, small, yet powerful commands today. After all, they are His will for you!

## THE CROWD AT THE CROSS

**John 19:17-20** — *"They took Jesus, therefore, and He went out, bearing His own cross, to the place called the Place of a Skull, which is called in Hebrew, Golgotha. There they crucified Him, and with him two other men, one on either side, and Jesus in between. Pilate also wrote an inscription and put it on the cross. It was written, 'JESUS THE NAZARENE, THE KING OF THE JEWS.' Therefore many of the Jews read this inscription, for the place where Jesus was crucified was near the city; and it was written in Hebrew, Latin and in Greek."*

Jesus was crucified in a public place for all to see. Who witnessed His death? First of all, the *two thieves* were there. One trusted Him for salvation while the other rejected Him (Luke 23:39-43). They represent all of mankind – saved or lost. Some *religious leaders* were present. The chief priests, scribes, and elders delighted in Jesus' death, hurling abuse at Him (Matthew 27:41-43). Some *Roman soldiers* were there. They routinely nailed Jesus to the cross and cast lots for His garments, indifferent to His pain and suffering. A few of His *disciples* were present. Jesus asked John to care for His aging mother, Mary (John 19:26-27). Mary Magdalene also witnessed His death (John 19:25). Surely Peter and others looked on "at a distance" (Matthew 26:58). *Mary*, Jesus' mother was there along with relatives (John 19:25). She had stood by Him as a baby, as a boy, throughout His life, and refused to leave Him at His death. Other *people* were there. Many had heard Jesus preach and had seen Him perform miracles. *God the Father* was there. Jesus prayed to Him from the cross (Luke 23:34, 46). Finally, *you and I* were there. Our sins nailed Jesus to the cross (Isaiah 53:6) and His love kept Him there.

As you think about those who were with Jesus at Golgotha, include yourself. Then thank the Lord for what He did for you on that day. When He was on the cross, you were not only on His mind – you were actually there!

## THE SWEETEST WORDS YOU WILL EVER HEAR

**Matthew 9:2** — *"And they brought to Him a paralytic lying on a bed. Seeing their faith, Jesus said to the paralytic, 'Take courage, son; your sins are forgiven.'"*

Words are powerful. They can make us laugh or cry. They can bring encouragement or discouragement. They can give hope or shatter dreams. What are the sweetest words you have ever heard? Perhaps your spouse spoke them at your wedding. Perhaps they were the first words of a child. The sweetest words I have ever heard are the words of our text. Like the paralytic, I heard Jesus say, "Son, your sins are forgiven."

The first time I heard those words, I was eighteen years old. I was a lost church member. I had joined the church as a boy, been baptized, and attended Sunday School, children's and youth choir. My dad was a deacon and my mom was a Sunday School teacher. But if I had died, I would have gone straight to hell. Then a wonderful thing happened during my freshman year of college. Some friends invited me to attend their meetings of the Fellowship of Christian Athletes. They later invited me to a revival service at a small, country church. The pastor preached that night, and I gave my heart to Jesus. I knelt down lost, prayed to Him, and stood up saved! I did not hear an audible voice, but in my spirit I heard Jesus say, "Take courage, son; your sins are forgiven."

If I live to be one hundred, I know that I have already heard the sweetest words I will ever hear. They still ring in my ear, and they will echo eternally in my soul as I walk hand in hand with the blessed One who spoke them – Jesus. He is a wonderful Savior. Has He spoken these sweet words to you? If so, rejoice today in His grace and mercy. Forget your past. It is under His blood. Move on from here assured of His forgiveness.

## THE LOVE OF GOD

**John 3:16** — *"For God so loved the world, that He gave His only begotten Son, that whoever believes in Him shall not perish, but have eternal life."*

John 3:16. For years I could quote it, but I had a hard time believing it. How could God love someone as sinful as *me*? I thought that God might love me more if I was more dedicated. So I spent more and more time reading my Bible, praying, fasting, witnessing, and memorizing Scripture. Then God began to show me that nothing I could do would make Him love me either more or less. He loved me simply because He chose to love me.

God's love is *divine*. "For *God* so loved." He initiates a love affair with every person on earth. That love originates in *His* heart. Those who love Him do so because He loved first (1 John 4:10, 19). God's love is *intense*. "God *so* loved." He loves us passionately, earnestly, and enthusiastically. We are His supreme creation, made in His image, and He loves us more than anything else He has created. His love is *universal*. "God so loved *the world*." God loves men, women, boys, girls, Hispanics, Orientals, blacks, whites, rich, poor, educated, uneducated, Baptists, Methodists, haves and have-nots. He loves *you*. God's love is *sacrificial*. "He *gave* His only begotten Son." God demonstrated His love when Jesus died for our sins (Romans 5:8). He did not just *say* He loved us; He *showed* us He loved us! God's love is *demanding*. "That whoever *believes* in Him." No one can be neutral about Jesus. A person must trust Him for salvation, or reject Him. God's love is *rewarding*. "Shall not perish, but have *eternal life*." The reward for trusting Jesus is abundant (John 10:10), everlasting life (John 14:1-6).

Imagine – God loves you. Your deeds cannot make Him love you more, or less. He has chosen to love you by His grace. By faith accept and enjoy His great love today.

## LIFTING HOLY HANDS

**1 Timothy 2:8** — *"Therefore I want the men in every place to pray, lifting up holy hands, without wrath and dissension."*

The worship service began. I was a new Christian. As we sang, several people closed their eyes and lifted their hands to the Lord in worship. Though it seemed awkward at the time, I joined them and immediately sensed an unusual intimacy with God that I had not known before. What does the Bible say about lifting holy hands?

**It Is Biblical.** Scripture refers to it frequently. "My lips will praise You...I will *lift up my hands* in Your name" (Psalm 63:3-4). "May my prayer be counted as incense before You; the *lifting up of my hands* as the evening offering" (Psalm 141:2). "I *stretch out my hands to You*; My soul longs for You, as a parched land" (Psalm 143:6). At His ascension, Jesus *"lifted up His hands"* and prayed over His disciples (Luke 24:50).

**It Is Sacred.** We are to lift "holy" hands to the Lord. To "ascend the hill of the LORD" requires "clean hands" (Psalm 24:3-4). We are also commanded to lift up our hands "without wrath and dissension." We must be right with both God and man.

**It Is Expressive.** Our hands are the most expressive parts of our body. When we lift holy hands to the Lord, we express *surrender* because it is a sign of yielding to a stronger person. We express *intimacy* like a young child lifting his hands to a parent. We express *respect* like a soldier saluting his superior. We also express *sacrifice* like a worshiper who offered up a sacrificial animal onto the altar with his arms extended.

Lifting holy hands is a wonderful, biblical form of worship for all Christians. It is to be done "in every place." Practice it in your prayer closet first and then in corporate worship. As you reverently reach up to Him, the Lord will lovingly reach down to you!

## THE NEEDY AND THE STRANGER

**Leviticus 19:9-10** — *"Now when you reap the harvest of your land, you shall not reap to the very corners of your field, nor shall you gather the gleanings of your harvest. Nor shall you glean your vineyard, nor shall you gather the fallen fruit of your vineyard; you shall leave them for the needy and for the stranger. I am the LORD your God."*

I sat in a young adult Sunday School class filled with affluent couples. The church was a different denomination than my own. I was an out of town guest, so I tried to remain low key. The class president began to try to raise an offering to send two orphan children to a summer camp. The class goal was $100. I saw men and women, most all of whom were wearing very expensive suits, give one to two dollars per couple. I whispered to my friend with whom we were staying, "I'll give fifty; you give the other half." He said, "What?!?" I said, "They are *orphans*! Pay up!" We gave and the "goal" (which should have been $1,000 for that bunch) was met. Some people can be stingy!

God had a built-in welfare program in the Promised Land. His people were not supposed to harvest all of their crops. Instead, they were to leave part of them in "the corners of (their) fields," as well as "the gleanings" (i.e. the leftover grain) for "the needy and the stranger." That is why Boaz allowed Ruth the Moabitess to "glean" in his fields (Ruth 2). God took care of the needy and the strangers, and He used His people to do it.

Today it is interesting to hear some people, especially politicians, talk about how much they want to help the poor, only to discover that they often give virtually nothing to charitable organizations, including their churches. How is your "charitable giving?" A portion of every paycheck you earn should go to those less fortunate. Many reputable charities, especially Christian groups, need your financial support. Do not be selfish. Your "gleanings" can still help "the needy and the strangers." You will never miss it.

## LEAVE AND CLEAVE

**Genesis 2:24** — _"For this reason a man shall leave his father and his mother, and be joined to his wife; and they shall become one flesh."_

Marriage is precious in the sight of God. He Himself performed the first wedding ceremony in the Garden of Eden. He escorted the first bride, Eve, down the first aisle, giving her away to the first groom, Adam. Moses commented on it in our text.

**A Married Person Must "Leave."** A husband and wife must "leave" their parents. That does not mean that they must move far away from them (although that might often prove helpful!). Rather, to "leave" means to transfer their primary loyalties from their parents to their new spouse. What their spouse desires and thinks is more important than what their parents desire and think. Married couples who "leave" their parents, in the biblical sense, are paving the way for a healthy marital union.

**A Married Person Must "Cleave."** After a married person "leaves" his parents, he must "cleave" to his spouse. This refers partially to the sexual union (see v. 25), but to cleave also means to be united emotionally and romantically as well as sexually. When it comes to cleaving, a couple must be careful to seek balance. On one hand, they must not smother each other. On the other hand, neither spouse should continue to live like he or she is still single. Their marriage must take priority over other friendships, hobbies, etc. Like two guitar strings playing harmoniously side-by-side, they are to operate in unison.

Someone once told me, "If couples don't 'leave' and 'cleave,' they will soon 'grieve.'" How true! In order to experience true intimacy and fulfillment in marriage, we must follow these God-given principals. Failure to do so will prevent the Lord from building our homes. We will then be laboring in vain trying to build them ourselves.

## PERPETUAL PRAISE

**Psalm 113:3** — *"From the rising of the sun to its setting the name of the LORD is to be praised."*

Years ago the people of England enjoyed boasting about the vastness of their empire by saying, "The sun never sets on the British Empire." Today that empire, like many before and after it, has faded in prominence. There is, however, an eternal kingdom that covers the entire earth. It is the kingdom of God within the hearts of those who know Jesus Christ as Lord and Savior. The sun never rises or sets anywhere without shining upon the loyal subjects of Christ who give Him perpetual praise. It may be under a tree in Africa, in a hut in Mongolia, in an apartment in Moscow, on a farm in Iowa, or in the projects of Chicago, but someone somewhere is praising King Jesus.

That song of perpetual praise began at creation. Adam sang it in Eden's Garden when he married Eve. Abel sang it when God accepted his sacrifice. Enoch sang it as he walked with God. Noah sang it as he sailed aboard the ark. Abraham sang it on Mt. Moriah. Moses sang it at the Red Sea. Joshua sang it at Jericho. David sang it when he slew Goliath. Elijah sang it as fire fell on Mt. Carmel. Daniel sang it in the lion's den. Peter sang it at Pentecost. Paul and Silas sang it in the Philippian jail. John sang it exiled on the Isle of Patmos. Luther sang it through the Reformation. Whitefield, Wesley, and Edwards sang it during the Great Awakening. Spurgeon sang it in London, while Moody sang it in Chicago. Billy Graham has sung it in great stadiums around the world.

Have you joined in this song of praise? Once Jesus redeems you, He places His song in your heart and you begin to give Him perpetual praise. Do not allow anyone or anything to keep you from singing to Jesus the eternal song of the ransomed and free.

## EVANGELIZING YOUR WORLD

**Acts 1:8** — _"But you will receive power when the Holy Spirit has come upon you; and you shall be My witnesses both in Jerusalem, and in all Judea and Samaria, and even to the remotest part of the earth."_

God loves all people and desires to save them (1 Timothy 2:3-4). He has commissioned His Church to evangelize the entire world. Before ascending back to heaven, Jesus told His followers to evangelize their world. How can we do that today?

**The People of Evangelism.** World evangelization is the responsibility of every Christian, not just the pastors, staff members, missionaries, evangelists, teachers, and deacons. All followers of Christ are commanded to share His Gospel verbally with lost people they encounter every day. Failure to do so is high treason against heaven itself.

**The Power for Evangelism.** The Holy Spirit empowers Christians to witness effectively. He indwells all believers (Romans 8:9; 1 Corinthians 12:13). As we stay filled with the Spirit (Ephesians 5:18), operating in His power, He convicts (John 16:8) and converts the lost (Titus 3:5). Effective evangelism requires the Holy Spirit's power.

**The Pattern for Evangelism.** We should follow the pattern given by Jesus in our text in order to evangelize our world. We must begin at our "Jerusalem" by witnessing to family, friends, and neighbors. We must then go to our "Judea and Samaria" and witness to those living near us and those of other races. We then can reach "the ends of the earth" by giving to missions' offerings, praying for missionaries, and going on mission trips.

At the age of 70, my father-in-law was trained in evangelism. He began to share Christ and people began to get saved. That is the way it works! Ask the Lord to lay the "lostness" of this world on your heart. It is not too late to begin evangelizing your world.

## GOD'S WORD IN YOUR HOME

**Deuteronomy 6:6-9** — *"These words, which I am commanding you today, shall be on your heart. You shall teach them diligently to your sons and shall talk of them when you sit in your house and when you walk by the way and when you lie down and when you rise up. You shall bind them as a sign on your hand and they shall be as frontals on your forehead. You shall write them on the door-posts of your house and on your gates."*

God loves the institution of the family. He created it before He formed the Church. Families that build upon the foundation of the Bible will survive the fierce storms of life. Therefore, God tells families to honor His Word. How can we do that?

**Meditate on God's Word.** "These words...shall be on your heart." God wants us to read, study, memorize, and meditate on His written Word. Husbands and wives, as well as parents and children should spend time absorbing Scripture. It must take priority over television, videos, music, and any other form of entertainment and recreation.

**Teach God's Word.** "Teach them diligently to your sons." Churches should assist, but parents are primarily responsible for teaching their children the Bible. They must teach it *diligently*, making it a priority, and also teach it *daily*. At home or on a trip, they should discuss the Bible. It must become a natural part of family conversations, affecting both actions ("sign on your hand") and thoughts ("frontals on your fore-head").

**Display God's Word.** "Write them on the doorposts of your house and on your gates." Scripture must be displayed in our homes. Plaques with Bible verses should be placed strategically in every room. Children will long retain the Word they see at home.

If you want to strengthen your family, build it on the foundation of Scripture. Make God's Word, the Bible, a centerpiece for your family's daily life. Meditate on it, teach it, and display it. That is the best way to pass your faith on to the next generation.

## RESPONDING TO SINNERS

**John 8:10-11** — _"Straightening up, Jesus said to her, 'Woman, where are they? Did no one condemn you?' She said, 'No one, Lord.' And Jesus said, 'I do not condemn you, either. Go. From now on sin no more.'"_

A politician is exposed for corruption. A church leader falls into sin. A college athlete is found guilty of taking steroids. How do you respond when secret sin is exposed? Do you throw stones of condemnation, or do you extend mercy like Jesus?

**Liberalism.** Liberalism, the response of the Sadducees, would have said to the woman caught in adultery, "I do not condemn you, either," but would not have added, "Go. From now on sin no more." It tries to lift up fallen sinners without also lifting up the standard of God's Word. It loves sinners but does not hate sin. It is a poor response.

**Legalism.** Legalism would have said, "Go. From now on sin no more," but it would not have added, "I do not condemn you, either." It tries to lift up the standard of God's Word without also lifting up fallen sinners. It hates sin without loving sinners. It was the Pharisees' response, whom Jesus rebuked. It values religion, not God's mercy.

**Love.** Jesus responded to the woman with love. He said, "I do not condemn you, either," and then added, "Go. From now on sin no more." Jesus lifted up both the sinner _and_ the standard of God's Word. He loved the sinner while He hated the sin. That is how Jesus treats us when we sin, and it is how we ought to treat other sinners also.

If a bridge is out, we must first care for the victims who have plunged into the ravine. But we must also warn others not to run off the bridge. That balance is the response of love, and _that_ is how we must respond to sinners. May we, like Jesus, love and lift up fallen sinners, and may we also encourage and warn them not to fall again.

## WHOM WILL YOU SERVE?

**Joshua 24:15** — *"If it is disagreeable in your sight to serve the LORD, choose for yourselves today whom you will serve: whether the gods which your fathers served which were beyond the River, or the gods of the Amorites in whose land you are living; but as for me and my house, we will serve the LORD."*

Man is incurably religious. We all worship something. Travel to any place in the world and you will discover evidence of man's religious nature. Mongolia has its hilltop altars, England has the rocks of Stonehenge, and Wall Street has its modern "golden calf" – a bull. These have been places where people worship idols. What are you worshiping?

Joshua was an old man. In his younger years he had led the people of God across the Jordan River into the Promised Land of Canaan. As the Israelites conquered the cities, they were exposed to many pagan cultures with various religious practices. Some of the Israelites eventually intermingled socially and religiously with the Canaanites. In our text, Joshua warned them of the dangers of idolatry. He challenged them to serve either the pagan gods their fathers had served before they entered the Promised Land, or the gods of the Amorites and the other inhabitants of the land where they were living. But these were not valid options for Joshua. He made a brave decision and a bold declaration. He and his family would serve the Lord – Jehovah! He took a stand for the Lord against paganism, and the people took notice.

The Lord is calling us to stand for Him in this generation. We must not blindly embrace the religious traditions of our ancestors if they are unbiblical. We must reject the pagan beliefs of humanism, atheism, or agnosticism, and shun cults like the Jehovah's Witnesses and Mormons. We must stand for Jesus Christ with our families, worshiping and serving Him alone. We will all worship someone. Whom will it be? Decide today.

## No Place For The Devil

**Ephesians 4:27** — *"And do not give the devil an opportunity."*

Satan is a diabolical adversary. He prowls about seeking someone to devour (1 Peter 5:8). He does all he can to prevent non-Christians from receiving eternal life in Christ. He also attacks Christians. Though he can never snatch us from God's hand and steal our salvation (John 10:27-29), he tries to enslave us with strongholds of sin. If allowed, he will use a Christian's disobedience to bring shame on the name of Jesus.

How can we overcome Satan? A lost person can only defeat him by surrendering to Jesus and becoming a Christian. A saved person can defeat him by utilizing spiritual weapons and biblical strategy in spiritual warfare. Our text tells us not to give the devil an "opportunity." The word means "place or foothold" (Greek *topos*). When we walk obediently with the Lord, Satan has no "place" in our lives. However, when we refuse to confess and forsake our sins, the Lord does not forgive us, we exist in a state of spiritual rebellion, and we give the devil a foothold to oppress and harass us. The devil cannot possess a Christian's spirit, but he can and will torment a believer mentally, emotionally, spiritually, and even physically if sin is stubbornly harbored and remains unconfessed. Until we get rid of the sin, we will not get rid of the devil's oppression.

Are you tired of Satan's harassment? If you are lost, repent and trust Jesus to save you. If you are saved, allow no unconfessed, unforsaken sin in your life. Confess it, repent of it, and renounce it right now. Jesus *will* forgive you (Proverbs 28:13; 1 John 1:9). Do not endure Satan's oppression another day. Take back the ground you have given him. Then post a permanent sign on your heart that says: "No Place for the Devil!"

## CHOSEN IN HIM

**Ephesians 1:4-5** — *"Just as He chose us in Him before the foundation of the world, that we would be holy and blameless before Him. In love He predestined us to adoption as sons through Jesus Christ to Himself, according to the kind intention of His will."*

What does the Bible mean when it says that Christians are chosen? Some say that it implies that before time began, God predestined some people to go to heaven and others to go to hell. But is that biblical doctrine, or is it fatalism? Dual predestination seems to deny the biblical concept of man's will. Is there another valid option?

When the Bible says that man is chosen or elected by God, it clearly qualifies that concept with the words "in Christ." For instance, in our text Paul says that God the Father chose Christians "in Him (Christ) before the foundation of the world." They were "predestined...to adoption" as God's children "through Jesus Christ." In other words, God did not choose individuals to be saved before they were born. Rather, He predetermined that everyone who would receive salvation would do so "in" or "through Christ." God chose a *plan* for salvation, not specific *people* whom He would save.

On several occasions I spoke with the late Baptist pastor, author, and theologian, Dr. Herschel Hobbs about our text. He gave an illustration, saying that it was as though God built a fence and that fence was Christ. All who enter that fence are saved because they are "in Christ." All who willfully remain outside that fence (i.e. Christ) are lost. The plan of salvation is predetermined, but the people who are actually saved are not.

God wants to save *all* people, not just some (1 Timothy 2:3-4). He never coerces anyone to be saved. Rather, He chooses those who choose His Son, Jesus. All who repent and believe on Christ will go to heaven. Why? Because we are chosen *in Him!*

## A GLIMPSE OF GLORY

**2 Corinthians 12:2-4** — *"I know a man in Christ who fourteen years ago – whether in the body I do not know, or out of the body I do not know, God knows – such a man was caught up to the third heaven. And I know how such a man – whether in the body or apart from the body I do not know, God knows – was caught up into Paradise and heard inexpressible words, which a man is not permitted to speak."*

The hospital room was dark and silent as my grandmother lay in the coma she had been in for several days. As my mother and aunt sat at her bedside, the door opened. My aunt's pastor, Adrian Rogers, had come with one of his deacons to visit and pray. After sharing Scripture, they joined hands and prayed for my "Granny" to slip peacefully into heaven. After they prayed, she sat up in bed with eyes wide open cooing like a dove – "Oooooh! Ahhhh!" Someone said, "She sees daddy!" Dr. Rogers responded, "No, she sees Jesus!" Everyone agreed. She never said another word. She lay down, and soon was with Jesus. But before she died, God allowed her to see a precious glimpse of glory.

In our text, Paul spoke of a man who had a glimpse of glory. Later in the text, he acknowledged that *he* was that man (v. 7). He was transported into Paradise. There he saw sights and heard sounds too holy to discuss. It changed his life forever. God had to give Paul a "thorn in the flesh" to prevent him from becoming proud spiritually. From then on, more than ever before, he lived totally abandoned to Jesus. Once he had seen the glories of heaven and the precious face of Jesus, this world lost its grip on him forever.

You may never catch a glimpse of the glories of heaven before you die as Paul did, but you can know for certain that heaven will be your home. If you have been born again, your name is in the book of life. You will not only get a *glimpse* of heaven's glory, but you will have the joy of *gazing* at Jesus, the true glory of God, forevermore!

## THE HOUSE WHERE GOD LIVES

**Isaiah 56:7** — *"Even those I will bring to My holy mountain and make them joyful in My house of prayer. Their burnt offerings and their sacrifices will be acceptable on My altar; for My house will be called a house of prayer for all the peoples."*

God does not live in temples made by human hands (Acts 7:48-49). He dwells in heaven (Psalm 11:4), within the bodies of individual Christians (1 Corinthians 6:19), and among His people who gather in His name to worship Him corporately (Matthew 18:20; 1 Corinthians 3:16). Since we are His house, what kind of "house" should we be?

We should be a house of *holiness*. God's temple must be "holy." He expects His people to be filled with His *Holy* Spirit and obey His commands. We are to be holy as He is holy (1 Peter 1:15-16). We should be a house of *joy*. God promised to make us "joyful" in His house. Christians should be full of joy. Our worship services should not be dull and boring. We are to shout to God, sing to Him joyfully, and serve Him with gladness (Psalm 100). His joy strengthens us (Nehemiah 8:10). We should be a house of *giving*. God spoke of "burnt offerings and sacrifices" being acceptable in His house. He wants us to give financially in a joyful manner (2 Corinthians 9:7) and become kingdom investors. We should be a house of *prayer*. God referred twice to His house as a "house of prayer." Prayer must become our priority (Colossians 4:2). When we pray, we see what *God* can do. Finally, we should be a house of *outreach*. God's house is for "all the peoples." Everyone who desires to worship Him through Jesus is welcome in His house.

God does not dwell in a building. He lives within redeemed humanity. When Christians assemble in His name, He manifests His presence. We will become the house that He desires when we come together with holiness, joy, giving, prayer, and outreach.

## JESUS, THE DOOR TO HEAVEN

**John 10:9** — _"I am the door; if anyone enters through Me, he will be saved, and will go in and out and find pasture."_

When I was young we had hardwood floors in our living room and main hallway. My brother and I loved to put on thick, white socks and run and slide across those floors. My parents eventually carpeted those areas, ruining our recreation! After the carpet was laid, my mother required everyone to enter our house through the back door in order to protect the carpet. _The_ way to enter our house was the back door. And woe to the foolish person that tried to enter any other way!

God has a specific way or "door" that people must enter if they want to enter His house in heaven. That door is His only begotten Son, Jesus Christ. Jesus referred to Himself as _the_ door. All who enter through Him receive God's merciful gift of salvation. All who refuse to do so will not be saved. Salvation is simple. In order to be forgiven of your sins, have a relationship with God, and go to heaven after you die, you must enter through Jesus Christ, God's door. You enter that door by repenting of your sin and trusting Jesus alone as your Savior. He is not the _best_ way to God; He is the _only_ way.

The Bible says that you can come close to heaven but miss it completely. Think of it – Judas, who betrayed Jesus for thirty pieces of silver, actually kissed Jesus on the cheek in the Garden of Gethsemane at Jesus' arrest. But Judas later died without being saved. He kissed the door to heaven and still went to hell!

Have you entered God's door to salvation? Have you surrendered your life completely to Jesus in repentance and faith? If so, you have walked into the wonderful realm of salvation. Enjoy God's blessings today as you go in and out of His refreshing pastures of abundant, everlasting life.

## THE HUMAN HEART

**Jeremiah 17:9** — *"The heart is more deceitful than all else and is desperately sick; who can understand it?"*

Is man good or evil by nature?  Is the human heart inclined toward righteousness or iniquity?  Do we gravitate naturally toward holiness or rebellion?  Are we innately sinners or saints?  What does the Bible say about the condition of man's heart?

**The Human Heart Is Deceptive.**  "The heart is more *deceitful* than all else."  "Deceitful" means "insidious."  A good slang word would be "sneaky."  The human heart is not naturally good.  Rather, it is subtle and sly, filled with trickery, fraud, and cunning guile.  Our hearts deceive others and are more than capable of deceiving us as well.

**The Human Heart Is Diseased.**  "The heart...is desperately *sick*."  Our hearts are infected with sin.  Jesus said, "From *within*, out of *the heart of men*, proceed the evil thoughts, fornications, thefts, murders, adulteries, deeds of coveting and wickedness, as well as deceit, sensuality, envy, slander, pride, and foolishness.  All these evil things proceed from *within* and defile the man" (Mark 7:21-23).  Our hearts need to be healed.

**The Human Heart Is Dumbfounding.**  "The heart...*who can understand it*?"  Someone might say, "I know my heart," but the fact is only God knows a person's heart (Jeremiah 17:10).  His Word is able to "judge the thoughts and intentions of the heart" (Hebrews 4:12).  He knows us better than we know ourselves.  He knows our hearts.

Man is a sinner by nature, prone to rebel against God.  Our hearts are deceptive, diseased, and dumbfounding.  Only God understands them, and only He can cleanse and change them by giving us a spiritual "heart transplant" through salvation (Ezekiel 36:26; John 3:3, 5).  Guard and take care of your heart.  Your life depends on it (Proverbs 4:23).

## PRIORITIES FOR GOD'S PEOPLE

**Mark 3:14-15** — _"And He appointed twelve, so that they would be with Him and that He could send them out to preach, and to have authority to cast out the demons."_

God wants every believer to live a disciplined life. Without discipline, we will live without purpose. Anyone can develop discipline by establishing priorities. Jesus had three priorities for His apostles, and they are still appropriate for Christians today.

**Worship.** "And He appointed twelve, so that they would _be with Him._" Jesus chose men who enjoyed His presence. He desired to _be_ with them, and wanted them to desire Him. God desires the same for us. He does not need our money, talents, or skills. He has set a table for two and invites us to dine daily with Him (Revelation 3:20).

**Witnessing.** "And He appointed twelve...that He _could send them out to preach._" These disciples witnessed after they worshiped. Spending time with Jesus caused them to desire to tell others about Him. Likewise, when we truly worship Him, we will desire to witness to a lost world. We talk about those we love. Whoever loves Jesus will tell others about Him. Passionate worship leads to compassionate witnessing.

**Warfare.** "And He appointed twelve...to have _the authority to cast out the demons._" These early disciples preached and then cast out evil spirits. They were authorized, or "deputized," by Jesus to tread upon serpents and scorpions (demons), and overcome all the power of the enemy (Luke 10:19). Believers have that same authority today. When we submit to God, we can resist the devil, and he _must_ flee (James 4:7)!

What are your priorities? Nothing could be more important than being with Jesus, telling others about Him, and helping them find freedom from satanic bondage. Embrace the apostles' priorities, and you too will turn your world upside down for Christ!

## BLOOD ON OUR HANDS

**Ezekiel 3:17-19** — *"Son of man, I have appointed you a watchman to the house of Israel; whenever you hear a word from My mouth, warn them from Me. When I say to the wicked, 'You shall surely die,' and you do not warn him or speak out to warn the wicked from his wicked way that he may live, that wicked man shall die in his iniquity, but his blood I will require at your hand. Yet if you have warned the wicked and he does not turn from his wickedness or from his wicked way, he shall die in his iniquity; but you have delivered yourself."*

We sat in the living room of a couple that had visited our church. After a few minutes, I asked them about their relationship with Jesus Christ and began to share with them how to become a Christian. I shared the Gospel politely, compassionately, and persuasively. When I finished, I asked if they would like to receive Jesus as their Savior. They respectfully declined. We courteously concluded the conversation and left.

On the way back to the church, the two church members who had gone with me were quiet. Finally one of them broke the silence and said, "Preacher, you were a little pushy with those people, weren't you? Why didn't you just invite them back to church and leave it at that?" I replied, "I *never* visit prospects to simply invite them to church. I *always* share the Gospel with them, and if I believe they are lost I try to win them to Christ. Jesus might return today, or one of them might die before he or she can come back to church. Go home and read Ezekiel 3:17-19 and you will see why I did what I did." That night they met me at church and said, "Pastor, you were right. If you had not witnessed to them, their blood would have been on your hands."

We must be willing to share the Gospel with lost people. Their souls are literally in the balance. We do not want to stand before Jesus with their blood on our hands. Obey the Spirit's prompting to witness. He who wins souls is wise (Proverbs 11:30).

## THE KISS OF FORGIVENESS

**Luke 15:20** — *"So he got up and came to his father. But while he was still a long way off, his father saw him and felt compassion for him, and ran and embraced him and kissed him."*

What is in a kiss? Kissing has always been an expression of love and affection. Married couples seal their wedding vows with a kiss. Likewise, the early Christians employed "a holy kiss" as a means of displaying brotherly love (Romans 16:16).

Our text speaks of a special kiss. The background is the parable of the prodigal son. In that story, the younger of two sons left his father, went to a distant country, and squandered his inheritance on sinful living. When he ran out of money, he was forced to feed swine. He became so hungry that he desired pig slop. No one gave him anything.

One day he "came to His senses." He decided to return home and apologize to his father. He planned to ask his father to take him back as a servant, not a son. His humility was indicative of his genuine repentance. He got up and started the long journey home. When the father went out that day and looked down the road, he saw a man approaching. Could it be his son? His boy had left with many possessions. This man walked alone and empty-handed. His boy had left healthy and well clothed. This man was hollow-eyed, thin, and in rags. But while the boy was still "a long way off," the father "*saw* him," "*felt compassion* for him," "*ran*" to him, "*embraced*" him, and "*kissed* him." *That* was the kiss of forgiveness! Though he did not deserve it, the father gave merciful grace.

If you have gone to the distant country of sin, God wants you to come home. The devil guarantees steak but serves slop. Come back to the Father today. Let Him kiss you with unconditional love, mercy, and forgiveness. You were created to live in His house.

## SPEAK TO THE MOUNTAIN

**Mark 11:22-23** — *"And Jesus answered saying to them, 'Have faith in God. Truly I say to you, whoever says to this mountain, "Be taken up and cast into the sea," and does not doubt in his heart, but believes that what he says is going to happen, it will be granted him.'"*

God is able to handle any problem we face. He knows how to slay every Goliath that attacks us. He owns the cattle on a thousand hills if we have a financial need. The Lord is still able to heal us when we are sick. He still serves manna to the hungry, and brings water out of the rock for those who are thirsty. In short, God is *still* God!

As Jesus entered Jerusalem one day, He saw a fruitless fig tree and cursed it. The next day when He and His disciples passed by, they marveled that it had completely withered. Jesus used that occasion to teach His disciples how to move any problem, or "mountain," they would face. To see a mountain moved, they needed to trust in God and speak to the mountain in faith. That simple act would move God's hand, cause the mountain's foundations to crumble, and it would be uprooted and cast into the sea.

God is able to move any mountain you face today. If you have the faith, He has the power. Stop focusing on the mountain, and start focusing on Jesus, the Mountain Mover. Ask Him to give you a "word," or promise, from Scripture to build your faith. Then, *speak* that word to your mountain! Tell it to be uprooted and moved in Jesus' name. Put your trust in Him, pray, and verbalize God's Word. God is great and good, omnipotent and gracious. He still works wonders for those who believe in His power, stand on His Word, and speak in faith to the obstacles they confront. May your faith be strengthened today. The Lord is still alive and able to relocate mountains into the sea!

# A GUARDED MOUTH

**Psalm 141:3** — _"Set a guard, O LORD, over my mouth; keep watch over the door of my lips."_

A wise person once said, "God gave us two ears and one mouth. If we will listen twice as much as we talk, we will excel in life." The Psalmist prayed for a divine guard to be placed over his mouth. He asked God to post the sentinel of His Spirit at the door of his lips to make sure that his every word glorified God. God wants to guard and guide our words as well. He changes us by altering our speech. How can we guard our mouths?

**We Should Avoid Words of Destruction.** The Holy Spirit watches over our mouths by encouraging us to refrain from sinful speech. He leads us to abstain from gossip and slander, as well as from speaking foul language, curse words, or questionable jokes. He always prompts us to use words in keeping with His holy and pure character.

**We Should Extend Words of Edification.** Harsh words tear down; good words edify and build up. Death and life are literally in the power of our tongues (Proverbs 18:21). Our words should give confidence to people rather than degrade them. We must ask the Lord to help us speak "a word in season" to the one who is weary (Isaiah 50:4).

**We Should Lift Up Words of Adoration.** The best usage of our tongues is to praise the Lord. God gives people breath to praise Him (Psalm 150:6), not to curse Him, complain, or be negative. We must offer the sacrifice of praise, the fruit of our lips, and give thanks to Jesus (Hebrews 13:15). We must praise Him _from_ our hearts _with_ our lips.

Do not underestimate the power and importance of words. God will judge every useless word you speak. By them you will be justified or condemned (Matthew 12:36-37). Let God set the sentry of His Spirit over your lips. He alone can tame your tongue.

## FOR FUTURE GENERATIONS

**Isaiah 59:21** — *"'As for Me, this is My covenant with them,' says the LORD: 'My Spirit which is upon you, and My words which I have put in your mouth shall not depart from your mouth, nor from the mouth of your offspring, nor from the mouth of your offspring's offspring,' says the LORD, 'from now and forever.'"*

God has a plan for your future. Most people either live in the past or become overwhelmed by present circumstances. Not God. He is concerned about today, but He is actively involved in determining tomorrow. That is especially true when it comes to reaching future generations with the Gospel of Jesus Christ. How can it happen?

**Pray for Future Generations.** We should pray for the next two generations – our children and grandchildren, and ask the Lord to give us scriptural promises that we can claim for their walk with Christ. As we bathe those future generations in prayer, God will pave the way for their salvation and spiritual growth in the years to come.

**Teach Future Generations.** God's Word is to be in our mouth, the mouths of our offspring, and the mouths of their offspring. We are to teach them the truths of the Bible. We must also set godly, Christlike examples for our children and grandchildren to follow. We must bring them up in the discipline and instruction of the Lord.

**Spend Time with Future Generations.** Spending time with our children and grandchildren must be a priority. We must be involved in their lives. We should avoid the temptation of spending too much time at the office, on the golf course, etc. Children grow up quickly. They need our time. Our investment in them will pay rich dividends.

Do you really want to impact the future? If so, make a positive spiritual impact on your children and grandchildren. Your greatest contribution to society should not be through your career, but through the godly generation you leave behind after you die.

## NO SHAME

**Isaiah 54:4** — _"Fear not, for you will not be put to shame; and do not feel humiliated, for you will not be disgraced; but you will forget the shame of your youth, and the reproach of your widowhood you will remember no more."_

Satan is like a boxer with a "one-two punch." He hits us first with _temptation_. Though he cannot make us sin, he entices us to do so by appealing to our fleshly nature. Once we yield to his temptation and commit sin, Satan then throws his second punch – _condemnation_. He actually condemns us for committing the very sin he tempted us with in the first place! He then proceeds to heap on us guilt, humiliation, and condemnation in order to torment us. Jesus Christ is the only One who can give victory over such shame.

Isaiah preached to the rebellious nation of Judah during a time when they had committed spiritual harlotry against the Lord by worshiping pagan idols in the land of Canaan. Isaiah spoke of a time when the people would repent and seek Jehovah's forgiveness. When they did, the Lord would redeem and deliver them from Satan's condemnation. They would "not be put to shame," thus they would no longer need to "feel humiliated." The Lord's mercy would prevent them from being "disgraced." Their former sins would be washed away so that they could "forget the shame of their youth," and "the reproach of (their) widowhood." In short, they would be delivered from shame.

Christ will do the same for us when we have been knocked down by Satan's "one-two punch" of temptation and condemnation. If we will run to the cross, repent of our sin, and confess it to Jesus, He will forgive, cleanse, and restore us. He will wipe away the basis for Satan's condemnation (Romans 8:1). Discouraged sinner, run to Christ. In Him there is no fear, no humiliation, no disgrace, no reproach, and above all, no shame!

## How To Slay A Giant

**1 Samuel 17:32** — *"David said to Saul, 'Let no man's heart fail on account of him; your servant will go and fight with this Philistine.'"*

Life is filled with challenges. We might call them "giants." David faced a giant named Goliath. He challenged Israel's army to a decisive dual. Whoever won would rule the opponent's nation. David killed Goliath, showing us how to slay our giants.

*Do Not Fear the Giant.* We must never give in to fear. Fear is not from God (2 Timothy 1:7). It short-circuits our faith and limits God's power. David feared God too much to be afraid of Goliath. David's mentality was "How dare he defy the army of the living God?" *Volunteer for the Fight.* Standing over nine feet tall, Goliath was quite intimidating. He was also a seasoned warrior. Even King Saul trembled in his presence. But David volunteered to fight him! That same brave spirit must be ours in any battle we face. *Use Your Own Talents.* Saul tried to force David to dress in his armor, but David refused. David chose stones, a sling, and a staff which he had used as a shepherd. In the same way, we must use our own gifts and talents to fight our giant, not the gifts of others. *Fight for God's Glory.* David shouted to Goliath, "I come to you in the Lord's name, that all the earth may know there is a God in Israel!" He fought for God's glory, not his own. Even so, our battles must bring honor to Him, not ourselves. *Run to the Battle.* When everyone ran away from Goliath, David ran toward him. They said, "He's too big to hit!" David said, "He's too big to miss!" We must confront our giant *head on* and not run away.

Regardless of what you face today, God desires to make you victorious. With Him on your side, you have all the power you need. Do not be intimidated. Run to the battle and engage the giant. One stone empowered by the Lord is an awesome weapon!

## THE WAY OUT

**Luke 9:30-31** — "*And behold, two men were talking with Him; and they were Moses and Elijah, who, appearing in glory, were speaking of His departure which He was about to accomplish at Jerusalem.*"

My wife and I once saw a movie about a group of mountain climbers that were overcome by an avalanche of snow. For several hours they were trapped in an icy cave before being located by a search team that made a daring rescue. The rescuers offered "the way out" to those desperate, dying people, and they were magnificently saved.

As Jesus prayed on a mountaintop one day, He was transfigured. His divine glory shone forth as Moses and Elijah appeared and talked with Him about His approaching "departure." That word in the Greek is *exodus*. *Ex* means "out of," and *odos* means "way." It was a reference to Jesus' death for sinners on the cross. The cross was Jesus' "exodus; way out of" this world! The only way He could go was by dying on the cross.

Christ's cross is our "way out" (exodus) too. When we come to Jesus for salvation, His cross cleanses us. The Jewish exodus from Egypt is a striking picture of salvation. In that exodus, God provided "the way out" by saving the Israelites. Likewise, God saves all those who come to Him through the exodus of the cross of His Son.

An old hymn says, "I must needs go home by the way of the cross, there's no other way but this; I shall ne'er get sight of the gates of light, if the way of the cross I miss. The way of the cross leads home!" Should Jesus tarry, you will depart from this world through death. Your only hope for spending eternity in heaven is the salvation that comes from Jesus' cross. Only through His shed blood can you be saved. The cross was Jesus' predetermined "way out" of this world. Make sure it is *your* way out as well.

## JEHOVAH-JIREH: THE LORD OUR PROVIDER

**Genesis 22:14** — *"Abraham called the name of that place The LORD Will Provide, as it is said to this day, 'In the mount of the LORD it will be provided.'"*

While in seminary, I had the privilege of hearing Pastor Manuel Scott preach in chapel. He told an illustrative story from his childhood. One day he asked his mother for a penny to buy a small sack of sugar cookies. His mother, however, did not have a penny to spare. Young Manuel took his "need" to the Lord, and asked God to help him find a penny. Walking along the sidewalks of Dallas, he suddenly spotted something. Someone had dropped a new penny on the ground. He looked up to heaven, thanked the Lord, ran to the store, and bought the cookies. All the way home he shouted, "Praise God, I found a penny!" From then on, he said, he never doubted that God would provide for him.

Abraham faced a severe test when God commanded him to sacrifice his son Isaac as a burnt offering. Though he did not understand, he faithfully obeyed God. When Isaac asked him where the lamb was for the sacrifice, Abraham, speaking in faith, said, "God will provide." He made the altar, bound his son, took the knife, and prepared to offer up Isaac. Suddenly a voice split the sky. God commanded Abraham to stop! He did not want Abraham to actually sacrifice Isaac. He simply wanted him to be willing to do so. Abraham looked up, saw a ram caught in a nearby thicket, and offered it in Isaac's place. He then named that mountain "The LORD Will Provide" (Hebrew *Jehovah-Jireh*)!

Child of God, do you have a need today? God is still able to provide for His children. He who blessed you with salvation will also meet your other needs (Romans 8:32). Do not worry about having enough. Rather, in faith, ask God to meet your needs. Then start looking around. The Lord's blessings always come at just the right time!

## THE PURPOSE OF TRIALS

**James 1:2-4** — _"Consider it all joy, my brethren, when you encounter various trials, knowing that the testing of your faith produces endurance. And let endurance have its perfect result, so that you may be perfect and complete, lacking in nothing."_

"My mother called and told me that my father just died." "The doctor diagnosed me today as having Muscular Dystrophy." "A good friend just told me that he and his wife have filed for divorce." What do we do with trials? God has a purpose for them.

**We Can Display Joy in Times of Trial.** We are to greet trials with "all (lit. supreme) joy." We can have "joy inexpressible" (1 Peter 1:8), like the early apostles did when they suffered for preaching the Gospel (Acts 5:40-41). Whenever we are squeezed by trouble, the joy of Jesus should come out. Lost people will see and take notice.

**We Can Develop Endurance in Times of Trial.** Times of testing produce "endurance." Endurance not only stubbornly withstands a trial, but also conquers it. Weight lifters break down the cells in their muscles. With rest, the muscles rebuild and grow back stronger and larger. Likewise, our trials build muscles of spiritual fortitude.

**We Can Demonstrate Maturity in Times of Trial.** "And let endurance have its perfect result, so that you may be perfect and complete, lacking in nothing." The word "perfect" refers to maturity. Trials help us grow in grace and in Christlikeness. When a believer is tested, it gives him the opportunity to respond maturely in faith and obedience.

Becoming a Christian does not exempt us from facing difficulties. We _will_ have tribulations in this world (John 16:33). Yet, Jesus is able to make us victorious. Are you discouraged by circumstances? Do not be. Count every difficulty as a glorious stepping-stone that will lead to joy, endurance, and maturity. God has a purpose in your trials.

## HIMPOSSIBLE

**Jeremiah 32:17** — *"Ah Lord GOD! Behold, You have made the heavens and the earth by Your great power and by Your outstretched arm! Nothing is too difficult for You."*

"Write down the word 'impossible' on a piece of paper. Now, write the letter 'H' in front of it." As I looked, it said *"Him*possible." In other words, what is impossible with man is possible when God takes control of any situation. Don Miller, from whom I have learned so much about prayer, had taught me a major lesson through his illustration.

The prophet Jeremiah had been commanded by the Lord to tell the people of Judah and Jerusalem that they would be defeated by the armies of Babylon and taken into captivity. Their idolatry and other iniquities had provoked the Lord to anger. He would discipline them using as His rod of correction a nation even more pagan and corrupt than they were. In the midst of those dismal, depressing days, God gave Jeremiah a promise as a ray of hope for Judah's future. Though the Babylonians had already constructed siege walls outside of Jerusalem and were literally starving the people to death, God told Jeremiah to purchase a piece of property that had belonged to one of his relatives. Then God told Jeremiah that after His people had been disciplined in captivity for a while, He would bring a remnant of them back to Jerusalem. There, they would again buy and sell land and live in freedom. In their hopelessness, God promised a better tomorrow. That promise would have been meaningless had an all-powerful God not given it.

There is nothing in your life that God cannot handle. All things are possible with Him (Luke 1:37; 18:27). Child of God, do not be discouraged today. Pray, obey God, and trust Him. Your problem may be too big for you, but with Jesus it is *Him*possible!

## WHERE HAVE ALL THE PREACHER'S GONE?

**2 Timothy 4:2-4** — _"Preach the word; be ready in season and out of season; reprove, rebuke, exhort, with great patience and instruction. For the time will come when they will not endure sound doctrine; but wanting to have their ears tickled, they will accumulate for themselves teachers in accordance to their own desires, and will turn away their ears from the truth and will turn aside to myths."_

Country musician George Jones sings a song entitled, "Who's Gonna' Fill Their Shoes?" In that song, he ponders who will replace the stars of the Grand Old Opry such as the late Hank Williams, Ernest Tubbs, and Patsy Cline. My response to his question is, "Who cares?" I am much more concerned about who will fill the shoes of the great Christian preachers of the past such as Peter, Paul, Augustine, Luther, Wesley, Edwards, Whitefield, Moody, Spurgeon, and Billy Graham. Where have all the preachers gone?

Preaching seems to have fallen on hard times. Today many pastors avoid preparing and preaching biblical sermons. They prefer to spend their time on leadership, counseling, administration, denominational work, visitation, Sunday school, and building programs. They strive to be seeker-friendly, but often avoid being Scripture-friendly, sermon-friendly, soul-friendly, Spirit-friendly, and Savior-friendly. This should not be!

Paul told Timothy to make preaching a priority. He warned of a coming day when people would not tolerate biblical sermons. Instead, they would secure hirelings to entertain them with pulpit pleasantries. Indeed, it is that time in much of America today.

If a pastor ought to do anything, he ought to preach the Bible! Today we have preacherettes who share sermonettes with Christianettes. May God send us some flaming _prophets_ who will cry, "Thus saith the Lord!" "Lord, raise up a generation of men who will boldly preach Your Word so that our pulpits may again blaze with the Spirit's fire!"

## THE PIT OF NOTHINGNESS

**Isaiah 38:17** — *"Lo, for my own welfare I had great bitterness; it is You who has kept my soul from the pit of nothingness, for You have cast all my sins behind your back."*

Satan hates every Christian. He longs to defeat and destroy us. While he cannot steal our eternal salvation, he can harass us as we seek to live for Jesus. Two of his most successful and powerful tools are *fear* and *discouragement*. Like a deadly viper, the devil seeks to paralyze us with those two venomous fangs. He wants us to walk in fear and anxiety, even though God has not given us a spirit of fear (2 Timothy 1:7). Satan also wants us to be depressed and discouraged. Discouragement is an enslaving dungeon, or pit, in which the devil will torment us if we let him. Jesus has given us all that we need to walk victoriously out of any pit into which we have fallen. He will lift us out of the miry clay, set our feet on a rock, and lead us forward on the pathway of conquering faith.

God told a very sick king named Hezekiah to "get (his) house in order" because he was about to die. At first, Hezekiah was very discouraged and afraid. He then turned his face toward the wall and began to ask God to heal him. The Lord heard his desperate cry, and told the prophet Isaiah to tell the king that he would be healed and would live for another fifteen years. Hezekiah rejoiced, and then wrote the words of our text. The Lord miraculously removed his bitterness and delivered him from his "pit of nothingness."

Have you fallen into a pit? Perhaps you are facing a crisis in your marriage, with your children, with your health, or with your finances. You may think there is no hope for your future, but all things are possible with God. Trust Him today. He can lift you out of your "pit of nothingness." He did it for King Hezekiah. He will also do it for you.

## IF THE WORLD HATES YOU

**John 15:18-19** — *"If the world hates you, you know that it has hated Me before it hated you. If you were of the world, the world would love its own; but because you are not of the world, but I chose you out of the world, because of this the world hates you."*

My children and I stood on a pier beside the lake watching the boats come and go. Some ducks near the dock were quacking, swimming, and fighting over pieces of bread tossed to them by vacationers. Suddenly, I felt an urgent tug at my shirt from my little girl. She asked, "Why are they picking on that one?" I then noticed a speckled duck being harassed by the others. His beak was deformed and his feathers were dull and spotted compared to the rest. They were jumping on his back, dunking him. When he tried to paddle away, they cut him off and bit him. He was literally being mobbed in the water in front of us. The owner of the marina said, "That's just the way ducks treat other ducks that are different than them. If he doesn't get away, they'll probably kill him."

Jesus' early disciples discovered that not everyone liked them. He told them not to be surprised. The world hated Him because He was different. If they followed Him, they would be hated also because they were no longer like the world. The world still despises Jesus and His followers. Why? Because we are different.

C. H. Spurgeon, once prayed, "Lord, I would not be a citizen in a land where You were an alien." Indeed, every Christian is an alien and stranger in this world (1 Peter 2:11). We are pilgrims passing through a world that is passing away (1 John 2:17). Since we are not of this world, it should not surprise us when the world turns on us.

We left the dock and the ducks. I never found out what happened to the "ugly duckling." But the longer I live in this sinful world, the more I identify with him.

## DYING TO LIVE

**Matthew 16:24-25** — *"Then Jesus said to His disciples, 'If anyone wishes to come after Me, he must deny himself, and take up his cross and follow Me. For whoever wishes to save his life will lose it; but whoever loses his life for My sake will find it."*

The Christian life is paradoxical. To receive, we must give. To be exalted, we must humble ourselves. To be loved, we first must love. Most importantly, to live, we must die. To the natural mind, such a notion is absurd. Yet it remains a glorious truth.

**We Must Die Initially to Experience Regeneration.** Regeneration is synonymous with becoming a Christian. Conversion requires taking up our cross and following Jesus. The cross was and is a means of execution. We must die to our old way of life to receive His eternal life. Becoming a Christian is nothing short of self-execution.

**We Must Die Daily to Experience Sanctification.** When we die at conversion, God sets us apart as His people and begins to mold us into Jesus' likeness. That process is called sanctification. For that to take place, we must die to and deny our selfish desires, take up our cross *daily*, and follow Jesus (Luke 9:23). Like Paul, we must wake up and "die daily" to allow Jesus' life to flow freely through us (1 Corinthians 15:31).

**We Must Die Physically to Experience Glorification.** As Christians, our home is not in this world. Rather, we are looking for an eternal city yet to come. When we leave this body through death, we will be present with the Lord in heaven (2 Corinthians 5:8). Our true life will begin when we behold Jesus and become like Him (1 John 3:2).

As long as you struggle to live, you will abide in a state of death. Only as you die can you truly live. If you save your life, you will lose it. If you lose it for Christ, you will find it. Decrease today, and let Jesus increase. Die, and begin to really live in Him.

## THE POWER OF REPENTANCE

**Jonah 3:10** — _"When God saw their deeds, that they turned from their wicked way, then God relented concerning the calamity which He had declared He would bring upon them. And He did not do it."_

Does God change His mind? God is indeed immutable and not capricious (James 1:17), yet there have been occasions when God _relented_ (i.e. changed His mind) and did not do something He originally had intended to do. Man's repentance caused Him to change His mind about judging sinners. Here we see the amazing power of repentance.

Nineveh was a large, Assyrian city filled with wicked, idolatrous people. God commanded the prophet Jonah to go and "cry against it" (1:2). Instead, Jonah rebelled and boarded a boat sailing for Tarshish. A storm arose at sea, and the crew threw Jonah overboard in an attempt to cause God's anger to subside. A giant fish prepared by the Lord swallowed Jonah and kept him isolated for three days and nights. When he was finally vomited out on the shore, "the word of the LORD came to Jonah a second time" (3:1). This time he obeyed God. He walked throughout the city saying, "Yet forty days and Nineveh will be overthrown" (3:4). The people of Nineveh repented and asked God to forgive them. When God saw their repentance, He relented and did not destroy them. Some may argue that He never intended to destroy them because He knew they would ultimately repent. But the text implies that He relented _because of_ their repentance.

Are you living in sin? Be not deceived. Unless you repent, you will perish (Luke 13:3, 5). The wages of sin is death. But God's good news is that if you will repent, He will relent and change His mind concerning the judgment He plans to send your way. Instead of discipline, He will give you His grace. _That_ is the power of repentance!

## GOD WILL MAKE A WAY

**Proverbs 3:5-6** — *"Trust in the LORD with all your heart and do not lean on your own understanding. In all your ways acknowledge Him, and He will make your paths straight."*

In high school, I was an offensive lineman on our football team. We had a great tailback named James Patrick. In one game that we were winning handily, our coach called a play in which James was supposed to run wide outside and then upfield. My job was to block the last defensive man so that James could score. I was lazy on that play and failed to block my man who, in turn, tackled James and prevented him from scoring. Our coach called me to the sideline and said, "We're going to call the same play, and if you don't get down field and block your man, you'll be sorry on Monday." I got his message! The ball was snapped. I ran down field, flattened the defensive back I was supposed to block, and James followed me into the end zone. I cleared the way for a great running back, and also saved myself from some painful wind sprints the next week.

God knows how to clear the way for His children. When we face obstacles in life, He says to us, "Let me block and clear a path for you. Just put your hand in Mine and I will take you where you need to go." That is what our text means when it says that God "will make (our) paths straight." He will clear a path for us by removing any obstruction in our way. He will level any hill or mountain, fill in any valley, straighten any crooked path, and smooth out any rough road (Luke 3:5). We must trust Him and walk by faith.

Are you facing an intimidating, threatening problem today? God is bigger than your problem. Do not let it tackle you. Allow God to block and clear the way as He escorts you on to victory. He will make a way for you though there seems to be no way.

## Is Anyone Among You Sick?

**James 5:14-16** — "_Is anyone among you sick? Then he must call for the elders of the church and they are to pray over him, anointing him with oil in the name of the Lord; and the prayer offered in faith will restore the one who is sick, and the Lord will raise him up, and if he has committed sins, they will be forgiven him. Therefore, confess your sins to one another, and pray for one another so that you may be healed. The effective prayer of a righteous man can accomplish much._"

The little girl clung to her father's neck as he and her mother walked into my office. Earlier that day a doctor had informed them that she had a hearing disorder. They asked our church staff to pray for her to be healed, and we gladly agreed to do so. After a wonderful time of reading Scripture and sharing together, we laid hands on her, anointed her with oil, and asked the Lord to work in her life. We asked Him to bless the doctors, and also to go beyond all that they could do and bring healing to her body. God's presence permeated the room. The father then prayed, "Lord, thank you for a church that still believes in Your Word and in Your power. Whatever you do, we give you praise."

I went downstairs to the sanctuary. Our mid-week prayer service had already begun. After the musical praise, I preached about how heaven will be a place void of sickness, pain, death, crying, or sorrow. At the end, several people came forward for prayer. A sad wife came with her husband. She had been diagnosed that day with cancer. She asked for prayer. We anointed her with oil, prayed, and again asked God for a miracle. He once more filled that place with His presence as He had done in my office.

Does God heal everyone all the time? No. But just as more people get saved in a church that preaches the Gospel faithfully, more people are healed in a church that prays according to our text. Many do not believe in miracles until they need one. God does heal. He is still Jehovah-Rapha (Exodus 15:26). Pray for someone to be healed today.

## How Long Will You Hesitate?

**1 Kings 18:21** — *"Elijah came near to all the people and said, 'How long will you hesitate between two opinions? If the LORD is God, follow Him; but if Baal, follow him.' But the people did not answer him a word."*

One morning while taking our children to school, a gray squirrel darted out into the street in front of us. At first he acted as if he would cross, but then he stopped, sat up, saw my wheels, and panicked. He turned to go back, then turned to cross again. My girls screamed, "Daddy, don't kill the squirrel!" I slammed on the brakes and barely missed him. That frightened squirrel's middle-of-the-road hesitation almost cost him his life.

One day Elijah told God's people to stop hesitating concerning whom they were going to worship and serve. They could not worship both the LORD ("Yahweh," or "Jehovah") and also Baal, the pagan, Canaanite fertility god. Elijah decided to have a spiritual showdown on top of Mt. Carmel. He told several hundred prophets of Baal to build an altar for their god while he built one for the LORD. A sacrificial animal would be placed on each altar, but no one could light a fire. Instead, they would each pray for fire to be sent from heaven. Whichever god answered by fire would be recognized as the true God! Baal's prophets prayed, but nothing happened. Elijah prayed, and fire fell, consuming the sacrifice. Baal's prophets were slain, and revival ensued. It happened when God's people stopped hesitating, and committed themselves totally to the LORD.

Are you hesitating between two opinions concerning Jesus Christ? "A double-minded man (is) unstable in all his ways" (James 1:8). Lukewarm Christianity nauseates God (Revelation 3:15-16). Stop hesitating between two opinions. Get out of the middle of the road. Live either for Jesus or for the devil. Either cross the street or stay out of it.

## HE SAVED US

**Titus 3:5** — _"He saved us, not on the basis of deeds which we have done in righteousness, but according to His mercy, by the washing of regeneration and renewing by the Holy Spirit."_

He stood on the corner of a busy intersection in Birmingham. The sign he held read, "Jesus Saves!" As people passed, he politely shared with them the good news of Jesus Christ. Some thought he was foolish. Yet his sign and words offered eternal life.

**The Fact of Salvation.** "He saved us." When we repent of our sin and call on Jesus in faith, He saves and transforms us completely. He transfers us out of sin's darkness into God's marvelous, holy light. Old things pass away and new things come.

**The Foundation of Salvation.** Jesus does not save us based on "deeds which we have done in righteousness," but "according to His mercy" and amazing grace (Ephesians 2:8-9). Our "righteousness" is like filthy rags compared to His perfection (Isaiah 64:6).

**The Forgiveness of Salvation.** We are saved by "the washing of regeneration." At conversion, Jesus bathes our sin-blackened souls in His powerful, redeeming blood (1 Peter 1:18-19) and we emerge forgiven, cleansed, and whiter than snow (Isaiah 1:18).

**The Filling at Salvation.** When we are saved, we experience the "renewing of the Holy Spirit." The Spirit baptizes, indwells, fills, sanctifies, and seals us at the point of conversion. Our bodies become His temple. His presence attests to our salvation.

Jesus came to seek and to _save_ that which is lost (Luke 19:10). If you are lost, call on Jesus today in humble repentance and childlike faith. He _will_ save you (Romans 10:13)! Then, once you become a Christian, or if you already are saved, you might consider joining that man on the street and tell others that it really is true – "Jesus Saves!"

## RETURN TO ME

**Zechariah 1:3** — *"Therefore say to them, 'Thus says the LORD of hosts, "Return to Me," declares the LORD of hosts, "that I may return to you," says the LORD of hosts.'"*

The old pickup truck lumbered down the road with the elderly couple inside. For more than fifty years, they had been married. As she looked at her aged husband, she could not help but notice how far apart they were sitting from each other. Her thoughts went back to a time when they were younger. Sadness filled her heart until finally she said, "Paw, what has happened to us?" "What are you talkin' about?" he sternly replied. "Paw, we used to sit so close together when we were young and in love. We never do that any more!" The old man never took his hands off the steering wheel. He thought and finally said, "Well, we may be apart alright, but I ain't the one that moved!"

Zechariah preached during the time of Judah's exile. He told God's people to repent and return to the Lord. If they would come back to Him, He would forgive, bless, and restore them to their land. However, if they refused to return, He would leave them in exile. The choice was theirs – return and be blessed, or rebel and be cursed.

Do you feel far away from God? If so, you are the one who has moved. God is right where you left Him – in that empty prayer closet, that unread Bible, that vacant pew at church. Jesus only goes where He is invited, and only stays where He is welcome. He never leaves or forsakes us. We are the ones who leave Him (Revelation 2:4). If you are away from the Lord today, return to Him. Confess and forsake your sin, and be cleansed by His grace. Draw near to Him and He will draw near to you. Do not follow Him at a distance. Any separation between you and God is your fault. Why? He has not moved!

## THE JOY OF SALVATION

**Psalm 51:12** — *"Restore to me the joy of Your salvation and sustain me with a willing spirit."*

Through the years I have spoken with Christians who believed they had lost their salvation. Because they felt defeated, and at times doubted their salvation, they decided that they were no longer actually saved. While it is not possible for a Christian to lose his salvation (John 10:27-29), it is possible for him to lose the *joy* of salvation. When a person is born again, he becomes God's child. Nothing can separate him from that *relationship* with his heavenly Father (Romans 8:38-39). However, if a believer sins and refuses to confess and repent of that sin, he can indeed lose a sense of *fellowship* with the Lord. When that happens, his joy vanishes and he becomes spiritually weak. Why? Because it is the joy of the Lord that gives strength to the child of God (Nehemiah 8:10).

David committed adultery with a woman named Bathsheba. He then had her husband killed to try to cover up his sin. The prophet Nathan confronted the immoral king, and David repented immediately. Psalm 51 is a record of David's confession to God. In the midst of his prayer, he asked God to restore "the joy of (His) salvation."

A joyless Christian is not lost, but he is weak and miserable. Do you need a fresh baptism of the joy of the Lord? If so, confess your sins to God, repent of them, and then forsake them. Ask the Lord to fill you with His Holy Spirit, who will produce His fruit in you, part of which is "joy" (Galatians 5:22-23). Your spiritual strength will soon return.

The Bible says that in God's presence there is "fullness of joy" (Psalm 16:11). You do not have to remain weak. Rather, you can "Rejoice with joy inexpressible and full of glory" (1 Peter 1:8). Let Jesus restore the joy of His salvation to you today.

## SILENT BEFORE HIM

**Habakkuk 2:20** — *"But the LORD is in His holy temple. Let all the earth be silent before Him."*

The choir flowed into the sanctuary from the left and right in two streams of grandeur. The white robed singers looked like angels. The aged pastor also entered as the organ began its soft and sacred tones. Then the glorious song began: "The Lord is in His holy temple, the Lord is in His holy temple; let all the earth keep silent! Let all the earth keep silent before Him! Keep silent! Keep silent, before Him!" To my young heart it was as though God Himself had walked into the room. Perhaps He had!

In Scripture, the Lord encourages His people to shout praises to Him, to sing joyfully, to clap hands, and to employ in our worship musical instruments such as tambourines, trumpets, and resounding cymbals. But the same God who desires for us to worship Him in these expressive ways also commands us to worship Him silently. There is a time to be silent as well as a time to speak (Ecclesiastes 3:7). Sometimes He wants us to come quietly into His presence and be still, knowing that He is God (Psalm 46:10).

When Peter saw Jesus transfigured, he talked when he should have kept silent. "Lord, this is awesome! Let me build three booths; one for You, Elijah, and Moses." Suddenly a cloud of glory appeared and the Father said, "This is My beloved Son; *listen* to Him!" He was telling Peter to be quiet and focus on Jesus' glory. That is good advice.

Today as you worship the Lord, try just sitting quietly in His presence, silently meditating on His greatness and goodness. Do not ask Him for anything. Do not make a commotion. Do not say a word. Just enjoy Him. Be content to worship Him in silent reverence. You just may become quiet enough to hear the sound of His still, small voice!

## BECOMING A GOD-PLEASER

**2 Corinthians 5:9** — *"Therefore we also have as our ambition, whether at home or absent, to be pleasing to Him."*

From time to time I have run across people who seem to have a desire to set some sort of agenda for my life. There are people out there that have a tendency to tell others what they "ought to do." The Lord has taught me that it is not a matter of whether or not my calendar is going to be filled. The real issue is *who* is going to be in charge of filling my calendar. Will I allow others to run my life and set my agendas, or will I seek the Lord's guidance each day and ask Him to show me what *He* wants me to do? You cannot please God if your primary goal is to please other people. You will never have the time, resources, or energy to do everything that *you* want to do, much less to do what *others* want you to do. But you will always have the time, energy, and resources to do what *God* wants you to do! Every Christian should seek to discover and do what pleases God.

The Apostle Paul did not worry about being a man-pleaser (Galatians 1:10). In our text he said that one of his chief ambitions in life was to please the Lord. He did not try to please other people at the expense of obeying Jesus. He spoke the Word of God even if its truth offended his audience. He planted churches in hostile areas even when people in those cities tried to stop him. When the authorities would persecute him, Paul refused to compromise the Gospel of Jesus. His goal was to live in such a way that he would one day hear Jesus say, "Well done, Paul, you good and faithful servant!"

Are you a man-pleaser or a God-pleaser? When all is said and done, *God* will judge you, not man. Your primary pursuit in life should be to please *Him.* May you be consumed today with a desire to bring joy to God, even if other people do not approve.

## THE FOURTH WATCH

**Matthew 14:25** — *"And in the fourth watch of the night He came to them, walking on the sea."*

God never sleeps and never gets tired. He is Spirit. Therefore, a physical body that grows weary does not limit Him. He is always awake, alert, and attentive to His children. He never slumbers, but watches over His children as they rest and sleep (Psalm 121). Since God never sleeps, He frequently comes to His children in the early morning hours to awaken them for prayer and fellowship in His Word. In our text, Jesus saw that His disciples were struggling at sea as they attempted to row to shore. He came to them in their distress, walking on the water in "the fourth watch," sometime between 3 a.m. and 6 a.m. He made their struggles cease, and gave them perfect peace.

Jesus will come to us during "the fourth watch" as well. Through the years, the Lord has often awakened me in the early hours before dawn with a deep desire to pray. There is something special about those early hours with God. While on earth, Jesus often prayed during that same time period (Mark 1:35). King David also offered His prayers to God early "in the morning" (Psalm 5:3). It is said of the great Methodist preacher, John Wesley, that he spent several hours in prayer and Bible study every morning before daybreak. Indeed, the sun should always rise on some Christian kneeling in prayer.

I often talk with Christians who complain about hectic schedules. They simply do not have time to pray. I tell them about "the fourth watch." The house is quiet, the family is asleep, and privacy is at a premium. Those early hours are for communion with God, not physical exercise. Go to bed early, and then rise early to meet with the Lord Jesus. He still comes to His struggling disciples in the early hours of "the fourth watch."

## DOING A GREAT WORK

**Nehemiah 6:3** — _"So I sent messengers to them, saying, 'I am doing a great work and I cannot come down. Why should the work stop while I leave it and come down to you?'"_

God has ordained certain good works for us to accomplish (Ephesians 2:10). Those tasks are vital to the advancement of Christ's Kingdom on earth. Every Christian is "doing a great work." We are to discover and complete those tasks before we die.

Nehemiah had an important work to accomplish. God called him to return to Jerusalem from exile to rebuild the great wall that had been leveled by the Babylonians. Though the task was immense, and his earthly resources were meager, Nehemiah knew God's will and was confident that God would do the work through him. When he arrived at Jerusalem, he saw the demolished wall around the Jewish temple that Zerubbabel had rebuilt decades earlier. He also met Ezra the scribe who had returned thirteen years earlier to teach God's Word. Nehemiah realized how desperately the Jews needed the protection of the city's wall if they were to prosper. God had given him "a great work."

Nehemiah faced severe opposition from the Gentile neighbors. Nevertheless, he refused to be distracted. Though they tried to lure him into a meeting so they could kill him, Nehemiah refused to leave the work. His classic response is given in our text – "I am doing a great work and I cannot come down!" Because of obedience and focus, the wall was completed in only fifty-two days! He finished the task God had given him.

If you are saved, God has a great work for you. It may seem insignificant to others, but that matters not. You must discover God's will for you and then go for it! Remember, God's work is a _great_ work. You must not come down until it is finished.

## THE MASTER'S MINORITY

**Matthew 7:13-14** — *"Enter through the narrow gate; for the gate is wide and the way is broad that leads to destruction, and there are many who enter through it. For the gate is small and the way is narrow that leads to life, and there are few who find it."*

"A loving God would never send anyone to hell." "If hell is real, its punishments are temporary, not eternal." "Everyone will go to heaven when he dies." People known as Universalists hold these views. They reject the notion that people must experience personal salvation in Christ to go to heaven. Jesus addressed this subject in our text.

Jesus taught about hell just as much as He did about heaven. In our verses, He invited His listeners to "Enter." They were on the outside of salvation and a relationship with God. He called them into that relationship through "the narrow gate." They could come to God only through Jesus. He is the only "gate" or "way" to the Father (John 14:6). Refusal to enter that way results in a dismal journey through this life on "the way that is broad." Jesus said, "Many enter through it," and its ultimate destination is "destruction," a reference to hell. But those who enter through Jesus will walk on "the way that is narrow that leads to life." This is a reference to abundant life on earth and everlasting life in heaven. Jesus noted that "there are few who find" the way to life. He said that more people walk down the broad road to hell than the narrow road to heaven! Universalists may not like that concept, but there is little doubt that Jesus taught it.

There are only two roads on which you can travel in this life: the broad and the narrow. They lead to either hell ("destruction") or heaven ("life"). Which road are you on? According to Jesus, the majority of people are walking blindly on the road to hell. You must not follow them. Make sure that you are part of "the Master's Minority."

## CLEAN AND BEAUTIFUL

**Ecclesiastes 3:11a** — _"He has made everything beautiful in its time."_

In 1996, our family vacationed for two weeks through New England. We toured the beautiful homes of Williamsburg, Virginia. We saw the historic sites of Washington D.C., and enjoyed the fireworks display sitting at the reflection pool by the Lincoln Memorial on the night of July Fourth. In Philadelphia, our children ran triumphantly up the steps in front of the museum just like "Rocky" did in the movies. In New York City, we attended a Broadway play, a church service at The Brooklyn Tabernacle, strolled through Central Park, and went to the top of The Empire State Building, the Statute of Liberty, and one of the World Trade Center buildings (5 years before their destruction). In Plymouth, Massachusetts, we saw where the Pilgrims landed in the early 1600s, and also saw more than a dozen Humpbacks on a whale watch. In Boston, we visited Paul Revere's boyhood home, the Old North Church, and Boston Harbor. Our final stop was Maine. We ate lobster in Kennebunkport and spent the night at The Beaches of York.

On the evening before we returned to Alabama, I had taken a shower, shaved, dressed, and entered the main area of our hotel room. Our three-year-old daughter, Bethany, climbed into my lap. Noticing that I had just showered, she put her little hands on my cheeks, looked into my eyes and exclaimed, "You're so clean and beautiful!" Our whole family enjoyed a belly laugh! It was a perfect climax for a wonderful trip.

Christian, God made you "beautiful" when He created you in His image (Genesis 1:27), and He made you "clean" when He recreated you at salvation (1 Peter 1:18-19). It matters not what people think of you today. In His eyes you are "clean and beautiful!"

## FIRE IN MY BONES

**Jeremiah 20:9** — *"But if I say, 'I will not remember Him or speak anymore in His name,' then in my heart it becomes like a burning fire shut up in my bones; and I am weary of holding it in, and I cannot endure it."*

We stopped our car in front of the Dairy Queen. I had been married for approximately four hours. I went inside smiling from ear to ear. I looked at the girl behind the cash register and said, "I just got married today! We're on our honeymoon and headed for Nashville!" She and everyone else in the room laughed and congratulated me. I went back to the car with our drinks and with a laugh, told Donna what I had just done. "I couldn't keep it in, babe. I just *had* to tell them the good news about us!"

Jeremiah was a prophet during a difficult period of Judah's history. Through the years, he faithfully delivered God's messages. The people would listen, but they would not heed God's warnings. Instead, they increased in wickedness. Jeremiah eventually became weary. In a moment of discouragement, he considered abandoning his ministry altogether. At that crucial moment, God's Word became a burning fire within his heart that had to be released. He discovered that he *had* to preach! Like Paul, he could say, "I am under compulsion; for woe is me if I do not preach the gospel" (1 Corinthians 9:16).

Does the Gospel of Jesus Christ burn within you? Grandparents find it impossible not to talk about their grandchildren. Newlyweds cannot refrain from speaking about their spouse. Victorious athletes exuberantly tell others about their victories. Likewise, true Christians find it difficult to hold back the fiery message of Jesus Christ. Ask the Lord to ignite a fresh flame of evangelistic zeal within your heart today. This world still needs to hear from one who shares passionately about Jesus with God's fire in his bones!

## WHY WILL YOU DIE?

**Ezekiel 33:11** — _"Say to them, 'As I live!' Declares the Lord GOD, 'I take no pleasure in the death of the wicked, but rather that the wicked turn from his way and live. Turn back, turn back from your evil ways! Why then will you die, O house of Israel?'"_

The God of the Bible is both holy and loving. He is absolutely righteous and altogether pure and sinless. He hates sin, and must punish it. The wages of sin has always been and always will be death. Yet, this same God is loving and merciful. He does not desire to punish sinners. Rather, He prefers to pardon and forgive them by His grace. He wants all who have disobeyed Him to repent and return to Him in a spirit of brokenness and humility through His Son, Jesus Christ. When a person repents, God immediately has mercy on him and forgives him of all iniquity.

Some teach that God predestines specific people for heaven and others for hell. They are convinced that all people have their eternal destinies determined by God's foreknowledge and there is nothing anyone can do to alter God's sovereign decision. The truth is that God does not foreordain or predestine anyone to go to hell. Rather, as our text clearly states, He wants people to turn from their sin and escape His divine wrath. He is not willing for anyone to perish but desires all people to turn to Him for forgiveness (cf. 2 Peter 3:9). Anyone who rejects Jesus Christ as Lord and Savior will go to hell, but not because God wills it. Rather, people go to hell because they choose to do so.

Are you a non-Christian? God does not desire your death, either physically, or eternally in hell. Repent today. Turn from your sin and turn to God for forgiveness through His only begotten Son, Jesus Christ. If you are a Christian living in sin, repent and return to the Lord. He desires life for you, not death. Why, O why, will you die?

## THE DAYS OF YOUR YOUTH

**Ecclesiastes 12:1** — *"Remember also your Creator in the days of your youth, before the evil days come and the years draw near when you will say, 'I have no delight in them.'"*

On my mother's refrigerator, there is a magnetic plaque that reads, "Life After 60: When Your Knees Buckle, but Your Belt Won't." All of us are aging. Life passes us by one day at a time. Like tiny grains of sand dropping through an hourglass, our days slip by and we seldom notice how many have passed, never to be lived again. When a person is young, thoughts about the brevity of life seem irrelevant. Younger people often live under the delusion that they have plenty of time left. They often resist a life of devotion to Jesus Christ for fear that they might miss out on the real enjoyment and thrills that the world has to offer. Consequently, they do not live for Him in the days of their youth.

King Solomon wrote the words of our text. He said that it is best for a person to remember the Lord while he is still young and in the prime of life. Failure to do so brings about evil days that have little delight in them. Indeed, the person who lives for Christ when he is young has fewer regrets than those living for the world. He also has more fulfilling and enjoyable memories. To follow Christ in the days of youth may put you in the minority, but the years will prove that you made the wisest choice. The seeds sown in the days of youth produce a life-long harvest. Make sure those seeds are good, not evil.

If you are young, live for Jesus Christ! It is a choice you will never regret. If you have wasted your youthful years, repent and ask the Lord to redirect you. He will change you and help you begin anew. It is never too late to start doing right! The earlier in life you follow Jesus wholeheartedly, the better. If possible, do it in the days of your youth!

## NAKED COME, NAKED GO

**1 Timothy 6:7** — _"For we have brought nothing into the world, so we cannot take anything out of it either."_

From birth until death, people struggle with selfishness and covetousness. Born with a sinful nature and innate self-centeredness, people desire to amass and stockpile the things and "stuff" of this world. Oftentimes that tendency to hoard and store treasures on earth is a sinful alternative to trusting God to supply one's needs. Savings accounts, investments, and possessions can quickly become that which we depend on to take care of us while we are on this earth. Mammon must not be our master. Gold should never take the place of God in our lives.

Paul reminded Timothy that God sends each person into this world utterly barren of possessions, and that is exactly the way we will leave it – empty-handed and naked. Truer words have never been spoken. As a parent, I witnessed the births of all four of our children. None of them had a wallet or portfolio in hand when they appeared kicking and crying. As a pastor, I have also performed hundreds of funeral services. Those people amassed possessions during their lives that were left behind completely at death. Someone has well said, "You will never see a U-Haul trailer attached to a hearse." Job said, "Naked I came from my mother's womb, and naked I shall return" (Job 1:21).

A modern bumper sticker says, "The One With the Most Toys in the End Wins." In God's view, that is the motto of a wasted life. Jesus calls us to seek first the kingdom of God. We are to use the earthly wealth and possessions God gives us to win people to Christ and spread the Gospel. We entered this world naked, and that is how we will leave it. May we live and die with open, giving hearts and hands.

## YET I WILL EXULT

**Habakkuk 3:17-18** — *"Though the fig tree should not blossom and there be no fruit on the vines, though the yield of the olive should fail and the fields produce no food, though the flock should be cut off from the fold and there be no cattle in the stalls, yet I will exult in the LORD, I will rejoice in the God of my salvation."*

Some people allow their feelings to be tied to the rise and fall of the economy. When financial systems surge, they are joyful. However, they become distressed when the stock markets plummet, companies lay off workers, food and gas prices soar, and retirement portfolios dwindle. Christians who walk by faith and not by sight do not allow financial ups and downs to defeat them. Rather, they choose to exult always in the Lord.

Habakkuk was a prophet who spoke to God's people around 605 B.C., just before the Babylonian armies came and deported them as exiles into captivity. During that time, the people of Judah were experiencing economic difficulties. Habakkuk explained that the Lord was using the down economy to discipline them because of their sin. They needed to repent, live righteously, and learn to live by faith in God (2:4). In our text, he reminded them that regardless of how bad the damage would be as a result of the Babylonian invasion, they should rejoice in the Lord. The figs, grapes, olives, and the rest of the crops might be devastated, along with the sheep and the cattle. Nevertheless, they needed to trust in the Lord, not in man or worldly possessions. If they would look steadfastly to Him for help, and learn to walk by faith, He would readily meet their needs.

God uses economic downturns and other catastrophes to cause us to stop focusing on finances and the things of this world, and to start focusing on Him. We must learn to rejoice in the Lord regardless of our circumstances, and trust Him. In spite of what the financial future may hold, our declaration of faith must be, "Yet I will exult in the Lord!"

## The Value Of Love

**Song of Solomon 8:7** — *"Many waters cannot quench love, nor will rivers overflow it; if a man were to give all the riches of his house for love, it would be utterly despised."*

Second only to my salvation in Christ, the greatest gift God has ever given me is my wife, Donna. I remember the first time I looked into her eyes. We were in the library at Union University. She was wearing a tan sweater with a loose, turtleneck collar. She was also wearing glasses. When she removed them and looked at me, it felt as though my heart had stopped! We soon went on our first date. Within a month we were in love. Within four and a half months, we were engaged. In June 1980, we married. Since then, we have endured many trials. Yet the threatening floods of life have not quenched the fire of our love. Such love cannot be purchased with money. It is a gift from God above.

Solomon wrote the Song of Solomon as a love song to his Shulamite bride. It is a story of romance between two young, married lovers. Their intimacy and affection is openly displayed throughout the book. Our text says two things about true love. First, it is indestructible. "Many waters cannot quench love, nor will rivers overflow it." Despite the difficulties a married couple encounter, love can see them through. As Paul says, "(Love) bears all things, believes all things, hopes all things, endures all things. Love never fails" (1 Corinthians 13:7-8a). Secondly, love is not for sale. "If a man were to give all the riches of his house for love, it would be utterly despised." True love cannot be prostituted. Rather, the lovers must give it to one another mutually and freely.

The blessing of romantic love that leads to a lifelong marriage is a gift from God. It weathers life's fiercest storms. It is more priceless than silver or gold. If God has blessed you with that gift, guard and cherish it. It is the most precious treasure you own.

## A PRAYER FOR PROSPERITY

**3 John 2** — *"Beloved, I pray that in all respects you may prosper and be in good health, just as your soul prospers."*

One of my heroes in the faith is the late Herschel H. Hobbs. He was a country boy from Coosa County, Alabama who became one of the greatest preachers, theologians, and leaders Baptists have ever known. Whenever he signed one of his many books, he always wrote "3 John 2" above his name. It is a prayer for prosperity.

**God Wants to Prosper Us Materially.** "Beloved, I pray that in all respects you may *prosper*." "Prosper" refers to material blessings. God will provide for our financial, material, and temporal needs. We are not to worry about what we will eat, drink, or wear. God feeds the birds, and He will take care of us. He loves to bless His children.

**God Wants to Prosper Us Physically.** "And be in *good health*." God heals spiritually, mentally, emotionally, and even physically. He does not promise perfect health in this life, but He does still heal people. When we are sick we should utilize doctors and medicine, but we should also ask God for His healing power (James 5:16).

**God Wants to Prosper Us Spiritually.** "Just as your *soul* prospers." God wants us to grow in grace and in the knowledge of our Lord and Savior Jesus Christ (2 Peter 3:18). He wants more of the fruit of His Spirit to be manifested in our lives. As we read the Bible, pray, witness, fellowship with believers, and worship, our souls will prosper.

God cares about every area of your life. He does not promise to make you rich, but He will prosper you materially, physically, and spiritually. Earthly fathers love to bless their children. How much more will our heavenly Father give what is good to those who ask Him? Pray this prayer of prosperity for yourself and for those you love today.

## JESUS, THE BREAD OF LIFE

**John 6:35** — _"Jesus said to them, 'I am the bread of life; he who comes to Me will not hunger, and he who believes in Me will never thirst.'"_

The crowds ate their food in amazement as they sat in groups of fifty. The disciples likewise were astonished as they gathered the twelve baskets filled with leftover food after the satisfied crowd of five thousand men and their families were finished eating. Moments earlier, the disciples had asked Jesus to send the crowd away to secure something to eat. The multitudes had been listening to Him teach for a long time and they were hungry. Jesus, however, told His disciples to provide them with food. When all they could manage to find was the lunch of a young lad, Jesus took it, blessed it, broke it, and told His disciples to distribute it among the people. The food miraculously continued to multiply as they all ate and were satisfied. A major miracle had taken place.

After the food and the effect of the miracle had worn off, the people chased after Jesus and asked for more miracles and meals. Jesus told them that their real need was spiritual food. He then told them that He was the "bread of life." Whoever partakes of Jesus in salvation is satisfied completely and eternally. Jesus had that in mind when He said that whoever hungers and thirsts for righteousness shall be satisfied (Matthew 5:6).

Everyone is hungry for something to fill the emptiness of his soul. Money cannot satisfy, nor can the things of the world. Even relationships with other people cannot bring the fulfillment we seek. Only a personal, intimate relationship with God through Christ can feed our spiritual natures. We must come to Jesus, receive Him as Savior, and then feast on Him daily through prayer, Bible intake, and worship. Jesus is the satisfying bread of heaven. Enjoy Him today. "Taste and see that the Lord is good" (Psalm 34:8)!

## WILL A MAN ROB GOD?

**Malachi 3:8-10** — *"'Will a man rob God? Yet you are robbing Me! But you say, "How have we robbed You?" In tithes and offerings. You are cursed with a curse, for you are robbing Me, the whole nation of you! Bring the whole tithe into the storehouse, so that there may be food in My house, and test Me now in this,' says the LORD of hosts, 'if I will not open for you the windows of heaven and pour out for you a blessing until it overflows.'"*

If you were in a church sanctuary and the offering was being received, what would you do if you saw someone take money out of the plate? You would probably notify someone in charge that a thief was in the crowd. While few would steal like that from an offering plate, many steal by failing to give as God commands. The Bible says it is the same as robbing from God Himself. Are *you* guilty of stealing from God?

In Malachi's day, God's people were ignoring their financial responsibilities to the Lord and His Temple. After several decades, they had returned from Babylonian captivity to Jerusalem. They built their houses, but failed to financially support the work of the Temple and the priests. When they refused to bring their tithes to the storehouse of the Temple, they were stealing from God. The Lord had cursed them for their financial disobedience, and refused to bless them until they repented and began again to tithe.

God still demands that His people tithe. He expects us to give 10% of our money to our local church's budget in an undesignated fashion. Both ministerial and lay leaders should be required to tithe. No one should serve as a minister, deacon, teacher, usher, committee member, or soloist in the church unless he tithes. A thief does not make a good leader.

Only two things open the windows of heaven — prayer (Luke 3:21) and tithing. Do we really trust God to save us and take our souls to heaven if we cannot rely on Him in this area? Trust God and tithe. An open heaven and His abundant blessings await you.

## WINE IS A MOCKER

**Proverbs 20:1** — _"Wine is a mocker, strong drink a brawler, and whoever is intoxicated by it is not wise."_

Our family sat together at the baseball game. We were on vacation in St. Louis to see the Cardinals play at Busch Stadium. The famous announcer, Jack Buck, had died that week and the game opened with a brief memorial service in his honor. It was a touching moment. I had listened to him call Cardinal games when I was a child.

Once the game began, stadium employees started yelling, "Cold beer! Get your cold beer here!" During the game, the young man sitting next to me drank six large glasses of beer. The thought of him driving home drunk scared me. Four men behind us were rooting for the Cardinal's opponents, the Anaheim Angels. The more they drank, the louder and more obnoxious they became. As I sat, I became oblivious to the game, amazed at the ugliness of the drunkenness around me. I watched those people become more and more intoxicated and I saw them become increasingly foolish and rude. Strong drink turned them into crude animals. They were slaves living in spiritual bondage.

Why should a person drink alcoholic beverages, even in moderation? What good comes from it? Alcohol damages brain cells. It also alters a person's personality, usually for the worse. Bars are places of fighting, drunkenness, immorality, and sometimes death. It is also difficult for a Christian to be a social drinker and a soul-winner.

When it comes to drinking alcoholic beverages, the best policy is abstinence. Drinking is not wise and it leads to sin. Nothing good comes from it. Get it out of your house, and out of your life. If you are thirsty, drink some water or a Coke. Better yet, drink deeply from God's Living Water, the Holy Spirit. That is what we are all thirsting for anyway!

## ACCORDING TO YOUR FAITH

**Matthew 9:28-30a** — *"When He entered the house, the blind men came up to Him, and Jesus said to them, 'Do you believe that I am able to do this?' They said to Him, 'Yes, Lord.' Then He touched their eyes, saying, 'It shall be done to you according to your faith.' And their eyes were opened."*

What causes God to act? What motivates Him to move in miraculous power? Are the events of this life already predetermined in some fatalistic fashion? Or is there a force that is only limited by God's sovereign will? There is, and that force is faith. Faith is not simply *hoping* that God will act, or even believing that He *can* do something. Faith *knows* that God both can and will act because it is His will to do so.

Jesus had just left Jairus' home where He had raised that man's twelve-year-old daughter from the dead. As He entered another home, two blind men followed Him requesting that He heal them. He asked if they believed He was able to do it. Note their answer — "Yes, Lord." It was a positive, faith-filled answer — "Yes!" It was also a humble, submissive answer — "Lord!" It secured Jesus' healing touch. As He touched them, He said that His power had flowed "according (in response) to (their) faith."

Faith touches the heart of God and moves the hand of God. Crying, complaining, and self-pity do not motivate God to act. Faith does. Our prayers are not powerful because they are long and elaborate. Rather, they are powerful only as we offer them to God in faith believing that He *will* act. Faith means, "Fully Assured, I Trust Him!"

What are you trusting God for today? Do you believe that He is able to do it? If so, pray the prayer of the blind men — "Yes, Lord." Then reach out and touch God's heart with your faith. His miracle-working hand will then touch you. Stop complaining, crying, and worrying, and start trusting. Your answer will come according to your faith.

## DWELLING TOGETHER IN UNITY

**Psalm 133:1** — _"Behold, how good and how pleasant it is for brothers to dwell together in unity!"_

As we drove along in our 1957 Chevy Belair, the noise from the backseat grew louder. "Stop looking at me!" "Move your foot!" "Mom, Ed just hit me." My mother leaned over the seat and said, "Guys, cut it out! You're ruining the trip for everyone!"

With four children of my own, I now know (times two!) what my parents went through on those family rides to Granny's house. It hurts a parent when his children bicker with one another. One day as I listened to my children talking unkindly to each other, I sensed the Lord saying to me, "Now you know how My heart aches when My children quarrel with one another." I had never thought of Christian disunity in that light.

Christians often have a knack for emphasizing their differences. It may be a particular style of music in a local church or an insignificant doctrinal difference between various denominations. The fact is, everyone who is born again is a child of God whether they agree with us on every matter or not. When we argue with one another, it grieves God's heart and also damages our witness with a lost world. That is why the Psalmist said that it is "good and pleasant" for God's children to live in harmony with one another. We must build bridges in Christ's body, not walls. Blessed are the peacemakers (Matthew 5:9). Cursed are the troublemakers (1 Corinthians 3:16-17). We must be "diligent to preserve the unity of the Spirit in the bond of peace" (Ephesians 4:3).

A fighting, fussing church and a factious Christian are both tools in Satan's hand. The world will know that we are Jesus' followers only when we love one another. Ask the Lord to give you a love for all Christians, even those with whom you differ.

## What To Do In A Down Economy

**1 Kings 17:14** — *"For thus says the LORD God of Israel, 'The bowl of flour shall not be exhausted, nor shall the jar of oil be empty, until the day that the LORD sends rain on the face of the earth.'"*

When things get tough financially, fear and discouragement seem to rule the day in the hearts of people. Most folks fret about the stock market, inflation, and dismal financial forecasts. Children of God, however, ought not to worry about such things.

The prophet Elijah lived during a severe economic downturn. God sent drought and famine to the land of Israel because of their sin. The heavens withheld rain, the food and water were depleted, the cattle were starving, and people were afraid and depressed. Yet, God was providing miraculously for His prophet. He led Elijah to live beside the brook Cherith. There He used ravens to bring him meat and bread twice a day. When the brook dried up, He led Elijah to the Gentile area of Zarephath where he met a widow who was emotionally and financially depressed. He asked her for water and bread, but she informed him that she had nothing but a small amount of flour and oil. She was about to prepare it for herself and her son so they could eat one last meal before they starved to death. Elijah told her not to worry. He knew that God loves to provide for those who trust and obey Him. She, her son, and Elijah ate miraculously for many days from a bowl and a jar that God continued to fill. God proved faithful to those who trusted Him!

Do you have a hard time trusting God financially? You should not. God allows the economy to go down at times to get our attention. Yet, He provides for His people who listen to Him and do what He says. Trust God today. He has not lost the recipe for manna. His resources are abundant. He has all the oil and flour you will ever need!

## SHOUT TO THE LORD

**Psalm 100:1** — *"Shout joyfully to the LORD, all the earth."*

Silence is not the only acceptable form of biblical reverence. It is also appropriate at times to *shout* to the Lord with a voice of praise. Sometimes God desires silence and stillness in His holy Temple (Habakkuk 2:20). At other times, He demands a shout!

When the armies of Israel invaded the Promised Land, the first fortified enemy city they faced was Jericho. Its walls were extremely tall and seemingly beyond penetration. Yet, God devised a military strategy theretofore unknown to man. God's people were to march silently around the city once a day for six days. Then on the seventh day they were to march around the city seven times. At the conclusion of the seventh lap, they were to shout unto God in praise. Notice: there was a time for silence and a time for shouting. They obeyed, and when they shouted, the walls of Jericho fell!

Jesus shouted, "It is finished!" (literally, "paid in full") just before He died on the cross. When He did, the great veil in the Jewish Temple that separated man from God was torn in two from top to bottom. Man forevermore had direct access to God through Jesus' shed blood. The Bible also says that Jesus will return for His children at the Rapture with both the sound of a trumpet and with the shout of the archangel.

It is appropriate for Christians today to be silent before the Lord in worship. But it is just as appropriate at times for them to shout joyfully unto Him. Both shouting and silence are "golden" to God. Creation began with a shout and it will end with a shout. The saints and angels in heaven shout endless praises to God. Heaven may be louder than we think. A good, strong "Amen," may be just what you and your church needs!

## A PRECIOUS PROMISE

**Philippians 4:13** — *"I can do all things through Him who strengthens me."*

Each of the thousands of promises in the Bible is a special gift from God to His beloved children. His promises give joy for sorrow, and hope for despair. Perhaps no promise is more quoted and claimed than the one in our text. What makes it so special?

It is a *personal* promise — "I can do." Notice that Paul said, "I." This was not something about which he had heard someone else speak. Rather, *he* knew what it was to have Christ for *his* support. We can place our name where Paul's "I" is in this verse, and make it ours today. It is also a *positive* promise — "I *can* do." Paul spoke positively, not negatively. He walked in faith and victory, not fear and defeat. We, too, have every reason for being positive in Christ. After all, every one of God's promises in Christ is "Yes," not "No" (2 Corinthians 1:20). The promise in this verse is also *productive* — "I can *do*." Paul was a worker. He was not lazy. He served God with his might as well as his heart. We also should work diligently and do good works that bring glory to Jesus (Matthew 5:16). It is also a *pervasive* promise — "I can do *all things*." Paul had learned how to thrive in both abundance and poverty. He was prepared to face any challenge. Even so, because of Jesus, we can experience victory in *all* areas. Finally, this promise is *powerful* — "...through Him (i.e. Christ) who *strengthens* me." Jesus empowered Paul for every deed he was required to perform. We too can depend on Christ to give us the necessary strength to live the Christian life and to obey all aspects of His perfect will for our lives.

The length of this promise may be short, but its depth is immeasurable. May these simple, yet profound words infuse you with God's supernatural power today.

## THE LORD WILL FIGHT FOR YOU

**Exodus 14:13-14** — _"Do not fear! Stand by and see the salvation of the LORD which He will accomplish for you today; for the Egyptians whom you have seen today, you will never see them again forever. The LORD will fight for you while you keep silent."_

When our son, Grant, was two years old, he began to bruise severely. His pediatrician shocked my wife and I one day when he made an appointment for Grant to see a specialist. He was to be tested for leukemia and several other life-threatening diseases. Needless to say, we could not sleep the night before his tests. Fear gripped our hearts like a vice. As I read my Bible, I came across our text. Moses and the Israelites were trapped between the Red Sea and the soldiers of Egypt with no apparent way out. The people looked to Moses for direction, and Moses wisely looked to God. The Lord parted the Red Sea so the Israelites could go to the other side on dry land. When the Egyptians chased them, God closed the Sea over them and they drowned. Moses and the people did not have to fear. They only needed to trust in God who fought for them.

As I read our text, God's peace overwhelmed me! I suddenly sensed that Grant would be fine. Before we drove to the hospital, I told my wife about the promise God had given to me. We rejoiced when the doctors tested Grant and discovered that he had a treatable blood disorder that he would soon outgrow. The Lord had fought for us as well.

Are you suffocating beneath a blanket of fear today? Perhaps you have lost your job, or you or one of your loved ones is sick, or you are facing a problem at school or in your home. Whatever your battle is, the Lord is with you and on your side. Go to His Word. Let His Spirit give promises of peace to your soul. He still parts the waters for His children. Trust Him and see. He will fight your battles today while you keep silent.

## CHARIOTS OF FIRE

**2 Kings 6:16-17** — *"So he answered, 'Do not fear, for those who are with us are more than those who are with them.' Then Elisha prayed and said, 'O LORD, I pray, open his eyes that he may see.' And the LORD opened the servant's eyes and he saw; and behold, the mountain was full of horses and chariots of fire all around Elisha."*

When I was in children's choir we sang a song that said, "All night, all day, angels watching over me, my Lord. All night, all day, angels watching over me!" I did not understand at that age the importance of angelic protection, but the older I become, the more I thank God for His ministering spirits and their "chariots of fire" around me.

Elisha the prophet and his servant appeared to be in trouble. A massive enemy army was heading their way. Elisha had been receiving divine revelation about the military strategies of Israel's opponents, and he was sharing that information with the leaders of Israel's army. As a result, Israel consistently defeated its opposition. When they discovered that Elisha was their problem, they came after him. His servant saw them coming, and in fear, told Elisha. Elisha told his servant not to worry, saying, "Those who are with us are more than those who are with them." Elisha prayed and asked God to "open his eyes" spiritually. Suddenly, his servant saw the spirit world, and beheld the angels of glory with swords drawn, riding on "horses and chariots of fire all around Elisha." God routed their enemies, and delivered the man of God and his servant.

The Lord's angels encamp around those who fear Him to rescue them (Psalm 34:7). If you or someone you love faces potential danger, ask God to open your spiritual eyes. Just as in Elisha's day, His angelic guardians are positioned and poised all around you in their chariots of fire! As long as they are present, no evil will befall you, nor will any plague come near your dwelling (Psalm 91:10-11). Thank God for His angels today.

## MAKING THE MOST OF YOUR TIME

**Ephesians 5:16** — *"Making the most of your time, because the days are evil."*

Time is a gift from God. To misuse it is to waste life itself. Time is life, and life is time. When someone says, "I'm just wasting time," he is really saying, "I'm throwing away my life." To squander time is incremental suicide. Paul told the Christians at Ephesus to walk wisely in this evil world (5:15). To do so, they needed to make the most of, or "redeem (their) time." How can we invest our time wisely and make the most of it?

**Do the Right Things.** Christians must prioritize. We cannot do everything we want to do, nor can we do everything others want us to do. God understands that. He wants us to do the *best* things. The main thing we are to do is to love God passionately and practically (Mark 12:30). Our second priority must be to love other people as we love ourselves (12:31). If we focus on these two areas, we will be doing the right things.

**Do the Right Things, the Right Way.** As Christians, we should do our very best in all that we do. God and other people deserve it. We must do what we do "with all our might" (Ecclesiastes 9:10). Service for Jesus demands our most excellent efforts.

**Do the Right Things, the Right Way, for the Right Reason.** We must do all that we do for Jesus' glory (1 Corinthians 10:31). He saved us to glorify Himself. We no longer belong to ourselves. He has redeemed and purchased us with His blood. Life is from Him, through Him, and to Him, and must be lived for His glory (Romans 11:36).

Many people are wasting their lives on frivolous, temporal matters. They are literally throwing away their lives. Do not be one of them. Invest your life in God's kingdom. "Only one life, it will soon be past; only what's done for Christ will last."

## GREAT IS YOUR FAITHFULNESS

**Lamentations 3:22-23** — *"The LORD's lovingkindnesses indeed never cease, for His compassions never fail, they are new every morning; great is Your faithfulness."*

Every day is a new beginning. Each night erases the previous day's events, causing them to be consigned forever to the grave of yesterday. Every sunrise offers a clean pad upon which fresh events may be written. Dawn brings a new consignment of God's gracious love and compassion, which He gladly distributes to His people.

Jeremiah, who penned these immortal words, lived during a dismal period of Judah's history. The invading armies of Babylon had destroyed Judah and Jerusalem. God's people had persistently engaged in idolatry and other odious sins, despite the Lord's solemn warnings through His prophets. When judgment finally came, the disaster was greater than anyone, even Jeremiah, could imagine. Homes, businesses, and even the Temple in Jerusalem were burned, leveled, and decimated. Men and women were murdered, and the young were deported as slaves into distant captivity. Yet God had promised Jeremiah that there was hope for Judah's future. After the people had suffered the discipline they deserved for several decades, the Lord would allow a remnant to return and rebuild Jerusalem. Jeremiah praised the Lord for His magnificent faithfulness that caused Him to bestow such love and mercy on the rebellious nation of Judah.

God is faithful to us as well. Though we are sinners by nature and choice, He consistently supplies a fresh batch of love and compassion for us each morning. Though we have not been faithful to Him, He remains ever faithful to us. He allows us to begin again.

Yesterday is gone. Today can be a new start. Praise Him for His mercy this morning. Shout Jeremiah's delightful doxology: "O Lord, *great* is Your faithfulness!"

## RENDER TO CAESAR

**Mark 12:17** — *"And Jesus said to them, 'Render to Caesar the things that are Caesar's, and to God the things that are God's.' And they were amazed at Him."*

"Politics makes for strange bedfellows." That saying was never truer than when, during the week prior to Jesus' crucifixion, the Pharisees united with the Herodians in order to question and ultimately trap Jesus to have Him arrested. Normally they hated one another. But their hatred for Jesus so superseded their ill feelings against each other, they were willing to lay aside their differences, at least momentarily. After flattering Him insincerely, they asked Jesus if it was "lawful" for Jews to pay taxes to the Roman Empire. They knew that if Jesus said, "No," they could have Him arrested for treason. Aware of their hypocrisy, He asked for a Roman coin. As He held it before them, He asked, "Whose inscription is on this?" They answered, "Caesar's." He replied, in effect, "Then give it to him. It belongs to him. Then give God what belongs to Him!" Jesus not only rebuked them for their love of money, but also emphasized that God's kingdom is not of this world (John 18:36). Amazed at His wisdom and insight, they left humiliated.

As Christians, we are citizens of an earthly kingdom. We owe taxes to our nation, and we should pay these dutifully (Romans 13:6-8). We are commanded to pray for our civil leaders (1 Timothy 2:1-2). We also owe respectful submission to the governmental authorities over us because they are ordained of God (Romans 13:1-5). We should rebel against their authority and defy them only if they tell us to disobey the Lord (Acts 5:29).

Christians have a dual citizenship. On one hand, we are citizens of an earthly country. But our primary allegiance is to Christ and His Kingdom. We should render to Caesar the things that are his, but only Jesus deserves our heart, soul, mind, and strength.

## First Class

**Luke 16:22** — *"Now the poor man died and was carried away by the angels to Abraham's bosom; and the rich man also died and was buried."*

As I approached the airport gate, I had higher than usual expectations for a pleasant flight. For the first time, I had a ticket in the First Class section. Due to a pricing special, my ticket in First Class was about the same price as one in coach. I took it, and was amazed at the difference. I boarded first, had plenty of room to store my carry-on bag, and I sat in a roomy seat. The stewardess hung my suit coat, and brought a beverage to me before we left the ground! It came in a real glass, not a plastic cup. Once in the air, I read, slept, and enjoyed it all. For at least that day, I was flying *First Class*!

Lazarus was a poor beggar. Too crippled to walk, he was carried daily from place to place to make a meager living. He was covered with sores that the dogs would lick as they passed by him. Before he died, he was stationed outside the house of a wealthy man. Though their worlds were very different, they soon shared a common experience — death. At that point, their circumstances reversed radically. The rich man went to Hades and suffered in tormenting flames. An angelic escort, however, took Lazarus to Paradise. He sat at Abraham's right hand with the saints of the ages and worshiped God. For the first time ever, the rich man suffered while Lazarus enjoyed "First Class" conditions.

God promises to meet our needs, but He does not guarantee us earthly riches. Our true treasures await us in heaven. Like Lazarus, we will go there accompanied by angels. We will live in mansions in a city with pearly gates, walls of jasper, and streets of gold. We will worship and serve our glorious King Jesus. If you are poor on earth, do not be discouraged. God loves you and has a seat for you in glory — and it is in "First Class."

## Heart Transplant

**Ezekiel 36:26** — _"Moreover, I will give you a new heart and put a new spirit within you; and I will remove the heart of stone from your flesh and give you a heart of flesh."_

Most people know someone who has suffered from some sort of heart disease. For instance, when a person's arteries do not allow a sufficient supply of blood to flow, he may have to undergo by-pass surgery. The surgeon severs the sternum and then replaces the bad arteries and veins with healthy ones from elsewhere in the body. They serve as alternate channels through which his blood can flow. There are times, however, when a patient has more than clogged arteries. A person's heart can be so diseased that he actually needs a heart transplant. That procedure calls for the removal of the bad heart followed by its replacement with a healthy heart from a donor. If the person's body accepts the new heart, he can potentially live a relatively normal life for many years.

Ezekiel prophesied about a coming day when God would perform spiritual heart transplants. That day was fulfilled in Jesus Christ. For those who repent of their sins and trust Christ to forgive them, God grants the gift of eternal salvation. Ezekiel's words in our text describe a three-fold result of such spiritual surgery: (1) God removes the person's sinful, hard heart; (2) He replaces it with a new, cleansed heart; and (3) He then fills that person's heart with the Holy Spirit. Now _that_ is a bona fide heart transplant!

Spiritually speaking, we need more than by-pass surgery. We need a transplant. Our hearts are evil (Genesis 6:5), deceitful and diseased (Jeremiah 17:9), and are the source of all the sin that defiles us (Matthew 15:18-20). You cannot restore your sinful heart. Give it to Jesus. He will replace it with a new heart that beats with love for Him.

## WHO IS THE LORD?

**Psalm 118:14** — *"The LORD is my strength and song, and He has become my salvation."*

The sovereign God of the Universe is referred to in the Old Testament as "the LORD," or "Jehovah." He is all-present, all-powerful, and all-knowing. His full identity as the Father of His only-begotten Son, Jesus Christ, is revealed in the New Testament. There is one God, and one Mediator between Him and all men — Jesus Christ (1 Timothy 2:5). In our text, the Lord is described and revealed in at least three ways.

**The Lord Is Our Strength.** The Psalmist viewed the Lord as the source of his power and strength. He knew that the Lord's will would only be realized through His Spirit's power (Zechariah 4:6). Like Paul, he could do "all things" through Christ who strengthened him (Philippians 4:13). Christ also gives us strength as we serve Him.

**The Lord Is Our Song.** The Lord not only empowered the Psalmist, but also filled his life with joy and celebration. Because of the Lord's bountiful grace and blessings, the psalmist celebrated with joyful singing and praise. Likewise, the Lord Jesus will become the melody of our heart and "keep (us) singing as we go."

**The Lord Is Our Salvation.** The Lord was the source of the Psalmist's strength and song because He had granted him eternal salvation. Even so, Jesus Christ has become our salvation. His name, "Jesus," means, "Jehovah is salvation." We are saved when we repent of our sins and place our faith in Christ alone to forgive and cleanse us.

If you belong to Jesus, He is the same to you as God the Father (Jehovah) was to the Psalmist. Make your good confession today. Say it loud, long, and confidently for all to hear: "Jesus is my strength and my song, and He has become my salvation!"

## LOVE ONE ANOTHER

**John 13:34-35** — _"A new commandment I give to you, that you love one another, even as I have loved you, that you also love one another. By this all men will know that you are My disciples, if you have love for one another."_

Christianity is based on the attribute of love. The greatest verse in the Bible is John 3:16. It tells us that God loved all the people of this world so much that He sent Jesus His Son to die as an atoning sacrifice for our sins so that we would be able to receive His gift of salvation, fellowship with Him in this life, and spend eternity with Him in heaven. When Jesus was asked what was the greatest of God's commandments, He immediately answered that it was to love God (Mark 12:30). The second greatest commandment is to love other people as we love ourselves (Mark 12:31). As Jesus' followers, we are even to love our enemies (Matthew 5:44). It should not surprise us, therefore, that our text teaches that our love for fellow believers is the primary indication that we are truly Christ's disciples. We are most like Jesus when we love one another.

The world is filled with hate, strife, conflict, bickering, war, and division. When non-Christians see true love among Christians, it causes them to desire to know more about Christ. They seldomly see compassionate, caring love. When they do, it catches them off guard. Christian love is the greatest testimony of the change Jesus brings to a person's life. Love is the bridge that must be built to carry the Gospel to our lost world.

Are you a Christian? Do others know that you are saved? Can they see the love you display toward God and other people, especially other believers? If we say that we love God, whom we cannot see, while we hate our Christian brother whom we can see, we are liars (1 John 4:20). Ask the Lord Jesus to fill you with His love for others today.

## No Compromise

**Daniel 3:17-18** — *"If it be so, our God whom we serve is able to deliver us from the furnace of blazing fire; and He will deliver us out of your hand, O king. But even if He does not, let it be known to you, O king, that we are not going to serve your gods or worship the golden image that you have set up."*

Many of us will never forget the tragic occurrence of the two teenage gunmen who walked through the hallways and classrooms of Columbine High School, leaving behind a wake of death and destruction. These ambassadors of the occult had as their mission to kill and maim as many of their fellow students as possible. In the midst of the chaos and carnage, one of the gunmen came upon a beautiful Christian girl named Cassie. Knowing of her faith in Christ, he placed the gun to her head and coldly asked, "Do you believe in God?" A student nearby heard Cassie answer, "Yes." It was a fatal reply. Immediately a shot was fired that left Cassie lying dead on the floor of her high school.

Many years earlier, three Jewish teenagers stood as the crowds around them lay prostrate in worship of a golden idol in Babylon. They were called before the king and threatened with death in a furnace if they did not join the others in idolatry. Like Cassie, they refused to compromise. They boldly affirmed that their God was mightier than any earthly king, and was also able to deliver them from the king's hand. But even if He did not, they refused to worship the golden image that had been set up. They were thrown into the furnace, but the Lord delivered them. The king saw it, repented, and worshiped the true God who had miraculously spared them and brought honor to His name.

Whether Christ spares us or not, we must never compromise our love and devotion to Him. The decision to stand for Jesus must be made *before* a gunman or king confronts us, not at the point of death. May we always be faithful to the God of Cassie.

## Growing In Grace

**2 Peter 3:18** — _"But grow in the grace and knowledge of our Lord and Savior Jesus Christ. To Him be the glory, both now and to the day of eternity. Amen."_

God desires for all of His children to mature spiritually. When a person becomes a Christian, he is born again (John 3:1-8) and becomes a spiritual babe who needs to grow and develop (1 Peter 2:2). Peter referred to this process in our text. A believer is to advance steadily in spiritual development by reading the Bible, praying, worshiping God, having fellowship with other believers, and witnessing to non-Christians.

The Christian's goal is to be conformed into the image of Christ (Romans 8:29). As he daily follows the Lord, he begins to think, talk, and act like Jesus. The fruit of the Holy Spirit (Galatians 5:22-23), which is indicative of Christ's nature, is increasingly displayed in the believer's life. Instead of hatred, there is love. Rather than bearing the weight of despair, he has joy. In place of anxiety comes peace. The believer cannot produce this fruit. Rather, it is the blessed by-product of abiding in Christ (John 15:1-5).

Our text teaches that as a Christian matures, at least two things will happen. First, he will "grow in the grace...of... Jesus Christ." He will become more merciful toward others. Legalistic condemnation will cease and he will extend forgiveness, restoration, and compassion to his fellow man. Second, he will "grow in the...knowledge of our Lord." He will not only know _about_ Jesus, but he will literally know _Him_. His increased intimacy with Christ will manifest itself both in passionate worship and obedient service.

Babies are cute, but it is tragic when someone advanced in years is not fully formed mentally or physically. How much more tragic when a believer is undeveloped spiritually. If you are saved, it is time to leave the nursery. It is time to grow in grace!

## SHE PUT IN ALL

**Luke 21:3-4** — *"And He said, 'Truly I say to you, this poor widow put in more than all of them; for they all out of their surplus put into the offering; but she out of her poverty put in all that she had to live on.'"*

I walked hurriedly into my office and saw the mound of mail in my box. As I sorted dutifully through the pile, most of which was "junk," I came across a personal note from one of the single ladies in our church. It contained a hand-written letter and also a check. In the letter, that precious sister in Christ told me that the Lord had prompted her to give to our church's building fund all that she had saved up as a down payment for a house she desired to purchase. She said that God had strongly impressed her to use that money to build His house, not hers. She knew that the Lord would take care of her need for a house, so with perfect peace, she gave "all that she had to live on" — $10,000.

As I looked at that letter and that check, I knew that I was standing on holy ground, holding "the widow's mite." I rejoiced that God had given that sweet lady such faith. I also evaluated my own level of trust and commitment to the Lord. Was I like the widow that Jesus honored, or like those who gave merely "out of their surplus"?

Do not feel sorry for that woman. And do not worry about whether or not she will get a house. God takes care of people like her. He always honors faithful obedience. She gave that money to Jesus, not to a building program. And *He* will certainly take care of her. She did not lose her senses. She was just thinking and acting in faith!

What kind of giver are you? Do you support the Lord's work at your church with your tithe and offerings? Are you afraid God will not take care of you? Take a lesson from two dear ladies: the one in our text, and the one in our church. They "put in all."

## GOD'S WEDDING RING

**Matthew 28:19** — *"Go therefore and make disciples of all the nations, baptizing them in the name of the Father and the Son and the Holy Spirit."*

That little ring felt like it was burning a hole in my pocket as I mustered up enough nerve to ask her "The Question." "Will you marry me?" I asked. She answered, "Sure," not aware of how serious I was. "Will you wear my ring?" I asked, as I handed it to her. Her mouth flew open as she opened the tiny box. She screamed, cried, and hugged me all at the same time, shouting, "Yes, yes, yes!!!" Boy, was I relieved!

Engagement and wedding rings are symbols of commitments and relationships that have been formed. Since that wonderful day when Donna put on my ring, I have had the privilege of performing many weddings for young couples. It always thrills me when they both give and receive rings as a symbol of their mutual love.

Did you know that God has a wedding ring? It is water baptism. The first commandment Christ gives to new Christians (i.e. "disciples") is to be baptized. Some advise new converts to wait for long periods of time before being baptized, but that is definitely *not* the New Testament pattern. Most people mentioned in the Book of Acts were baptized within the same hour they were saved! It is also noteworthy that the Bible knows nothing of infants being sprinkled. That is man's idea, not God's. Baptism is for believers only. Also, baptism does not save anyone. Only Jesus' blood can do that.

Baptism shows that Christ has already saved you. Even as married people should wear their rings to let others know they are married, Christians should be baptized to let others know they are saved. We will never mature spiritually until we obey God's first command for new believers. Be baptized, and put on God's wedding ring for all to see.

## A Natural Man

**1 Corinthians 2:14** — *"But a natural man does not accept the things of the Spirit of God, for they are foolishness to him; and he cannot understand them, because they are spiritually appraised."*

There are three categories of people — natural, spiritual, and fleshly or carnal. Paul refers to these in 1 Corinthians. The "natural" man is lost and not a Christian. The "spiritual" man is a Christian who is seeking to live for the Lord and do His will. The "carnal" man is also a Christian, but he is walking in disobedience to the Lord.

Regarding the natural man, Paul says that he is unwilling to accept "the things of the Spirit of God." Indeed, they are "foolishness to him." That is why lost people do not understand believers. I once talked with a man who was saved while listening to the preaching of Dr. John MacArthur on the radio. He told me that his wife, who was not yet a believer, was having problems with his newfound faith in Christ. She did not understand why he wanted to go to church regularly and even take notes when the minister preached. She was concerned that he was going "overboard" with religion. Her response was, in a word, *natural*. She was responding as the Bible said she would — she did not understand.

If you have been saved and you seek to live a godly life for Jesus Christ, be assured that your lost family members, friends, classmates, co-workers, neighbors, and other associates will not understand what has happened to you. They may even believe that you have a problem, when in reality just the opposite is true. *They* are the ones with the problem. They are lost, without Christ, without hope, and without God in this world. Love them, pray from them, be patient with them, and keep sharing Christ with them. They are talking and acting the way "natural" people do — they simply do not understand.

## A SPIRITUAL MAN

**1 Corinthians 2:12** — *"Now we have received, not the spirit of the world, but the Spirit who is from God, so that we may know the things freely given to us by God."*

Have you ever been near someone who truly walks with God? That person is so in tune with the Lord that you can sense His presence when you are with him. He literally "reeks" of God. God's anointing is on him and the fragrance of that anointing is apparent. Billy Graham is like that. Years ago I was present when he was scheduled to preach at the annual meeting of the Southern Baptist Convention, which was in Atlanta. As we were waiting on Dr. Graham to enter the Georgia Dome, a holy hush suddenly fell across the congregation that had assembled. It was as though God had entered to say, "I just want all of you to know that my servant, Billy, is about to speak My Word to you!"

Every Christian should desire to become a *spiritual* believer. A spiritual man crucifies his carnal, fleshly nature each day and yearns to live a holy life. He stays filled with God's Spirit, so he is able to discern accurately and walk in the things of God. He speaks spiritual words (1 Corinthians 2:13) and appraises life from a spiritual vantage point (1 Corinthians 2:15). His thoughts are spiritual because he possesses "the mind of Christ" (1 Corinthians 2:16). He loves God, walks obediently to His will, hates sin, and loves righteousness. He is a spiritual man in a natural world — and God blesses him!

Is that the kind of Christian you are? That is the type of Christian you should desire to become. Many Christians live such *subnormal* lives that when they finally meet a *normal*, spiritual Christian, they think he is *abnormal*! Christianity is more than just getting saved and going to heaven. Abundant victory, joy, peace, and unimaginable blessings await you. But they are blessings reserved exclusively for *spiritual* believers.

## A CARNAL MAN

**1 Corinthians 3:1** — *"And I, brethren, could not speak to you as to spiritual men, but as to men of flesh, as to infants in Christ."*

There are two kinds of Christians — spiritual and carnal. The spiritual Christian loves the Lord passionately and seeks to do His will completely. The carnal, fleshly Christian lives in a state of rebellion. He is saved, but harbors unconfessed sin in his life. He is double-minded (lit. "two-souled") and unstable in all his ways (James 1:8).

The worst enemy of Christ's Church is the carnal Christian, not the natural, lost man. A lost man is admittedly indifferent toward and disinterested in the things of God. He makes no pretense of being concerned about spiritual matters related to Jesus. He does not play the role of a religious play-actor, or hypocrite. Rather, he is open and honest about his spiritual indifference. A carnal, fleshly Christian, on the other hand, is the epitome of hypocrisy. While the lost man is spiritually cold, and the spiritual man is hot, the carnal man is lukewarm. Such halfhearted loyalty sickens Jesus (Revelation 3:16).

Are you a carnal Christian? Have you been born again but remained a spiritual babe who refuses to grow in grace and in the knowledge of Jesus? God has more in store for you than that! He wants you to repent and return to Him so that your sins will be wiped away and He can send seasons of refreshing and renewal to you. He desires to restore all that the enemy's locusts have devoured in your life. If you will be honest, confess and forsake the sin you have been holding on to, draw near to God, and resist the devil, then the Lord will draw near to you and bless you. Though your sins have been as scarlet, you will become as white as snow. Your spirit is willing, but your flesh is so weak. Crucify your flesh. Say "Yes" to God's Spirit, and declare war on carnality today!

## THE LIGHT OF GOD'S WORD

**Psalm 119:105** — *"Your word is a lamp to my feet and a light to my path."*

I could barely see the road as I drove our van. A dense morning fog had settled across the road. The sun had not yet risen as I progressed slowly and steadily with my lights on. As I traveled forward, my visibility was limited to approximately 40-50 yards. I could see ahead just far enough to continue traveling safely. My headlights were giving the sufficient light I needed. Eventually I emerged from the fog with the morning sun shining down. When my ability to see improved, I increased my speed and drove ahead.

Knowing and doing God's will is a lot like that. Sometimes the Lord reveals only a portion of His will to us. Our spiritual vision is limited to only a tiny path before us. But as we read His Word, our way is enlightened. The Bible is our lamp that illumines our way. Through it, God shows us just enough to enable us to move forward. As we advance, He faithfully gives us more visibility. We make slow, steady progress as we seek Him in Scripture, standing on His precious promises. Eventually, the fog of the unknown is lifted and He reveals His complete will for that portion of our journey. While we were in the fog of uncertainty, He guided us with the light of His Word. Then when the fog was lifted, He continued to light our way through Scripture like the sun shining in its brightness. His Word is indeed a lamp to our feet and a light to our path.

Perhaps you are traveling through a dark and hazy time in life. Do not be alarmed. God's Word is the lamp you need to light your path for a successful journey. Take time to read your Bible today. A Christian who neglects his Bible gropes in darkness. You do not have to travel in the dark. Reach down and turn on His light!

## AUTHORITY OR ANARCHY?

**Judges 21:25** — *"In those days there was no king in Israel; everyone did what was right in his own eyes."*

I grew up during the 1960s and 70s. Those were days of rebellion in our nation. Hippies ushered in the drug culture, while our streets were rocked with race riots. John Kennedy, Robert Kennedy, and Martin Luther King were assassinated. The Supreme Court outlawed the Bible and prayer in our schools, while, ironically, they legalized the murdering of unborn babies by abortion. Vietnam divided our nation. Colleges saw students express their frustrations with "the establishment" by engaging in "sit-ins" during which they would boycott classes and hold so-called "freedom-forums." The cries of that era were: "Do Your Own Thing," "Down with the Establishment," "Question Authority," and "If It Feels Good, Do It!" Rebellion was in, and authority was out.

What kind of country would we have if everybody "did his own thing?" The biblical book of Judges tells us. It describes some of the darkest days of Israel's history. After entering the Promised Land, the godly generation of Joshua and Caleb died. A new generation arose that turned its back on the Lord and embraced idolatry and a pagan, secular lifestyle. God disciplined them with oppressive, foreign invaders. Israel would repent and ask God for mercy. He would then send one of the Judges to rescue them. A time of peace would ensue, but soon the people again grew restless and returned to their sin and rebellion. The biblical writer described the entire era with the words of our text.

When we reject God's authority and commandments, the certain result is anarchy and chaos. Peace and fulfillment only come through submitting to Jesus Christ. Which do you want — authority or anarchy? Choose wisely and be prepared to live with your choice!

## COMMITMENT

**Ruth 1:16-17** — _"But Ruth said, 'Do not urge me to leave you or turn back from following you; for where you go, I will go, and where you lodge, I will lodge. Your people shall be my people, and your God, my God. Where you die, I will die, and there I will be buried. Thus may the LORD do to me, and worse, if anything but death parts you and me.'"_

Two broken women wept as they reflected over the recent tragedies they had experienced together. Naomi had suffered the death of her husband, Elimelech, as well as the deaths of her two sons, Mahlon and Chilion. Her sons had taken wives, Orpah and Ruth, from the land of Moab. After those deaths, Naomi decided to return to Israel. At that point, her daughter-in-law Orpah kissed her good-bye and returned to the land of Moab. But Ruth refused to leave. She clung to Naomi as she quoted the words of our text. She told Naomi that she loved her and that she was committed to her until death.

The Lord rewarded Ruth's loyalty. When she and Naomi returned to Israel, they came to Bethlehem where they met a prosperous, wealthy man named Boaz. His mother was Rahab, a former harlot who had assisted the Israelites when they conquered Jericho (Joshua 2; Matthew 1:5). Though Boaz was older, he and Ruth fell in love and married. He provided abundantly for his new wife and mother-in-law. But the greatest blessing came through their future generations. Boaz and Ruth had a son named Obed, who had a son named Jesse, who had a son named David, who became Israel's greatest king.

Our family members, especially our spouse and children, should know that we are devoted to them for better for worse, for richer for poorer, in sickness and in health, to love and to cherish, until death separates us. We must be loyal, regardless of changing feelings or unexpected circumstances. We are committed — we _cannot_ let them down.

## THE MOTTO OF A FOOL

**Luke 12:19** — *"And I will say to my soul, 'Soul, you have many goods laid up for many years to come; take your ease, eat, drink and be merry.'"*

The late Janis Joplin was a rock star from the hippie culture of the 1960s. She was sexually immoral, addicted to drugs, but immensely popular. Her music was wild and reckless. At times she screamed more than she sang. One song that was typical of her musical message was entitled, "Get It While You Can." The song encouraged people to freely indulge their every fleshly appetite, especially sexually. The rationale was that this life is short, and this life is all there is. Nothing exists beyond death, so whatever enjoyment you plan to experience must be done on earth, i.e. "Get It While You Can!"

That was the same philosophy of someone Jesus called a fool. The man was a farmer who had enjoyed a bumper harvest of crops. His success was not the problem. Rather, how he reacted to his success is what got him into trouble with God. He decided to save all of his wealth for himself. Eleven times in three verses (Luke 12:17-19) he used either "I" or "my." He never thanked God for his blessings, nor did he entertain the idea of giving anything back to the Lord. Neither did he consider helping his fellow man with some of his holdings. He only thought of himself. He then uttered a saying from ancient Epicurean philosophy: "Eat, drink, and be merry!" But he left off the last part: "For tomorrow we die." And die he did — immediately after God called him a fool.

God is the source of our blessings. He will guide us to be faithful caretakers of what He gives us. He blesses us so we can be a blessing. We are not to live to indulge our fleshly pleasures. We are to live to glorify Jesus. "Get It While You Can?" "Eat, drink, and be merry?" No way! Those are merely the mottos of a fool.

## CALLED TO HOLINESS

**Leviticus 20:26** — _"Thus you are to be holy to Me, for I the LORD am holy; and I have set you apart from the peoples to be Mine."_

God is holy. He is perfectly pure. He is light and in Him there is no darkness. It is incomprehensible that He would ever think, do, or say anything remotely sinful. He is high and lifted up, and majestically set apart as the only truly Holy One of the Universe.

God also desires for His children to be holy. The only people who can ascend the Lord's hill and stand in His holy place are those whose hearts and hands have been cleansed and purified by the blood of Jesus through regeneration. God must make us holy by His grace through faith in His Son, Jesus. When He grants us salvation, He sanctifies us and sets us apart from other people to be His. We become delightfully different from the world. He causes us to love Him and despise the lust of the flesh, the lust of the eyes, and the pride of life, all of which are of the world and not of the Father.

Holiness is a rare topic in contemporary churches. Few pastors are willing to preach on it because few church members desire to hear it. Preaching _for_ righteousness and _against_ sin is often considered legalistic, archaic, and mean-spirited. Yet, God demands and delights in holiness. Without it, no one will see the Lord (Hebrews 12:14).

Child of God, you have been saved to belong distinctly to God. He has called you out of this world to be a vessel of honor for His glory. You are in it, but not of it. The evil world system that is anti-Jesus, anti-church, and anti-Bible must not determine the way you act, think, speak, or dress. Friendship with the world is hostility against God. Jesus is holy and He expects holiness from you. Today, ask God to create a clean heart within you. His holiness will bring you true happiness. May you be holy as He is holy.

## SATISFACTION FOR THE THIRSTY SOUL

**Psalm 107:8-9** — *"Let them give thanks to the LORD for His lovingkindness, and for His wonders to the sons of men! For He has satisfied the thirsty soul, and the hungry soul He has filled with what is good."*

As the rain fell steadily just before daybreak, I was reminded that the Lord loves to bless His people. Rain is a blessing sent from God. When an area has experienced a period of severe drought, and it finally rains, the ground absorbs the water like a sponge.

Just as dry soil thirsts for rain, man's soul thirsts for God's blessings. The Psalmist knew that when he penned our text. He thanked the Lord for some of His most precious blessings that still satisfy man's thirst for God today. What are they?

**God's Lovingkindness.** The word "lovingkindness" (Hebrew *chesed*) is similar to a Greek word for "love" (*agape*). It refers to sacrificial love. God's lovingkindness caused Jesus to die for our sins. Thus, God's unmerited love is His greatest blessing.

**God's Wonders.** God works "wonders" among His people. He is still in the miracle business today. There has never been a *day* of miracles. Rather, there has always been a *God* of miracles. He still saves, heals, delivers, and sets the captives free.

**God's Goodness.** God also satisfies the thirsty soul with "what is good" (lit. His "goodness"). God's goodness causes Him to provide temporal blessings such as clothing, food, and shelter. But He also meets our deeper, spiritual needs for intimacy, love, joy, peace, and hope. Satisfaction is found in Jesus, not in another person or possession.

Is the Lord satisfying your thirsty soul? Stop drinking from the broken cisterns and empty wells of this world. Come to Jesus, who gives living water. There you may drink freely, frequently, and fully. And when your thirst is satisfied, give Him thanks!

## JESUS IS LORD

**Philippians 2:11** — *"And that every tongue will confess that Jesus Christ is Lord, to the glory of God the Father."*

The early Christians' primary belief was — "Jesus is Lord!" Many were martyred in Roman amphitheaters because they refused to say, "Caesar is Lord." Their primary allegiance was to Jesus, not Rome. What caused them to be willing to die for their *Lord*?

**Jesus Was Lord Before He Came to Earth.** Before time as we know it began, Jesus existed as God's divine Son. Before He came to earth, He reigned in heaven. He is fully God — co-equal, co-eternal, and co-existent with the Father and the Holy Spirit.

**Jesus Was Lord While He Was on Earth.** During His years on earth, Jesus was Lord. He was Lord over nature, the devil and demons, disease, and death. Thus, He could calm the stormy Sea of Galilee, cast out demons, heal the sick, and raise the dead.

**Jesus Was Lord on the Cross.** No one took Jesus' life from Him. He laid it down willingly. He prayed on the cross. He forgave a thief. At the end, Jesus offered up His spirit to the Father and died. He was Lord and totally in control even at His death.

**Jesus Will Be Lord When He Returns.** Jesus *will* return to this earth! He will come as an exalted King, not a lowly carpenter. He will ride a white horse, not a donkey. On that day, every knee will bow to Him, and every tongue will confess that He is *Lord*!

Is Jesus *your* Lord? Have you bowed and surrendered your life to Him? Is He the Master of your life? Scripture says that whoever will call upon the name of the *Lord* will be saved (Romans 10:13). If you are not yet a Christian, bow today and receive Jesus as your Lord and Savior. Then shout the greatest news of the ages — Jesus is Lord!

## WHO CAN BUT PROPHESY?

**Amos 3:7-8** — *"Surely the LORD God does nothing unless He reveals His secret counsel to His servants the prophets. A lion has roared! Who will not fear? The LORD God has spoken! Who can but prophesy?"*

This world is in need of God-called prophets. Too many of today's pulpits are filled by religious "professionals" who can "get up" a sermon. Those messages may be homiletically crafted and presented with fantastic oratorical skill. Yet they lack God's power to change the lives of their listeners. We need real preachers who will preach.

Amos was a shepherd whom God called to prophesy to the people of Israel. He loved the Lord and spent time with Him. God revealed "His secret counsel" to Amos. It was a harsh message of discipline. God told Amos to tell His people that He was going to judge their surrounding neighbors for their sins. The people of Damascus, Gaza, Tyre, Edom, Ammon, Moab, and even Judah would be punished. But then God said that He would also punish Israel for its sins! He had chosen and blessed Israel above all nations, yet they had rebelled against Him, committing idolatry. Because they had been given much, God required much from them. Amos heard God's revelation as clearly as the roaring of a lion. He therefore said, "Who can but prophesy?" Like Jeremiah, God's message was like fire in his bones. Like Paul, Amos said, "Woe is me if I don't preach!"

We need men like Amos to fill the pulpits of our Christian churches today. We must have preachers who know God and know how to receive His secret counsel from His Word. They must then be willing to speak that Word, even if it is not pleasant. If you hear a true prophet of God, you may not like what he says. But please do not get mad at him. The Lion of Judah has roared, he has listened, and he simply has to prophesy!

## LITTLE CHILDREN

**Jeremiah 19:5** — _"And (they) have built the high places of Baal to burn their sons in the fire as burnt offerings to Baal, a thing which I never commanded or spoke of, nor did it ever enter My mind."_

"Jesus loves the little children, all the children of the world." That preschool song presents a simple, yet profound truth. While on earth, Jesus took time to tenderly lay His hands on little children and bless them. Jesus loved children, and they loved Him.

It should not surprise us that the devil hates whatever Jesus loves, including little children. The Lord told Jeremiah to go to the Valley of Ben-hinnom, outside Jerusalem. He was to prophesy against the idolatrous atrocities that God's people were committing there. The most heinous act they were performing was child sacrifice. They were giving their children as burnt offerings to Baal, the Canaanite fertility god. They believed that Baal would send rain and bless them with abundant crops if they would offer their children at his altar. God was horrified, saying that He never commanded such a thing, nor did it ever enter His mind. That thought originated in the perverted mind of Satan.

Satan hates little children. He prompted Pharaoh to drown Hebrew babies in the Nile River in Moses' day. He incited Herod to massacre the male children two years old and younger in Bethlehem at the time of Jesus' birth. He master-minded the murders of over one million Jewish children during the Holocaust in the 1930s and 1940s. Satan is also behind every act of child abuse today, including the damnable practice of abortion.

The Bible says that children are a gift from God, and the "fruit of the womb" (i.e. a little child) is a "reward" (Psalm 127:3). Children are a blessing, not a blight. Today, take time to show genuine love to a child. The Lord Jesus loves them. So should we.

## CRYING OUT TO GOD

**2 Chronicles 18:31** — *"So when the captains of the chariots saw Jehoshaphat, they said, 'It is the king of Israel,' and they turned aside to fight against him. But Jehoshaphat cried out, and the LORD helped him, and God diverted them from him."*

One of the great kings of Judah in Old Testament times was Jehoshaphat. He loved the Lord and refused to participate in pagan worship. Because he obeyed God's commandments, the Lord blessed him abundantly, making him a rich and powerful king.

Along the way, however, Jehoshaphat made a foolish mistake by aligning himself with Ahab, the wicked king of Israel. Ahab enticed him to join with him to fight against the King of Aram. Ahab's hired prophets told them to go and conquer the Arameans. Only one real prophet, Michaiah, was willing to tell Ahab and Jehoshaphat that their battle would be ill fated. He prophesied that Ahab would be killed in the battle. Ahab had Michaiah arrested. He then convinced Jehoshaphat to dress in full kingly array while he (Ahab) dressed in the clothes of a common soldier. Ahab hoped that the opposing armies would attack righteous Jehoshaphat while he would go unnoticed.

When the battle began, the Arameans chased Jehoshaphat thinking that he was Ahab, the King of Israel. Just when they were about to kill him, Jehoshaphat cried out to the Lord. The Lord defended and delivered him. An arrow shot randomly by one of the enemy warriors, however, struck Ahab, fatally. By sundown, the wicked king was dead.

What made the difference? A righteous man called out to the Lord God and he was rescued! If you need help today, pray passionately to the Lord. When you do, He will divert Satan's arrows that are aimed at your soul. Fervent prayer still moves the heart and hand of our heavenly Father. Lift up your voice and cry out to Him in prayer today!

## MOTHS AND RUST

**Matthew 6:19** — _"Do not store up for yourselves treasures on earth, where moth and rust destroy, and where thieves break in and steal."_

As we pulled into the driveway, my wife and I noticed the peeling paint on our home. It had been painted just three years before, but now it was showing signs of age again. I smiled and said to her, "Everything in this world is either rotting or rusting."

Indeed, while we live on this earth, we are constantly putting patches on a ship that will eventually sink. God did not design this world to last forever. In fact, the Lord placed many unique reminders in this life to help us realize how nonpermanent it is. Jesus mentioned two of them in our text — "moth(s) and rust." If you have ever had moths infest your home, you understand how damaging they can be, and also how hard they are to exterminate and eliminate. Those tiny, winged creatures multiply rapidly and eat ravenously. Before they are even detected, they can often damage and destroy clothes, drapes, and other expensive items. Then there is rust. Everything metal, from automobiles, to tools, to gutters on the house, must be repainted regularly. Moths and rust are God's reminders to us of how temporary and transient this life really is.

God has other "reminders" such as mildew, and (heaven help us) wrinkles! All we really have to do is look in a mirror to recognize that things on this earth are deteriorating. Even though people all around us live like they and this planet will last forever, one thing is certain — you and I are passing through a world that is passing away.

Do not hold this world or its things too tightly. If you do, you will discover that what you are holding will rot. Only Christ's kingdom is eternal. Allow Jesus to be your supreme treasure. Then give this world and its things back to the moths and the rust.

## IT PAYS TO FOLLOW JESUS

**Psalm 1:3** — *"He will be like a tree firmly planted by streams of water, which yields its fruit in its season and its leaf does not wither; and in whatever he does, he prospers."*

Someone once told me, "It *pays* to follow Jesus." How true that is. When we follow Christ closely, He rewards us beyond our wildest imagination. The benefits of loving and obeying Jesus are incalculable. Psalm 1 says that the righteous person does not "walk...stand (or) sit" with "the wicked...sinners, (and) scoffers" (v. 1). Rather, he meditates on God's Word "day and night" until it becomes his "delight" (v. 2).

That person soon experiences several benefits: (1) *Stability.* "He will be like a tree firmly planted by the streams of water." The righteous person is not easily shaken. He is not "up" one day and "down" the next. He walks in consistent strength and steadiness. (2) *Productivity.* "Which yields its fruit in its season." The life of the righteous person produces good things for God's glory. The fruit of the Spirit ("love, joy, peace, etc.") is manifested in his life. Also, his acts of obedience testify of his sincere love for the Savior. (3) *Longevity.* "Its leaf does not wither." The righteous believer leaves a lasting legacy. He reaps a harvest of eternal rewards. He seeks Christ's Kingdom, which lasts forever. (4) *Prosperity.* "In whatever he does, he prospers." The righteous person "prospers," or succeeds because the Lord's blessing and favor are upon him. When others fall, he stands. When others retreat, he advances. When others fail, he succeeds.

Are you living a holy and righteous life? God rewards obedience. If you will sow seeds of righteousness, you will reap a blessed life on earth and an eternity of rich rewards. Though it costs you complete commitment, it always *pays* to follow Jesus!

## HAS GOD SAID?

**Genesis 3:1** — *"Now the serpent was more crafty than any beast of the field which the LORD God had made. And he said to the woman, 'Indeed, has God said, "You shall not eat from any tree of the garden?"'"*

Satan was the original liberal theologian. He was the first to question God's Word. God placed Adam and Eve in the lush paradise of Eden. He gave them a vast array of beautiful and fruitful plants and trees to enjoy aesthetically and also to serve as a source of food. The only one from which they could not partake was the tree of the knowledge of good and evil. God warned them that consumption of its fruit would result in spiritual and physical death. Despite God's abundant provision, Eve and Adam were drawn to the forbidden tree. When they looked at its fruit, Satan, in the form of a serpent, was present to tempt them. The sinister tone of his perverted voice is easily identifiable in the words, *"Indeed,* has God said?" In other words, "Are you sure you heard God correctly? Do you think He really meant to be that strict?" Satan not only questioned God's Word, but also exaggerated God's prohibition. He purposefully ignored the fact that God permitted them to eat from any tree but one when he said, "Has God said, 'You shall not eat *from any tree of the garden?'"* He later denied God's Word by saying, "You surely will not die" (v. 4). Satan was, is and will always be a liar who hates and distorts what God has said.

Today in our world of cultural and moral relativism, few people believe in absolute, non-negotiable truth that applies to all people. But the Bible is perfect, eternal truth that relates to every person of every generation. Though it is disobeyed, doubted, and despised by infidels, liberals, and other rebels who echo Satan's original question, Christians must face their culture and boldly declare, "Indeed, our God *has* said!"

## WHERE ARE YOU?

**Genesis 3:9** — *"Then the LORD God called to the man, and said to him, 'Where are you?'"*

The first question God ever asked was, "Where are you?" He asked that question while He was seeking His rebellious children, Adam and Eve. He had explicitly told them not to partake of the fruit of the tree of the knowledge of good and evil, warning that if they did they would die. Nevertheless, Eve was drawn to the tree. As she gazed at its fruit, the serpent (lit. "shining one"), who was Satan himself, engaged her in dialogue. At first, he questioned whether or not Eve had correctly heard God's prohibition. Then he denied God's warning altogether. He said that the Lord knew that if she and Adam ate of its fruit they would become like God, knowing good and evil. The more they talked, the more appealing the forbidden fruit appeared to her. At last, she took and ate. She then gave the fruit to Adam and he ate. Their eyes were opened, but their innocence was lost. Ashamed of their nakedness, they tried to cover themselves with leaves.

Eventually the guilty pair heard the Lord as He walked through the Garden of Eden. Though they tried to hide from Him, the Lord continued to call out for them. He knew exactly where they were hiding, nevertheless He asked, "Where are you?" He was really asking, "Where are you spiritually now that you have disobeyed Me?" He wanted them to confess their sin so He could forgive them and begin the process of restoration. Though their sin caused them to be punished, God faithfully called them back to Himself.

The question, "Where are you?" is precious indeed if you are either lost or have wandered away from Jesus. Are you hiding from God? It is an exercise in futility. He knows where you are, and He is calling out your name. Run to Him today in repentance.

## AM I MY BROTHER'S KEEPER?

**Genesis 4:9** — *"Then the LORD said to Cain, 'Where is Abel your brother?' And he said, 'I do not know. Am I my brother's keeper?'"*

The first question man ever asked was both sad and selfish — "Am I my brother's keeper?" A murderer named Cain, who still had the blood of his only brother, Abel, on his hands, asked it. Cain's anger originated and flared when he and his brother presented their offerings to the Lord. Cain brought a gift to the Lord from the fruit of his crops. Abel, however, gave "of the *firstlings* of his flock and of their *fat* portions" (v. 4). The biblical language suggests that Cain gave a token, nominal offering which cost him little, while His brother, Abel, gave a gift that cost him much. That is the primary reason God accepted Abel's offering and refused Cain's. Cain began to pout and became jealous of his brother. He then asked him to go out into a field with him. There, away from their parents, Cain committed the first murder by slaying Abel. His anger led to murder.

Just as God came looking for Adam and Eve when they committed the first sin in the Garden of Eden, God came looking for Cain. He asked him a straightforward question, "Where is Abel your brother?" God knew exactly what Cain had done because He later told Cain that Abel's blood was "crying to (Him) from the ground" (v. 10). Cain lied and said, "I do not know." Then he arrogantly answered with the question, "Am I my brother's keeper?" He should have been, but instead he was his brother's killer!

God tells us not to look out for ourselves only, but also for the affairs and interests of others (Philippians 2:3-4). We are to do good to others, especially to fellow Christians (Galatians 6:10). True "joy" comes when you think of **J**esus first, **O**thers second, and **Y**ourself last. You *are* your brother's keeper. Minister to someone in Jesus' name today!

## WHAT SHALL I DO WITH JESUS?

**Matthew 27:22** — *"Pilate said to them, 'Then what shall I do with Jesus who is called Christ?' They all said, 'Crucify Him!'"*

The angry crowd grew restless as they impatiently awaited Pilate's verdict. The Jewish religious leaders, jealous of Jesus' increasing popularity among the masses, had prompted the mob to request His crucifixion. Pilate, the Roman Governor of Judea, was all that stood between Jesus and the cross. At that critical moment, Pilate asked a very important question that each of us must answer: "What shall I do with Jesus?"

**Some Condemn Jesus as a Liar.** Atheists, infidels, and other liberals often say that Jesus was deceitful. They refer to Him as an overzealous rabbi at best, or a cunning deceiver at worst. They doubt the validity of His miracles and denigrate His teachings. In their opinions, He was certainly not who He claimed to be — the almighty Son of God.

**Some Classify Jesus as a Lunatic.** Still others believe that Jesus was simply some sort of a religious extremist who manipulated crowds. According to them, He may have actually believed He was God's Son, but mistakenly so. They categorize Jesus as an ancient Jim Jones or David Koresh who, as a madman, attracted weak, gullible people.

**Some Crown Jesus as Lord.** To those who believe the Bible, and have met Jesus personally in salvation, He is Lord. His miracles and teachings are not only real and true, but they are also available and applicable today. These people are Christians.

What will you do with Jesus? Your answer to that question is most important. Read the Bible and weigh the evidence. Jesus is no liar or lunatic. He is Lord. Crown Him as *your* Lord today. If you have already done so, then share His Gospel with others. Each person's eternal destiny hinges on his answer to Pilate's pivotal question.

## WHAT MUST I DO TO BE SAVED?

**Acts 16:30-31** — *"And after he brought them out, he said, 'Sirs, what must I do to be saved?' They said, 'Believe in the Lord Jesus, and you will be saved, you and your household.'"*

The blood ran down their backs as the clock struck midnight. Paul and Silas had been arrested and beaten by the civil magistrates of Philippi for preaching the Gospel. Yet the two men prayed and worshiped God (Acts 16:25). The Lord sent an earthquake, the chains fell off, and the prison opened. The jailer was about to take his own life when Paul assured him that all was well. The jailer then asked: "What must I do to be saved?"

**The Requirement for Salvation.** "Believe." God grants salvation "by grace...through *faith*" (Ephesians 2:8). Faith means "to believe, commit, and trust." We must *believe* the facts of the Gospel, *commit* ourselves completely to Jesus, and *trust* Him to save us. He justifies us by faith (Romans 5:1). We then stand clean before God.

**The Object of Salvation.** "In the Lord Jesus." Only Jesus can give salvation. The Philippian jailer could not place his faith in Paul or Silas. He had to trust Jesus *alone* before he was converted. It was not enough to "believe." He had to "believe *in the Lord Jesus*," not Jesus plus baptism, church membership, good works, or anything else!

**The Assurance of Salvation.** "You will be saved, you and your household." Paul and Silas did not say, "Believe in Jesus and you *might* be saved." They said, "You *will* be saved!" Christ does not give a "hope-so salvation," but a "know-so salvation."

God did not make salvation complex. In fact, a child can understand the answer that these men gave the jailer. "Believe in Jesus and you will be saved." That is how to be saved. We must not complicate it. Rather, we are to share it with a world that is lost.

## WHO IS YOUR PAUL?

**1 Corinthians 11:1** — *"Be imitators of me, just as I also am of Christ."*

Years ago I heard Howard Hendricks say, "We all need a Paul." He was saying that we all need a Christian who is more mature than us to help mentor us spiritually. God uses people to impact people. Who has God chosen to disciple and influence you?

From the beginning of my Christian pilgrimage, I have been blessed with godly people whom the Lord has used to mold me spiritually. Bob Orr, my pastor when I was young, was a compassionate, godly role model who loved the Lord, His Word, and other people. After I went to college, men like Bob Agee and Denzel Dukes made positive impacts on my life. Dr. Agee taught me to be a soul-winner. He and Brother Dukes helped me learn how to be a pastor by guiding me in areas such as hospital visitation and conducting weddings and funerals. Both men also gave me opportunities to preach. At seminary, God used several professors to mentor me, especially Roy Fish and Al Fasol. Dr. Fish helped develop within me a yearning for revival, while Dr. Fasol showed me how to develop and deliver sermons. Later on, God used Don Miller to teach me the priority of prayer. Fred Wolfe taught me more about walking in the Spirit and loving people. Adrian Rogers has shown me how to become a more effective leader, an expository preacher, and a better husband. These "Pauls" have shaped my life forever.

Who is your Paul? If you want to grow more as a Christian, you should find a more mature believer and learn from him. God will use different people to teach you in various areas. They will guide you and help you develop and grow. Be open to God's leadership. Stay teachable. Follow your "Pauls," and you will become more like Jesus!

## WHO IS YOUR BARNABAS?

**Acts 4:36** — _"Now Joseph, a Levite of Cyprian birth, who was also called Barnabas by the apostles (which translated means Son of Encouragement)."_

An old western song says, "Home, home on the range, where the deer and the antelope play; _where seldom is heard a discouraging word_, and the skies are not cloudy all day" (italics mine). Like "the range," local churches should be places devoid of discouraging actions and words. We all need encouragement. The world, our flesh, and the devil diminish our courage and sap our spiritual strength. We must be "encouraged," which means we need to have our courage restored and replenished. God uses His Word, His Spirit, and His people to encourage us. Those people become our "Barnabases."

Joseph was a First Century Christian who encouraged other believers so much that the apostles renamed him "Barnabas," or "Son of Encouragement." In the context of our verse, he sold a piece of land and gave the proceeds to help needy Christians. Later, he assisted Paul in being accepted by the disciples in Jerusalem who were skeptical of the sincerity of Paul's conversion in Damascus (Acts 9:26-28). Barnabas also encouraged the new Greek believers in Antioch to remain true to Christ (Acts 11:20-24). He and Paul were the first missionaries (Acts 13:1-5). Barnabas also salvaged Mark's ministry when Paul had turned that young preacher away (Acts 15:36-41). Had Barnabas not been an encourager, Mark might not have written the second Gospel!

You need a Barnabas who is similar to you in spiritual maturity. Though he knows you well, he should still love you unconditionally. He is to spur you on, and you are to reciprocate by lifting him up when he falls. As iron sharpens iron, you will make each other more effective. If you lack a Barnabas, ask God to give you one today.

## WHO IS YOUR TIMOTHY?

**2 Timothy 2:2** — *"The things which you have heard from me in the presence of many witnesses, entrust these to faithful men who will be able to teach others also."*

Christians are to be spiritual reproducers. Mature believers should seek to disciple those who are younger in Christ. The Apostle Paul was a master at mentoring. He rarely traveled alone. Instead, he sought to take others with him so they could watch him worship, witness, and work. Those people always learned valuable lessons. Paul's most famous "student" was Timothy. Paul poured his life into that young preacher and helped him immeasurably in his spiritual progress. Christians today must do the same.

Jesus established this discipline while He ministered on earth. He chose twelve "disciples," who were His "students" or "learners." They lived in His presence for three and a half years. They "caught" as much as they were "taught." They learned as much observing Jesus' actions as they did listening to His teachings. Among the twelve, Peter, James, and John, received special attention. They constituted Jesus' "inner circle." They were the only ones who saw Jesus raise Jairus' daughter from the dead. They alone were present on the mountain when Jesus was transfigured. They also traveled farther than the others into the Garden of Gethsemane the night Jesus prayed prior to His arrest and betrayal. Jesus mentored small groups in order to eventually reach the masses.

If you have been growing in the Lord for some time, ask Him to give you a "Timothy." Spend time with that person. Teach him to pray, read God's Word, witness, tithe, and serve the Lord faithfully in a godly, local church. Be genuine and transparent, allowing him to see your strengths and weaknesses. Freely you have received; freely you should give. Pour your life into others, and watch Jesus reproduce His life in them.

## A PROMISE MADE, A PROMISE KEPT

**Genesis 21:1-2** — _"Then the LORD took note of Sarah as He had said, and the LORD did for Sarah as He had promised. So Sarah conceived and bore a son to Abraham in his old age, at the appointed time of which God had spoken to him."_

God keeps His promises. If He says He will do something, He does it. He is not a human being who is capable of lying. Rather, God is truthful, trustworthy, faithful, and utterly dependable by nature. No one can accurately accuse Him of deceit or infidelity.

One day God promised an elderly couple named Abraham and Sarah that they would have a son in their old age. Years passed and the promise went unfulfilled. In their impatience, Abraham and Sarah decided to "help God out" by devising a plan of their own. They decided that Abraham should unite with Sarah's maid, Hagar, in order to have a son. Hagar conceived and bore Ishmael. But God had promised the couple a biological son named Isaac. Time passed and God's plan was eventually realized. Abraham was one hundred years old and Sarah was ninety years old when Isaac was finally born. Our text says that God "took note of Sarah _as He had said,_ and the LORD did for Sarah _as He had promised."_ Isaac was born _"at the appointed time_ of which God had spoken to him." The words mean "at the predetermined time." God's timetable is not necessarily ours. Although He never gets in a hurry, He is always right on time!

Has God given you a promise? If so, wait on Him to answer. Do not take matters into your own hands. God does not need your help. He wants you to enjoy a timely Isaac, not a premature, illegitimate Ishmael. The Lord is faithful. He will not stop thinking about you. He always fulfills His promises, and you are always on His mind. Remember that God loves you, and that with Him, a promise made is a promise kept.

## OUR FATHER WHO IS IN HEAVEN

**Matthew 6:9a** — *"Pray, then, in this way: 'Our Father who is in heaven.'"*

One Friday night I was eating supper in Jerusalem. Friday night is the beginning of the Jewish Sabbath, so the restaurant was filled with Jewish families celebrating their weekly day of rest and worship. The men wore dark suits, and their wives wore elegant, dark dresses. The children were clothed formally as well. As I stood at the buffet table, I heard a young, Jewish girl in a high chair call to her father. She shouted, "Abba! Abba!" He affectionately responded in Hebrew. In English, her cry means, "Daddy! Daddy!" She loved her father, and he readily acknowledged her when she called him by that name.

Jesus referred to God the Father as "Abba" when He prayed in desperation and anguish in the Garden of Gethsemane just before His arrest (Mark 14:36). Likewise, Paul encouraged the early Christians to cry to God by calling Him their "Abba," because God's indwelling Spirit had made them children of God (Romans 8:15; Galatians 4:6).

In the Model Prayer, Jesus told His disciples to "Pray, then, in this way: 'Our *Father* who is in heaven.'" He told them to address God as "Father," because they were His beloved children. That concept was never taught throughout the Old Testament. In fact, to most Jews in Jesus' day, it seemed blasphemous to refer to God as one's "Father." Yet, those who have received Christ as Savior have indeed become children of God (John 1:12). We are to be intimate with Him, even as that little Jewish girl was with her daddy.

God is not distant and impersonal. Rather, He is a "very *present* help" (Psalm 46:1). What touches your heart touches His heart. You are His precious child, and He loves you dearly. When you pray today, thank Him that He is your heavenly Father.

## HALLOWED BE YOUR NAME

**Matthew 6:9** — *"Pray, then, in this way: 'Our Father who is in heaven, hallowed be Your name.'"*

Once we become children of God through Jesus Christ, we desire to praise Him. We are to worship Him, taking into consideration the names ascribed to Him in Scripture. Each name indicates an aspect of His nature. He is holy. Thus, His name is "hallowed."

Several of the names in the Old Testament that refer to God are very helpful to us as we worship Him. He is *Jehovah-Jireh: The Lord Who Provides* (Genesis 22:14). He supplies all our needs according to His riches in glory in Christ Jesus. He is *Jehovah-Rapha: The Lord Who Heals* (Exodus 15:26). He is still the Great Physician who heals us spiritually, emotionally, and physically. He is *Jehovah-Nissi: The Lord Our Banner* (Exodus 17:15) who fights for us while we silently trust Him. He is *Jehovah-Mekadesh: The Lord Who Sanctifies* (Leviticus 20:8). He sets us apart from the inhabitants of this world to be His chosen people. He is *Jehovah-Shalom: The Lord Our Peace* (Judges 6:24). As we trust and obey Him, He gives us incomprehensible peace. He is *Jehovah-Rohi: The Lord Our Shepherd* (Psalm 23:1) who leads, protects, feeds, and sustains us as His sheep. He is *Jehovah-Tsidkenu: The Lord Our Righteousness* (Jeremiah 23:5-6) who forgives our sin, and covers us with the righteousness of Jesus. He is also *Jehovah-Shammah: The Lord Who Is Present* (Ezekiel 48:35). He will never leave or forsake us.

These and other names are ascribed to our heavenly Father in the Bible. The more we study them, the more specific and intimate we can be in our worship of Him. God is holy. He loves to hear us praise Him using His biblical names, each of which is also holy. Praise Him today. He still loves to hear us say, "Hallowed be Your name!"

## YOUR KINGDOM COME

**Matthew 6:10a** — *"Your kingdom come."*

Bill Gaither has written many wonderful songs that have been an encouragement to the body of Christ. One of his songs, entitled, "There's Something About That Name," contains these lyrics: "Kings and kingdoms will all pass away, but there's something about that name!" Of course, "that name" is the name of Jesus who is the King of kings.

**Jesus Is Our King.** When we pray for God's kingdom to come, we can be certain that Jesus Christ is our King. The prophets predicted that the Messiah would be a reigning king (Isaiah 9:6-7; Daniel 7:13-14). When Pilate asked Jesus if He was a king, He said, "You say correctly that I am a king. For this I have been born" (John 18:37).

**Jesus Has a Kingdom.** While Jesus stood before Pilate, he also said, "My kingdom is not of this world" (John 18:36). Jesus' kingdom is not similar to a fleshly, temporal, earthly kingdom. Rather, His kingdom is spiritual and eternal. Flesh and blood cannot inherit it (1 Corinthians 15:50). To enter His kingdom, you must be born again.

**Jesus' Kingdom Will Come.** To pray for God's kingdom to come is to ask that His spiritual kingdom will expand on earth until Christ returns and establishes His Millennial Kingdom. God's kingdom expands as people receive salvation. When Jesus returns, He will reign powerfully and peacefully in His kingdom on earth for a thousand years. Then the earth will be destroyed by fire and we will live in New Jerusalem.

Earthly kingdoms will come and go, but Christ's kingdom is forever! Are you part of it? If not, trust Jesus as your Savior, and join His kingdom today. Then pray for His kingdom to come until that glorious day when we see Him, King Jesus, face to face!

## YOUR WILL BE DONE

**Matthew 6:10b** — *"Your will be done, on earth as it is in heaven."*

My good friend and mentor, Fred Wolfe, once told me, "Ninety percent of discerning God's will for your life is being totally surrendered and obedient to whatever He wants." To that I say, "Amen!" Jesus taught His disciples to ask God to let *His* will be done in their lives "on earth as it is in heaven." Submission is the key to discernment.

Jesus grew up seeing this kind of submission to God's will in the life of His mother, Mary. After all, when the angel, Gabriel, told her that God had chosen her to bear the Messiah even though she was still a virgin, she had responded by saying, "Behold, the bondslave of the Lord; may it be done to me *according to your word"* (Luke 1:38). Though she knew that her obedience would result in being misunderstood and ridiculed by those who would think she had been immoral, she was willing to endure it all in order to experience God's perfect plan for her life.

Jesus Himself prayed a similar prayer just hours before His crucifixion. As He "fell on His face" in agonizing prayer in the Garden of Gethsemane, He prayed, "My Father, if it is possible, let this cup pass from Me; *yet not as I will, but as You will"* (Matthew 26:39). He prayed this two more times before He graciously embraced His death on the cross for sinners. Because He surrendered to God's will, He was able to discern it. We too must follow His example by yielding totally to God's plans for us.

To know God's will, you must first submit and surrender to it. An old hymn might help: "Have Thine own way, Lord, have Thine own way; Thou art the potter, I am the clay. Mold me and make me *after Thy will* while I am waiting, yielded and still!"

## OUR DAILY BREAD

**Matthew 6:11** — *"Give us this day our daily bread."*

God promises to supply the needs of His children (Philippians 4:19). He gave us His Son, Jesus, to pay the atoning ransom for our sins. He will, therefore, along with Jesus, freely give us all things (Romans 8:32). He is simply waiting for us to ask Him.

Our text is a petition requesting God's provision. It is a *morning* prayer — "Give us *this* day." The day obviously lies directly before the person who is praying. God wants us to begin each day communicating with Him (Psalm 143:8). Morning prayers result in blessings all day long. It is a *daily* prayer — "Give us this *day* our *daily* bread." These words literally mean, "Our bread for tomorrow." We are to take one day at a time. We must not ask for vast storehouses for the future. God desires for us to walk by faith, day-by-day. It is a *selfless* prayer — "Give *us* this day *our* daily bread." We are to pray for ourselves and for others, asking the Lord to meet their needs too. It is a *simple* prayer — "Give us this day our daily *bread*." We are not to ask for steak, but for bread! God will provide all our *needs*, but not all our *greed*. God often gives us our "wants," but we must be content with clothing, shelter, and food (1 Timothy 6:8). Finally, it is a *specific* prayer. We are not to pray a vague, meaningless "Lord, bless me." Rather, we are to pray for specific blessings. God is more than able to handle any request we bring to Him!

Often, we do not receive what we need because we simply do not request God's help (James 4:2). He desires for us to ask Him to provide our necessities. Though He will not answer if we pray greedily (James 4:3), He will grant what we require. What do you *need* today? Your Father is just waiting to hear from you. Go ahead. Ask!

## Forgive Us Our Debts

**Matthew 6:12a** — *"And forgive us our debts, as we also have forgiven our debtors."*

When a person becomes a Christian, he is a new creation. Old things have passed away and new things have come (2 Corinthians 5:17). God cancels his sin debt, forgives him, and secures his salvation forever (John 10:27-29). But what does a person need to do when he sins *after* he becomes a Christian? He should ask God for forgiveness.

Before a person can pray for forgiveness, *conviction* must come. The Holy Spirit causes the believer to be aware that he has sinned. The Spirit convicts lost people of sin, righteousness, and judgment (John 16:8). He is also grieved when God's people sin (Ephesians 4:30). *Confession* must come next. When the believer sins, God expects him to confess and repent (1 John 1:9). Such confession does not maintain his *relationship* with the Lord (i.e. his salvation). Rather, it restores his *fellowship* with Him. After confession, God brings *cleansing*. When God forgives, the iniquity is purged and the person becomes "whiter than snow" (Isaiah 1:18). The believer can then *claim* his forgiveness. The devil tries to make him think that God did not actually forgive him when he confessed. Nevertheless, regardless of how he feels, he is to stand on God's promises in faith and accept His forgiveness. The final aspect is *calmness*. God grants the believer a confirmation in his heart that he has been restored and that all is well.

The forgiven person is a blessed person (Psalm 32:1-2)! God loves to forgive, but He only does so when we repent, confess our sin to Him, and humbly ask Him to pardon our iniquity. Ask the Holy Spirit to bring to your attention any unconfessed sin in your life right now. Jesus is ready to restore. Repent and He will forgive your sin debt today.

## WE FORGIVE OUR DEBTORS

**Matthew 6:12b** — *"As we also have forgiven our debtors."*

Those who are forgiven should forgive. If you have received God's mercy through His Son, Jesus Christ, you are called to extend that same mercy to others who have wronged you. Unless you forgive them, God will not forgive you (Matthew 6:15).

Jesus tells a parable (Matthew 18:23-35) about a man who owed a king 10,000 talents (about $3 billion today). One talent was worth fifteen years of a common man's wages. It would have taken 150,000 years for him to earn that much money! When the man could not pay, the king sentenced him and his family to be sold as slaves. He begged for mercy and the king amazingly forgave all his debt! But then the forgiven man left the king's presence and found a man who owed him 100 denarii (approximately $8,000 today). To put that into perspective, for every dollar the man owed him, he had owed the king about $350,000! When the man could not repay him, he had him thrown into prison. The king found out what had happened and sentenced that wicked man to be tortured until his original $3 billion debt was paid. Jesus then warned his listeners that God would do the same to anyone who refused to forgive his brother "from (his) heart."

Jesus forgave those who crucified Him (Luke 23:34). They did not ask for forgiveness, nor did they deserve it. His forgiveness did not mean that He approved of their actions. He forgave them because He refused to be controlled by a bitter spirit.

If someone has hurt you, release him from the cage of unforgiveness. Choose to forgive him and let him go free. Pray for God to bless him. Then grant him the mercy you desire from God. Prove that you are forgiven by forgiving others from your heart.

## DO NOT LEAD US INTO TEMPTATION

**Matthew 6:13a** — *"And do not lead us into temptation."*

One privilege we have as Christians is to ask the Lord to give us guidance in life. He has promised to lead us in "paths of righteousness for His name's sake" (Psalm 23:3). Jesus also tells us to ask our heavenly Father to keep us from any path that might lead us into temptation. This preventive petition must become part of our daily prayers.

Jesus is not implying in our text that God would ever entice a person into temptation. Scripture says explicitly that God never tempts anyone to sin (James 1:13). Rather, this prayer is simply asking God to help us avoid temptation throughout the day. All of us are tempted by our own selfish lusts (James 1:14), the evil world system (Romans 12:2), and the devil (Matthew 4:1). We are tempted in three spheres: the lust of the flesh, the lust of the eyes, and the pride of life (1 John 2:15-16). Adam and Eve were tempted in all of these areas (Genesis 3:6), as was Jesus (Luke 4:1-13). We are also.

We must pray to avoid temptation so that we can also avoid sin. Temptation is being enticed to sin. Sin is yielding to that temptation. Temptation itself is not sin. Jesus was tempted, but He never sinned (Hebrews 4:15). If we avoid the temptation, we will avoid the sin as well. If we do not want to fall down, we must not walk in slippery places!

How can we avoid temptation? We must live in the Bible (Psalm 119:9-11), pray (Matthew 26:41), seek God's "way of escape" (1 Corinthians 10:13), tear down strongholds of sin (2 Corinthians 10:3-5), dedicate the members of our body to God (Romans 6:12-14), avoid the appearance of evil (1 Thessalonians 5:22), and flee from ungodly lusts (2 Timothy 2:22). Ask the Lord to shelter you from temptation today!

## DELIVER US FROM THE EVIL ONE

**Matthew 6:13b** — *"But deliver us from evil."*

Prayer is spiritual warfare. Though God is infinitely superior to the devil, He expects us to pray in order to be delivered from Satan's schemes. The word "evil" in our text is actually, "the evil one." Jesus was not telling us to pray for power over evil in general, but to ask God to give us victory over the devil. How can that happen?

First, we must understand that we are in a spiritual battle. Our struggle is not with people, but with demonic forces (Ephesians 6:12). We must stop wasting time fighting with people and start praying instead. We must also learn that we are seated with Jesus in heavenly places (Ephesians 2:4-6). Since He is Lord of all, in Him we have authority over demonic forces (Mark 3:14-15; Luke 10:19). Christ within us is more powerful than Satan in the world (1 John 4:4). We are to put on God's whole armor each day through prayer in order to fight the enemy (Ephesians 6:10-18). We must tear down mental strongholds and take our thoughts captive to prevent Satan from deceiving us with his lies (2 Corinthians 10:3-5). We must bind evil spirits by evoking the name of Jesus (Acts 16:18), and also overcome them by pleading the shed blood of Christ (Revelation 12:10-11). We must constantly quote Scripture and watch God use the sword of the Spirit to obliterate the enemy's works (Luke 4:1-13; Ephesians 6:17). Finally, we can defeat even the mightiest demonic forces with the disciplines of fasting and prayer (Matthew 17:21).

In these dark days, we must not be ignorant regarding spiritual warfare. God wants us to fight and win the good fight of faith. We live on a battlefield and we must be prepared. God is able to deliver us from the evil one. Our victory is only a prayer away.

## Yours Is The Kingdom, Power, And Glory

**Matthew 6:13c** — _"For Yours is the kingdom and the power and the glory forever. Amen."_

Jesus taught His disciples how to pray. In the Model Prayer (Matthew 6:9-13), He told them to begin their prayer time with praise — "Our Father who is in heaven, hallowed be Your name." They were then to offer up prayers of submission, confession of sin, intercession (praying for others), and petition (praying for their needs). They were to seek God's guidance, as well as His protection from the evil one. Their prayers were to conclude just as they had begun — with heartfelt worship.

**The Lord's August Kingdom.** God's children praise Him when they say, "Yours is the kingdom." As was mentioned in an earlier devotional (5/20), God is King of all kings. He reigns majestically over the Universe, lofty and exalted. Angels encircle Him and offer Him perpetual praise. His children should do the same.

**The Lord's Absolute Power.** We also praise the Lord by saying, "Yours is the power." God is omnipotent. No one can usurp or overthrow His eternal, righteous government. Every human and angelic being is subservient to Him. He is in complete control. The Lord is the immutable, absolute authority over the Universe.

**The Lord's Awesome Glory.** God is majestic in His royal, eternal splendor. Thus, we worship Him by saying, "Yours is the glory forever." God reigns in glory. Christ will return to earth in breathtaking, glorious grandeur. Our God is indeed glorious!

The Model Prayer ends with, "Amen," which means "truly," or "so be it." In this model, Jesus both inspired and informed His disciples concerning prayer. It should serve as a daily guide for all of us as we commune personally and passionately with our Lord.

## EXAMINE YOURSELF!

**2 Corinthians 13:5** — *"Test yourselves to see if you are in the faith; examine yourselves! Or do you not recognize this about yourselves, that Jesus Christ is in you — unless indeed you fail the test?"*

Sometimes church members have serious doubts regarding the certainty of their salvation. Paul advises such people to "test" and "examine" themselves to see if they are truly "in the faith." What traits should characterize a true Christian? What questions should we ask ourselves in order to discern whether or not we are really saved?

**Does the Spirit Lead Me?** True Christians are "led by the Spirit of God" into spiritual maturity (Romans 8:14). They may experience temporary setbacks, but habitual backsliding indicates lostness (1 John 2:19). Christians should grow in grace.

**Do I Enjoy Obeying God?** True Christians want to keep God's commandments (1 John 2:3). If you can disobey God without being grieved in your spirit, you are not really saved. Those who know Christ have a burning desire to do His will (Luke 6:46).

**Do I Love Other Christians?** Genuine Christians also love other believers (1 John 2:9-11; 4:7-8, 20). Those who perpetually criticize other Christians and never have a desire to attend church are not saved, despite any "religious experience" they have had.

**Do I Have Inner Peace?** If we are saved, the Spirit within us "testifies with our spirit that we are children of God" (Romans 8:16). He gives us the inner assurance and peace that Christ knows us (John 10:27-29) and that God is our Father (Romans 8:15).

Other questions can be asked, but these are sufficient to see if you are truly "in the faith." Is Christ in you? Be honest. Do not cheat. No exam matters more than this one. Failure brings death and hell. Passing brings life and heaven. Examine yourself today.

## YOUTHFUL LUSTS

**2 Timothy 2:22** — _"Now flee from youthful lusts and pursue righteousness, faith, love and peace, with those who call on the Lord from a pure heart."_

The greatest Christian testimony is not of a rebellious life changed radically by a dramatic conversion. Far better to come to Christ as a youth and live an entire life for His glory. Such a person avoids the scars of "youthful lusts." How can that happen?

**Flee from Youthful Lusts.** Paul told Timothy, a younger pastor, that the only appropriate response to youthful lusts is to "flee!" Other sins we may fight, but when it comes to lust, the only safe response is to run away! Like Joseph who was tempted by Potiphar's wife, we must escape before we succumb to immoral desires (Genesis 39:12).

**Pursue Righteousness.** Once we say "No" to sin, we must say, "Yes" to godliness. The best defense is a good offense. We must aggressively seek the Lord, His kingdom, and His righteousness (Matthew 6:33). We must let His virtue flow through us, learn to walk by faith, extend His love, and abide in His incomprehensible peace.

**Establish Godly Relationships.** We need the encouragement of other believers who also seek the Lord and desire to live holy lives. With them, we can "call on the Lord" with hearts purified by Jesus. Like iron sharpening iron, so other believers will establish and encourage us in our pursuit for personal purity (Proverbs 27:17).

Can we have victory over "youthful lusts?" Yes, if we will run away from them, aggressively pursue the Lord and His righteousness, and establish spiritual relationships with other committed Christians. "Youthful lusts" may provide brief moments of enjoyment, but they also lead to years of pain, guilt, bondage, and regret. The seeds we sow today will determine our future harvest. Let us sow wisely.

## PUT YOUR TRUST IN HIM

**Psalm 56:3** — *"When I am afraid, I will put my trust in You."*

God has not given His children a spirit of fear or timidity (2 Timothy 1:7). Yet fear paralyzes many Christians in states of hopelessness, torment, and uselessness. The opposite of fear is faith. When we are tempted to fear, we must put our trust in the Lord.

**We Can Trust God Exclusively.** The only Person who will never let you down is Jesus. He is absolutely dependable. All people, even those you love and cherish the most, are sinners filled with flaws. Even the best of people are capable of disappointing you. The Lord alone is worthy of your complete trust. He is the wholly faithful One.

**We Can Trust God Entirely.** You can trust God in every situation. Fear can only grip you in its vice of despair and doubt if you let it. You can trust God with your salvation, your prayer requests, and your personal needs. Nothing is too large or small to bring to Him in prayer. No matter what you face, you can depend on Him.

**We Can Trust God Eternally.** Not only can you trust God exclusively and completely in this life, but you can also trust Him in eternity. Should Jesus tarry in His return, all people will encounter death. Regardless of how healthy, wealthy, or wise you are, you will share in the common experience of death. As a Christian, death should not cause you to fear. When you are at last absent from your body, you will be present with the Lord. In His presence there is no fear; only abundant life and joy forevermore!

Are you tempted to be afraid? You do not have to be. Instead, you can depend on Christ exclusively, entirely, and eternally. What man does to you does not matter if your hope is in Jesus. Walk in faith, not fear. Lean on the One who is worthy of your trust!

## Religious Titles

**Matthew 23:8** — *"But do not be called Rabbi; for One is your Teacher, and you are all brothers."*

Some religious leaders prefer to be addressed by various titles. For instance, in Jesus' day, the scribes and Pharisees were fond of being called "Rabbi" by the people in the marketplaces (Matthew 23:7). Jesus warned His disciples at this point, telling them not to encourage others to call them by titles such as "Rabbi," "Father," "Leader," or "Teacher" (23:8-10). Why? Because they were "all brothers." They each stood on level, common ground at the cross of Christ. To be distinguished among their peers, they needed to do one thing — be faithful servants (23:11). Demanding to be called by titles was a sign of self-exaltation, which God would discipline with humiliation. Jesus' followers were to humble themselves. Only then would He bless and exalt them (23:12).

Today there are Christian leaders who feel they *must* be referred to by religious titles. There is nothing innately wrong with calling someone by a title, but when that person demands it, something is terribly wrong. Such an attitude surely grieves our Lord. Jesus certainly never demanded a title. The early Christians, even the apostles, related to one another on a first name basis. As a rule, believers today should do the same. None of us should insist on being called "Doctor," "Father," "Bishop," or "Reverend."

W. A. Criswell, longtime pastor of First Baptist Church, Dallas, Texas, made a humorous statement that applies here. He said, "Ph.D., D.Min., Litt.D., Ed.D., and D.D. Put it all together, and in God's sight it adds up to Fiddle-De-Dee." Education is desirable. Nevertheless we should remember that it is usually the common man who will hear Jesus gladly (Mark 12:27). Jesus alone is worthy of being exalted. Man is not.

## SOWING THE WORD

**Mark 4:14** — *"The sower sows the word."*

When I was a boy, my father bought a farm. One day he placed on my shoulders a seed-bag with a crank-handle and a flywheel at the base. As I walked and turned the handle, the seed was broadcast in all directions. When dad took me back to look at the field a few weeks later, I could not believe my eyes. The barren field was now covered with bright green grass. I was overwhelmed. I had sown seed and reaped a harvest!

Jesus told a parable about a sower who went out into the fields to sow. He sowed the same seed on different types of soil. Some of the soil was hard, some was shallow, some was thorn-infested, and some was good and fertile. The parable explains how a Christian is to share the Word of God with others. Every Christian is to sow the seed of God's Word, not human opinions, human philosophies, or man-based doctrines. Like the soils, not every person will receive God's Word and bear fruit. Some will harden their hearts and Satan will steal the Word away before it produces fruit. Others will receive God's Word, but when persecution arises they will wither away. Other seed will fall among the thorns of worldliness that will choke out God's Word and its fruit. The good news is that if we continue to share God's Word, some will listen and receive it. They will be saved, grow in grace, and bear much fruit for God's glory. These people make the process of sowing God's Word worth all the difficulties we as sowers experience.

Some never see anyone saved because they never sow Gospel seed. God's seed will not leave the barn or the seed bag on its own. A sower must sow it. Christian, share God's Word today. The Lord of the Harvest is calling you to labor faithfully in His field.

## HOLY GROUND

**Exodus 3:5** — _"Then He said, 'Do not come near here; remove your sandals from your feet, for the place on which you are standing is holy ground.'"_

Wherever God sovereignly and graciously meets with man, that place becomes a hallowed spot. It matters not if it is a beautiful cathedral, or a simple setting in nature. The road to Damascus became a high and holy temple when Jesus confronted Saul (Paul) there (Acts 9). Jacob's well in Sycar became a cathedral when Jesus dealt with the woman from Samaria (John 4). Whenever God touches down on earth, that site forever becomes sanctified and set apart from the commonplace in the heart of the worshiper. The place in and of itself is not holy, but the Lord's presence makes it "holy ground."

Moses was born a Hebrew slave. Through divine intervention, he was rescued from death as a baby and reared in the house of Pharaoh, the King of Egypt. Eventually he murdered an Egyptian taskmaster whom he saw mistreating a Hebrew slave. When Pharaoh learned of Moses' deed, he tried to kill him. Moses fled from Egypt to Midian. There he settled, married, and became a shepherd. For forty years he tended sheep in an isolated desert. Then one day, as an eighty-year-old man, Moses saw a bush that was on fire, but it was not being consumed. When he turned aside to see the strange sight, God called to him from the bush. Moses was on "holy ground." He removed his sandals out of reverence for the Lord, and received his call to be Israel's deliverer.

Wherever God meets with us becomes a sacred spot. Abraham had Bethel; Elijah had Mount Carmel. We will have special places as well. We must not worship the sites themselves. Rather, we must worship God who meets us there. If He is calling you from a burning bush, remove your sandals! Why? You are standing on "holy ground."

## GOD'S COMMENDABLE WORD

**Acts 20:32** — *"And now I commend you to God and to the word of His grace, which is able to build you up and to give you the inheritance among all those who are sanctified."*

When I became a Christian, my college roommate had a New American Standard Bible. Until that time, I had never read the Bible very much. When I did it had been primarily from the King James Version, which sounded awkward to me. As I began to read the N.A.S.B., I began to grow spiritually. My hunger for God's Word increased. The more I read, the more I knew why the Bible is indeed God's commendable book.

**The Bible Leads Us to Salvation**. Paul referred to the Word of God as "the word of His grace." The Bible tells us how to be saved. It gives us "the wisdom that leads to salvation through faith which is in Christ Jesus" (2 Timothy 3:15). It tells us to repent of our sin (Acts 3:19), and trust Jesus alone as our Savior (John 1:12).

**The Bible Helps Us Mature.** Paul said that God's Word would "build...up" the Ephesian pastors whom he was addressing. As they spent time in Scripture, they would grow in Christlikeness. The same is true for us. The more time we spend reading, studying, memorizing, and meditating upon Scripture, the more we become like Jesus.

**The Bible Gives Us an Inheritance.** God's Word gives us "the inheritance among all those who are sanctified." We inherit salvation (Hebrews 1:14), the promises of God (Hebrews 6:12), and other wonderful blessings from above (1 Peter 3:9). One day, because of God's Word, we will also inherit eternity in heaven (Revelation 21:7).

The Bible helps you become a Christian (regeneration), enables you to mature (sanctification), and gives you a heavenly inheritance (glorification). Do you want to be a triumphant Christian? If so, "I commend you to God and to the word of His grace!"

## FOR SUCH A TIME AS THIS

**Esther 4:14** — _"For if you remain silent at this time, relief and deliverance will arise for the Jews from another place and you and your father's house will perish. And who knows whether you have not attained royalty for such a time as this?"_

There once was a beautiful girl named Hadassah, also known as Esther. The Babylonians had taken her and many other Jews from Jerusalem as captives. Her parents had died in the invasion, and her cousin Mordecai became the only parent she ever knew. Eventually the Medes and Persians overthrew the Babylonians, and Ahasuerus became king. His queen, Vashti, was beautiful, but she was a rebel. When the king vanquished her from her royal position, a search was made, and the stunning Esther was chosen as his new queen. God's reason for putting her in that position would soon be obvious.

Ahasuerus had a wicked head prince named Haman who hated Mordecai the Jew because he refused to bow down before him. Haman planned Mordecai's death and built a gallows 75 feet tall upon which to hang him. Haman then scheduled a day to annihilate all the Jews in the kingdom, not knowing that Queen Esther was a Jew, and that Mordecai had once saved King Ahasuerus from assassination. Mordecai told Esther that God had placed her in her royal position "for such a time as this." God had blessed her with prominence so she could be a blessing to her people. She informed the king of Haman's wicked plans, and he was appropriately hung on the gallows he had erected for Mordecai!

God has placed each of His children on this earth for a reason. He has a perfect will for all of us (Romans 12:2). We each have been strategically located in life in order to achieve certain accomplishments. Have you discovered your life's purpose? Ask the Lord to reveal it to you. Like Esther, God has positioned you "for such a time as this."

## THE DIGRESSION OF SIN

**Psalm 1:1** — *"How blessed is the man who does not walk in the counsel of the wicked, nor stand in the path of sinners, nor sit in the seat of scoffers!"*

How does someone become an atheist? Often a person who claims to be an atheist grew up with some exposure to religion. Perhaps he was taught about Jesus Christ. Yet somewhere along the way that person began to sink downward in the digression of sin.

**The Counsel of the Wicked.** The downward spiral of sin begins with "the counsel of the wicked." A person begins to take guidance, advice, and direction from "wicked," ungodly people instead of God and His Word. He becomes indoctrinated with worldly wisdom, which is "earthly, natural (unspiritual), (and) demonic" (James 3:15).

**The Path of Sinners.** Once that person believes the lies of "the counsel of the wicked," he becomes more willing to associate with "sinners." As a person thinks, so he will act. His godless beliefs based on man's wisdom produce sinful behavior. The more he sins, the harder his heart becomes toward Jesus and the things of God.

**The Seat of Scoffers.** Unless a person accepts Jesus as his Lord and Savior, he can potentially become a "scoffer." A "scoffer" is someone who is not merely hard toward the things of God. He literally becomes hostile. He is an atheist who hates Jesus Christ, the Bible, and Christians. He wants no mention of Jesus in the public arena. He mocks Christianity and hates God's truth. Today, such "scoffers" are ruining our nation.

Sin has a downward pull. It begins when someone embraces ungodly counsel. Such counsel leads to sinful living. If left unchecked, the person can even become an atheist — a mocker of Jesus and His church. Do not go near this downward path. Rather, let Jesus lift you and set your feet on the rock of the eternal truth of His Word, the Bible.

## WHEN I SEE THE BLOOD

**Exodus 12:13** — *"The blood shall be a sign for you on the houses where you live; and when I see the blood I will pass over you, and no plague will befall you to destroy you when I strike the land of Egypt."*

Egypt lay in ruins. God had sent devastating plagues upon the country, yet their king, Pharaoh, had hardened his heart and refused to let his slaves, the people of Israel, leave the land. Pharaoh warned Moses not to appear before him again unless he wanted to die. At that point, the Lord let Moses know about the final plague He intended to send.

God told Moses to command every household of Israel to take an unblemished one-year-old male lamb, kill it, and with a hyssop branch, spread its blood on the lintel and doorposts of their house. Then at evening time they were to roast the meat and eat it, along with unleavened bread and bitter herbs. It would be their "Passover meal." The Lord would send His death angel during the night and kill the firstborn of every Egyptian household, from the house of Pharaoh to that of every slave. However, whenever the angel would see the blood of a lamb on the doorposts and lintel of a house, he would pass over it and no one there would die. The people obeyed, the destroying angel came, the Egyptians' firstborn were killed, the Hebrews' firstborn were spared, and Pharaoh finally allowed the people of Israel to depart from the land. The lambs' blood saved God's people!

Christian, God has cleansed and covered you with the blood of Jesus, God's holy Lamb. When He sees you, He no longer sees your sin. Rather He sees the righteousness of Jesus! Those covered by His blood escape God's wrath. Those who are not, will suffer eternally in hell. Be sure to thank the Lord today for Christ's precious, protective blood. How blessed we are that when God sees it, He still "passes over" in mercy!

## THE CHRISTIAN'S COUNSELOR

**Psalm 119:24** — *"Your testimonies also are my delight; they are my counselors."*

Every Christian holds within his hand a supernatural source of flawless advice, guidance, and counsel. The Bible, God's perfect Word (Psalm 19:7), contains divine instruction for any situation we face in life. One of the benefits of regular Bible study is being exposed to the eternal thoughts and supreme wisdom of God regarding any given subject. Through Scripture, the child of God receives the guidance and encouragement he needs. The person who immerses himself in the biblical text discovers that the Lord Jesus, through His sacred writings, is indeed the "Wonderful Counselor" (Isaiah 9:6).

Unfortunately, many believers ignore the discipline of consistent Bible intake. Instead of feeding daily upon the milk and meat of God's Word, they indulge in the "junk food" of worldly entertainment. Godless television programming, movies, and music fill their minds with profane, unbiblical thoughts and suggestions. Not only do they waste their time, but they also become spiritually anemic. Filled with fear, discouragement, and depression, they lack the information and strength required to live a victorious life. What they need is more influence from God's Word and less from the world. They should "unplug" from Hollywood, and "tune in" to heaven. They need to take a Bible bath!

To be sure, human counselors have their place (Proverbs 11:14). But they should never serve as a substitute for the counsel of Scripture. Before you consult with a human therapist or counselor, open God's Word. Read it and meditate on what it says. It is a perfect treasure of divine wisdom just waiting at your fingertips. The doctor is in if the patient is ready. His counsel is free. What are you waiting for? Read your Bible today.

## WHAT GOD REQUIRES

**Micah 6:8** — _"He has told you, O man, what is good; and what does the LORD require of you but to do justice, to love kindness, and to walk humbly with your God?"_

"Pastor, how can I know God's will for my life?" Through the years, I have been asked that question many times. Whenever the subject of knowing God's will pops up, I ask the person about his Bible reading habits. I encourage him to begin a systematic, daily Bible reading program. Why? Because God's will is revealed in His written Word. Many times, as in our verse, God's will is clearly stated. Notice God's will in this text.

**We Are to Act Justly.** The Christian is to "do justice," or "do what is right" (New Living Translation). God is a holy God, and He desires for us to live holy lives. Our actions should be aligned with the precepts of His holy Word. He wants every believer to think, speak, and act in a righteous, just, pure, Christlike manner.

**We Are to Love Mercy.** The word "kindness" is best translated "mercy." God has been merciful to us by giving forgiveness to us through His Son, Jesus. Likewise, we are to be kind and merciful to others. Jesus taught that those who want to receive mercy should themselves extend it to other people (Matthew 5:7).

**We Are to Walk Humbly.** God does not bless arrogant, boastful know-it-alls. We must walk as Jesus did — in humility (Philippians 2:3-8). No one can exalt himself and Jesus Christ at the same time. We must decrease and let Jesus increase in our lives.

Knowing God's will is as simple as knowing God's Word. His will is found in the Bible. It is His will for every Christian to act justly, love mercy, and walk humbly. Now that you know His will, do it. Failure to do so is nothing short of sin (James 4:17).

## THE KEY TO ANSWERED PRAYER

**John 15:7** — *"If you abide in Me, and My words abide in you, ask whatever you wish, and it will be done for you."*

One of the greatest joys of the Christian life is to see God answer our prayers. How awesome it is when we take something to the Lord in prayer, and He, through His Word, reveals to us His will regarding that matter. Then we can pray for Him to act according to His will until it becomes a reality! That is the process that Jesus had in mind in our text. If we abide in Him and His Word abides in us, our prayers *will* be answered!

**We Must Abide in Jesus.** Every Christian is "in Christ" (2 Corinthians 5:17). The moment we are saved, the Holy Spirit baptizes us into Christ's body (1 Corinthians 12:13). To "abide" in Christ means that once we are saved we *walk in harmony* with Christ and His desires for us. The abiding Christian is filled with the Holy Spirit. He loves Jesus, and is surrendered completely to His Lordship, readily obedient to His will.

**Jesus' Word Must Abide in Us.** The abiding Christian spends much time reading and studying the Bible. God's Word dwells richly within him (Colossians 3:16). He treats the Scriptures as a priority, not in a perfunctory fashion. God's Word becomes more important to him than physical food (Matthew 4:4). He begins to think biblically. God's desires become his desires. He is then able to pray in accordance with God's will. When that happens, God graciously hears and answers his prayers (1 John 5:14-15).

When is the last time God answered a prayer for you? The secret is to take your request to the Lord, ask Him to reveal His will through His Word, and then pray in accordance with His Word and will until the answer comes. Abide in Him and let His Word abide in you today. Then go to Him in humble prayer. The results will amaze you!

## THE DANGER OF NUMBERS

**1 Chronicles 21:1** — _"Then Satan stood up against Israel and moved David to number Israel."_

King David lived an interesting life. He began as a simple shepherd. As a young man, he fought and defeated a Philistine giant named Goliath. From then on, David's influence grew in Israel. He led that nation to become the most powerful military force on earth. All of Israel's enemies were defeated and forced to pay financial tribute. At the height of David's success, he committed a sin that devastated the nation. It was so severe that God punished Israel and its king by killing 70,000 of their finest soldiers. What sin was it? You may be surprised. It was not David's adultery with Bathsheba. Nor was it his murder of her husband, Uriah. As treacherous as those sins were, this particular sin resulted in far more deaths among God's people. What was the sin? David numbered his army. His motive for counting his army was to indulge his pride. He wanted to be the biggest and best. He flexed his muscles to astound others, but God was not impressed.

Christians need to be both balanced and cautious at this point. It is wrong to disregard numbers totally. Some do so because their churches are lifeless and ineffective. No one is being saved and few are in attendance. No wonder they do not like to talk about numbers! But growing churches can place too much emphasis on statistics. The size of our budgets, the number of our baptisms, and how many we have in Bible study and worship may not accurately measure God's power in our midst. We must be careful!

We should not only ask, "How many people are here?" We must also ask, "How much of God's manifest presence is here?" We are called to focus on Jesus and people. If we do what we do for God's glory, He will give us the numbers He wants us to have.

## THE PRAYER GOD ALWAYS ANSWERS

**Luke 18:13** — *"But the tax collector, standing some distance away, was even unwilling to lift up his eyes to heaven, but was beating his breast, saying, 'God, be merciful to me, the sinner!'"*

There is a prayer that *always*, without exception, reaches the ear and heart of God. Of all the thousands of prayers ascending heavenward each second, this prayer takes priority. It is not a long prayer, nor is it complex. It consists of seven simple words: "God, be merciful to me, the sinner!" Those words immediately attract God's attention.

Jesus addressed some people, probably Pharisees, who "trusted in themselves that they were righteous" (Luke 18:9). Unsurprisingly, they "viewed others with contempt" because they were *self*-righteous, arrogant, and condescending. Jesus told a parable about two men who went to the temple to pray. One, a Pharisee, prayed a sophisticated prayer in which he elaborated about his righteous deeds such as tithing and fasting. At the end of his "prayer," he thanked God that he was not like other people, especially the tax collector who was standing some distance away. The tax collector prayed differently. He was not impressed with his own righteous-ness. He knew that he was a sinner. He "was even unwilling to lift up his eyes to heaven." Instead, he "was beating his breast" in earnest repentance. The word "saying" in our text implies that he prayed this prayer repeatedly. He confessed his sin, asked for mercy, and God graciously answered.

All of us know what it is like to pray and wonder if we are "getting through." At times we question whether or not our prayers are rising higher than the ceiling above us. But we can always be certain that God will hear and answer the simple prayer mentioned in our text. Do you need God's mercy today? Ask for it and He certainly will answer!

## WRESTLING WITH GOD

**Genesis 32:24** — *"Then Jacob was left alone, and a man wrestled with him until daybreak."*

Jacob was in trouble. His angry brother, Esau, whom he had defrauded twenty years earlier, was coming toward him with an army of four hundred men to kill him. Jacob, fearful for the sake of his family and himself, sent them across the Jabbok River. That night he wrestled with a Man whom he later realized was God (Genesis 32:28, 30). The wrestling match changed Jacob's life. What happens when we wrestle with God?

**God Breaks Us.** Jacob struggled for quite some time until the Man touched and dislocated the socket of his thigh. He "broke" Jacob. God must also break us before He can use us. He must empty us of all our self-reliance. His best vessels are broken ones.

**God Bridles Us.** The Man then made Jacob tell Him his name. That was the equivalent of making him say, "Uncle! I give up!" All of his life, Jacob had advanced by being a deceiver and a manipulator. Now he had met more than his match. He surrendered, and let God take control. We must do the same. God must bridle us before He can use us.

**God Blesses Us.** The Man then changed Jacob's name to "Israel," which means, "He struggles with God." Jacob wrestled with God, God won, and Jacob was blessed. From then on Jacob walked with a limp, but every step reminded him of God's goodness. When Esau arrived, the brothers fell into each other's arms, wept, and forgave each other.

God turned Jacob's problem into a blessing. Likewise, He allows us to "wrestle" with Him so that He can break, bridle, and bless us. The pathway to blessedness is brokenness. Has God broken you? If not, go ahead — wrestle with Him. Surrender quickly! Allow Him to break, bridle, and bless you. You will cherish your limp forever.

## THE GOOD NEWS OF THE GOSPEL

**1 Corinthians 15:1-2** — *"Now I make known to you, brethren, the gospel which I preached to you, which also you received, in which also you stand, by which also you are saved, if you hold fast the word which I preached to you, unless you believed in vain."*

This world does not hear much good news. Newspapers and news magazines bring steady reports of chaos and turmoil in society. Wickedness is rampant. Christians have been entrusted with the "Gospel," or "good news," and people need to hear it!

**The Gospel Must Be Preached.** Paul devoted his life to the proclamation of the good news of Jesus. He was not ashamed of the Gospel. It is God's power that saves (Romans 1:16), and Paul was under compulsion to declare it (1 Corinthians 9:16). In this sense, all Christians are "preachers." We must verbally share Christ with lost people.

**The Gospel Must Be Received.** When Paul preached to the Corinthians, they willingly "received" the Gospel. God did not force them to do so. His grace is resistible. Today, people must still receive Christ. Merely believing facts about Jesus does not save. Demons do that (James 2:19). We must believe in and also *receive* Christ (John 1:12).

**The Gospel Brings Salvation.** Paul "preached" the Gospel, the Corinthians "received" it, and as a result, they were "saved." Their salvation made them "stand" spiritually. Many of them had lived wickedly before being saved, yet the Gospel had changed them completely. That same Gospel will transform people in our day as well.

This world needs to hear some good news, and Christians have the best news available! We simply need to communicate it. Many will listen to the Gospel because it is so delightfully different and pleasantly positive compared to what they regularly hear. Open your eyes and see those people. Then open your mouth and share the good news!

## WHAT GOD HAS JOINED TOGETHER

**Matthew 19:6** — _"So they are no longer two, but one flesh. What therefore God has joined together, let no man separate."_

Marriage is a sacred covenant between one man and one woman for life. It is not to be treated frivolously or lightly. God ordained marriage to be the foundation for the family. In our text, Jesus shares some powerful thoughts concerning the marriage union.

**Marriage Is a Literal Union.** "So they are no longer two, but _one flesh_." When two people marry, they become one. In marriage, one plus one equals one. Husband and wife are to share everything. Unless they are willing to do so, they are not ready for the marriage altar. Words like "mine" or "yours" must be abandoned for the word "ours."

**Marriage Is a Divine Union.** "What therefore _God_ has joined together." God, not the preacher, unites a husband and wife. The two of them make a covenant with one another and also with God. He presided at the first wedding in the Garden of Eden with Adam and Eve. Only He can cause two people to become one.

**Marriage Is a Permanent Union.** "Let _no man_ separate." Since God unites people in marriage, no human being has the right to separate that union. God does not hate divorced people, but He does hate the damage that divorce causes (Malachi 2:16). When people divorce, they can never again become two individuals. Rather, they become two broken pieces of one flesh. Marriage should end only by way of death.

If you are single and desire to be married, ask the Lord to send you the right spouse in His time. If you are divorced, ask God to cleanse, restore, and guide you in the future. If you are married, ask God to help you love your spouse biblically. Whoever you are, hold marriage in high esteem. Remember, it is what _God_ has joined together.

## GOD'S PERFECT WORD

**Psalm 19:7a** — *"The law of the LORD is perfect, restoring the soul."*

I am a Christian first, and a Baptist second. Anyone who is born again by God's Spirit is on his way to heaven, regardless of what church he attends. Nevertheless, I am grateful to be part of a denomination that has steadfastly affirmed its conviction that the Bible is the inspired, inerrant, infallible Word of God. As Southern Baptists, we believe that the Bible not only *contains* God's Word, but that it *is* God's "perfect" Word.

**The Precepts of God's Word.** Scripture is "the *law* of the LORD." The Bible does not offer God's "suggestions" to mankind. Rather, it proclaims His authoritative precepts and laws, which are standards for all people of all times. The chaos of relativity is dismissed in light of God's law. What the Bible says is true for everyone!

**The Perfection of God's Word.** The Bible is "perfect." It is flawless truth, completely free of error. When it speaks, it speaks with pure, untainted accuracy. Even if it speaks scientifically or historically, it speaks truthfully. The Bible is trustworthy. It is perfect because it comes from a perfect God who cannot lie or mislead.

**The Power of God's Word.** The Bible benefits the believer by "restoring (his) soul." The soul includes one's mind and emotions. We rejuvenate ourselves mentally and emotionally by bathing in the healing, uplifting waters of God's Word. It is milk for our spiritual thirst, ointment for our wounded hearts, and manna for our hungry souls.

The Bible offers all the wisdom we need to lead fulfilling, productive lives. It is God's perfect standard. It will replenish our spiritual strength and give us daily guidance. Best of all, the Bible will point us to our heavenly home through Jesus Christ our Lord.

## HUSH, BE STILL

**Mark 4:39** — _"And He got up and rebuked the wind and said to the sea, 'Hush, be still.' And the wind died down and it became perfectly calm."_

The weary disciples climbed into the small fishing boat with their Lord. Jesus had been teaching and ministering to the vast multitudes beside the Sea of Galilee, and He and His men were retreating to the other side of the Sea for some well-deserved rest. En route, a strong wind began to blow, causing the waves to swell and rock their boat. Water began to fill the vessel's hull, so much so that the disciples, some of whom were veteran fishermen, were fearful for their lives. When they looked at Jesus, they could not believe their eyes. He was fast asleep at the rear of the boat! Shouting, they awoke Him saying, "Teacher, do You not care that we are perishing?" (v. 38). Jesus rose from His rest, looked at the wind, and said, "Hush!" He then looked at the waves and said, "Be still!" Both obeyed immediately! The disciples, amazed and fearful, said, "Who then is this, that even the wind and the sea obey Him?" (v. 41). He was and is, Jesus, the Son of God, through whom God created the Universe (John 1:1-5). Creation had to obey Him!

Are you experiencing a storm in your life? Remember, Jesus still speaks to storms and says, "Hush, be still." Before the storm, Jesus told the disciples to get into the boat so they could "go to the other side" (v. 35). He knew the storm was coming, but He also knew that they were going to make it to the other side! He will do the same for us. If Jesus is with us, we will pass victoriously through our storm, no matter how bad it is.

Child of God, do not grow weary. The calming of your storm is at hand. The wind will not blow much longer. The waves will not sink your vessel. Listen! The Master is standing and is about to say, "Hush, be still!" Rest with Him. He is in control.

## GET BEHIND ME, SATAN

**Matthew 16:23** — *"But He turned and said to Peter, 'Get behind Me, Satan! You are a stumbling block to Me; for you are not setting your mind on God's interests, but man's.'"*

Quite often, spiritual mountaintops are followed by severe temptations, tests, or trials. The devil is a sore loser. He hates to see Christians experience victory. He seeks to attack us shortly after a breakthrough or a blessing in order to catch us off-guard and pour cold water on our fire. Jesus had just had a great, mountaintop experience. He had asked His disciples to tell Him who they believed He was. Peter, guided by the Holy Spirit (v. 17), answered correctly and said, "You are the Christ, the Son of the living God" (v. 16). That confession was a turning point in Jesus' ministry. When His disciples finally realized who He was, Jesus began to openly reveal to them the primary reason for which He had come to earth — to die for man's sins on the cross (v. 21). But when Jesus began talking about death, Peter rebuked Him and said, "God forbid it, Lord!" (v. 22).

At that point, Jesus spoke the words of our text. Recognizing Satan's temptation resounding through Peter's words, He said, "Get behind me, Satan!" It can also read, "Get away from Me!" Peter was being a "stumbling block" (Greek *scandalon*). Peter was not thinking about what was best for the kingdom of God. Rather, he selfishly wanted Jesus to live and not die. But Jesus would have none of it. He knew that in order to be able to save man from sin, He had to die on the cross as a substitutionary sacrifice.

Is the devil harassing and tempting you to put your desires above the will of God? If so, follow Jesus' example. Look the enemy dead in the eye, and say, "Satan, get behind me — *now!*" When we submit to God and resist the devil, he *will* flee (James 4:7).

## My Presence Shall Go With You

**Exodus 33:14** — _"And He said, 'My presence shall go with you, and I will give you rest.'"_

The people of Israel were sad and frightened as they awaited the Lord's verdict from God's servant, Moses. They had rebelled while he was on top of Mount Sinai receiving the Ten Commandments from the Lord. When he tarried for many days, the people grew impatient. They persuaded Aaron, Moses' brother, to make an idol shaped like a calf. They offered sacrifices to it and proclaimed, "This is the god that brought us out of Egypt!" They then engaged in a drunken orgy. Idolatry and immorality are notorious companions. The Lord told Moses to leave the mountain and return to the people because they were committing a great sin. As Moses and his servant, Joshua, approached Israel's camp, Joshua mistook the roar he heard for the sound of battle. But Moses rightly discerned that it was the sound of singing and dancing. When Moses saw the decadent debacle, he became furious. He threw down the tablets which had the Ten Commandments written upon them, breaking them on the ground. He then ordered the Levites to kill the ringleaders of the rebellion. Three thousand fell in one day.

After Moses rebuked the people, he went before the Lord and interceded for their forgiveness. The Lord disciplined His people severely, but He did not abandon them. In our text He promised that His manifest presence would remain among them and that He would give them rest, a reference to their eventual entrance into the Promised Land.

God mercifully allows us to experience His manifest presence and replenishing rest. Even when we sin, He remains faithful to us. He _will_ discipline us, but He _will not_ abandon us. His sweet presence and rest graciously await any sinner who truly repents.

## GOD'S HEDGE OF THORNS

**Hosea 2:6-7** — *"Therefore, behold, I will hedge up her way with thorns, and I will build a wall against her so that she cannot find her paths. She will pursue her lovers, but she will not overtake them; and she will seek them, but will not find them, then she will say, 'I will go back to my first husband, for it was better for me then than now!'"*

The prophet Hosea sat with his three children, weeping and in shock. His wife, Gomer, had abandoned them not only for another *man*, but for other *men*. She had literally become a harlot. But God told Hosea that He would put a spiritual "hedge of thorns" around Gomer so that whenever she reached out to her lovers, something would go awry, and she would not be able to engage in immorality. Likewise, whenever her would-be lovers would reach out to her, their wicked overtures would be unsuccessful.

One day the Lord told Hosea to go into town so that he could find his estranged wife. Gomer was being sold as a slave. The Lord commanded Hosea to buy her back and bring her home. Hosea forgave her and loved her as he had before her infidelity. Through those events, God reminded the prophet and his listeners that although His people had been unfaithful to Him through idolatry, He was willing to buy them back and forgive them. The message is for us today also. Through Christ's death, God has paid the price to buy us back regardless of our waywardness. He loves us despite our sin!

Do you know someone who is straying from the Lord? Perhaps they are even involved in sexual immorality like Gomer. Pray that God will put His "hedge of thorns" around that person so that when they reach out to sin, they will not be successful. Pray that they will return to Jesus, like Gomer returned to Hosea. They may be running wild now, but the Lord *can*, and *will*, bring them back to Himself with His hedge of thorns!

## GOD'S REMEDY FOR LAZINESS

**2 Thessalonians 3:10** — *"For even when we were with you, we used to give you this order: if anyone is not willing to work, then he is not to eat, either."*

While I was a student in seminary, I worked at a grocery store in Fort Worth, Texas. One of my responsibilities was to sack customers' groceries and take them to their automobiles. I often met people who would pay for their groceries with food stamps, but they also drove new, luxurious cars. I once took a large load of groceries purchased with food stamps to a new, top-of-the-line Lincoln Continental Sedan that still had the new car sticker on the window. Something was dreadfully wrong with that picture!

Many people today are able to work, but because of laziness, they refuse to do so. When people are not physically or mentally capable of holding down a job, they deserve food stamps or any other kind of help they can receive until they get back on their feet. But those who expect some sort of governmental supplement that encourages them to continue in their slothfulness ought to repent and get a job. Society owes them nothing.

Paul told the church at Thessalonica to deal firmly with the lazy people in their congregation. Some of them were refusing to work because they said they were waiting for the Lord to return. Yet they believed that the church should feed and take care of them. Paul said, "No way! If they *can* work but *will not*, then do not allow them to eat!"

If you are physically able to work, God expects you to do so. God told Adam to work in the Garden of Eden *before* he and Eve sinned (Genesis 2:15). Laziness is not only a sin, but it is a very poor witness. If you are healthy, no one owes you a living. You need to be industrious and work as unto the Lord. If you refuse to do so, then you deserve God's remedy for laziness — hunger. It is a great motivator for idle people.

## THE BLESSING OF PHYSICAL REST

**Psalm 127:2** — *"It is vain for you to rise up early, to retire late, to eat the bread of painful labors; for He gives to His beloved even in his sleep."*

God's people are not supposed to live hectic, frenzied lives. A "frantic Christian" in an oxymoron (i.e. a contradiction of terms). God wants us to enjoy and enter into His rest (Hebrews 4:11). The first type of rest He provides for His children is physical.

**God Gives Us Nightly Rest.** Our text condemns being a "workaholic." It is injurious to our health to "burn the candle at both ends." If you get up early, you should also go to bed early. If you go to bed late, you should get up late. You must not get up early and go to bed late on a regular basis. Someone might say, "I had rather *burn* out than *rust* out!" Either way you are *out*! Sometimes one of the best things you can do is to get a good night's sleep. Our text says, "He gives to His beloved *even in his sleep."* It can also be rendered, "He gives to His beloved *sleep."* God blesses us both *while* we sleep, and *with* sleep. He makes sleep "sweet" (Proverbs 3:24) and "safe" (Psalm 4:8).

**God Gives Us Weekly Rest.** In the Old Testament, God's people worked six days, and rested on the seventh day (Saturday), which was the "Sabbath." After Christ's resurrection, Christians began to worship on the first day of the week (Sunday) to commemorate the day on which Jesus was raised from the dead (Acts 20:7). While Christians do not observe Jewish Sabbath laws, we should follow God's plan to rest one day out of seven. For most, it should be on Sunday, "the Lord's Day" (Revelation 1:10).

You will never have time to do all that *you* desire to do. Nor will you be able to do everything that *others* want you to do. But you will have time to do what *God* wants you to do. Slow down, prioritize, and get some rest. It is God's precious gift to you!

## THE BLESSING OF SPIRITUAL REST

**Matthew 11:28-30** — *"Come to Me, all who are weary and heavy-laden, and I will give you rest. Take My yoke upon you and learn from Me, for I am gentle and humble in heart, and YOU WILL FIND REST FOR YOUR SOULS. For My yoke is easy and My burden is light."*

The greatest type of rest is spiritual. It comes only to those who have received Christ as Lord and Savior. When He saves us, we have peace *with* God (Romans 5:1). After that, we also begin to experience the restful peace *of* God (Philippians 4:7).

Our text contains one of the greatest invitations Jesus ever offered to mankind. He invites those who are "weary and heavy-laden" to "come to Him." Jesus Himself is the source of our peace and rest (Ephesians 2:14). He invites us to enter His "yoke" and "learn from (Him)." Jewish rabbis in Jesus' day referred to their relationship with their students/disciples as being yoked together with them. When we "take (His) yoke upon (ourselves)" we begin to learn from the One who is truly "gentle and humble in heart." Our souls begin to find rest and calmness in Him. His "yoke" is not hard, but "easy." The "burden" He calls us to bear is not heavy, but "light" because He shoulders the brunt of it (Psalm 55:22). Indeed, "we who have believed enter that rest" (Hebrews 4:3a).

We can maintain this rest in several ways. First, we can focus on the Lord. When we do, He keeps us in "perfect peace" (Isaiah 26:3). Also, when we pray instead of worry, His incomprehensible peace guards our hearts and minds (Philippians 4:6-7). Finally, we can "cease striving (i.e. relax) and know that (He) is God" (Psalm 46:10).

There is no rest or peace for the wicked (Isaiah 48:22). Christians alone have spiritual rest. If you are tired of life's turmoil, come to Christ. He is your answer. In His arms of grace you will find redemption, restoration, and most importantly, spiritual rest.

## THE BLESSING OF ETERNAL REST

**Revelation 14:13** — *"And I heard a voice from heaven, saying, 'Write, "Blessed are the dead who die in the Lord from now on!"' 'Yes,' says the Spirit, 'so that they may rest from their labors, for their deeds follow with them.'"*

Christians today do not think, talk, teach, write, sing, or preach enough about heaven. Many believers seem to be convinced that to emphasize heaven at all is to become "so heavenly minded that they are no earthly good." How sad. With the Church's tragic de-emphasis on heaven, we have forfeited the precious hope and reality that one day we will leave this wicked, weary world and rest eternally in the arms of Jesus. God not only gives His children physical and spiritual rest, but also eternal rest!

**We Will Rest in Our Heavenly Home.** Jesus is preparing a place for us in the "Father's house" where we will dwell forever (John 14:1-6). Nazareth's Carpenter is also heaven's Architect and Builder. There we will rest in mansions made by our Master.

**We Will Rest in God's Presence.** When we die, we will be "absent from the body and present with the Lord" (2 Corinthians 5:6-8). Regardless of what we see before we leave this earth at death, the moment we slip away from here into eternity, we will see the blessed face of Jesus and abide in His glorious, peaceful presence forevermore.

**We Will Rest in a Place Void of Sin, Sickness, and Suffering.** In heaven, there will be no tears, no death, no crying, and no pain. These "former things" will have all passed away (Revelation 21:4-8). Heaven will bring joy, peace, comfort, and rest!

You can only enter heaven through Jesus Christ (John 14:6; Acts 4:12; 1 Timothy 2:5). If He is your Savior, you have spiritual rest now, but you also have God's guarantee that one day you will experience eternal rest with Him in a land that is fairer than day.

## SWEET HOUR OF PRAYER

**Matthew 26:40** — *"And He came to the disciples and found them sleeping, and said to Peter, 'So, you men could not keep watch with Me for one hour?'"*

The old hymn, "Sweet Hour of Prayer," begins with these words: "Sweet hour of prayer, sweet hour of prayer, that calls me from a world of care, and bids me at my Father's throne make all my wants and wishes known. In seasons of distress and grief, my soul has often found relief, and oft' escaped the tempter's snare by thy return, sweet hour of prayer." What beautiful words! But do we hear what they are saying?

Jesus was facing the cross. Judas and an angry mob were on their way to arrest Him in the Garden of Gethsemane. Jesus had taken His disciples to that special place for prayer. When He returned from praying, He found His disciples, not interceding, but sleeping! He rebuked them with the words of our text, and told them to watch and pray.

Would we have done any better? When is the last time you spent an hour with the Lord in prayer? God wants more than "quality time" from us. He also wants "quantity time." Jesus prayed in the early morning (Mark 1:35), often in the wilderness (Luke 5:16) and at least once He prayed for an entire night (Luke 6:12). If we want to emulate Jesus, we must experience and enjoy sustained periods of private prayer with the Father.

God gives you twenty-four hours every day. You should dedicate one of those to prayer. Read your Bible (20 minutes), worship and sing to the Lord (5 minutes), thank Him for His blessings (5 minutes), pray for others (10 minutes), pray for your needs (10 minutes), pray for your church and our nation (5 minutes), and end by being quiet in His presence (5 minutes). Have you noticed that time flies when you are with someone you love? Spend an hour with Jesus. It will become the "sweetest" part of your day.

## THE POWER OF PRAISE

**2 Chronicles 20:22** — *"When they began singing and praising, the LORD set ambushes against the sons of Ammon, Moab and Mount Seir, who had come against Judah; so they were routed."*

Jehoshaphat was a man of God. He served as Judah's king at the same time that Ahab and wicked Jezebel reigned over Israel. Jehoshaphat stayed faithful to Jehovah throughout his life. Even so, he came under attack by three powerful nations — the Moabites, the Ammonites, and the Meunites. Their armies comprised a vast host that threatened to devastate the relatively small army of Judah. Jehoshaphat turned his attention to the Lord, proclaimed a nationwide fast, gathered all the people, and cried out to God in prayer. He told the Lord that he and the people were helpless and did not know what to do to defend themselves. Nevertheless, he said that they were looking to Him for help. God was listening. He sent a prophet who told the king not to fear because the battle belonged to the Lord! He told Jehoshaphat to assemble the singers who led worship at the temple. They were to go before Judah's army singing praises as they entered the battle. Our text tells us that as they did, the Lord routed the opposing forces. By the time Judah's army arrived, their opponents were either slaughtered or dispersed. They named that field, "The Valley of Beracah," or "The Valley of Blessing." God transformed their battlefield into a blessing when they trusted and praised Him!

Are you in some sort of battle? Has the devil sent his evil forces to thwart your progress as a Christian? Do you feel helpless and uncertain about what to do next? Fear not. You need not fight the enemy on your own. Worship God! He will show you the amazing power of praise. Remember, the battle you face is not yours; it is the Lord's!

## JESUS, THE RESURRECTION AND THE LIFE

**John 11:25** — _"Jesus said to her, 'I am the resurrection and the life; he who believes in Me will live even if he dies.'"_

Sadness and the stench of death were in the air in the small town of Bethany. Lazarus, brother of Martha and Mary, had passed away four days earlier. His sisters had sent for Jesus to come and heal him before he died, but the Lord purposefully delayed. Lazarus' death was allowed because Jesus intended to perform a miracle that would bring glory to God and deeper understanding to His disciples. When the sisters met Jesus outside the tomb, He told them that Lazarus would rise again. Martha thought He was referring to the resurrection of the dead in the distant future. Jesus spoke the words of our text informing her that the resurrection is not only a future event, but also a present, divine Person. Jesus Himself is the resurrection! In Him is life. All that has come into existence has Jesus as its creative source. Furthermore, whoever believes in Jesus for salvation will continue to live even after he experiences physical death! Jesus created each of us and will also recreate us so that we will continue to live in heaven after we die.

Someone has well said that if a person is born only once, he will die twice. But if he is born twice, he will die only once. How true that is! Whoever is only born physically will die twice, in that his body will die physically and then his spirit and soul will die spiritually in hell. But whoever is born again in Jesus Christ has been born twice — once at physical birth and once at salvation. He will taste physical death, but will never experience spiritual death in hell. Because of Jesus, he will live even after he dies.

Rejoice today, child of God. You have everlasting life. You are delivered from the power of death, hell, and the grave. Jesus Himself is your resurrection and life!

## WHEN YOU FAST

**Matthew 6:17-18** — *"But you, when you fast, anoint your head and wash your face so that your fasting will not be noticed by men, but by your Father who is in secret; and your Father who sees what is done in secret will reward you."*

There is a Christian discipline that brings significant spiritual power to those who practice it. That discipline is fasting. Some Christian leaders who do not understand its significance often discourage its practice. They say that only religious extremists and fanatics do it. Is that true, or are we missing something by not fasting in our day?

Jesus taught His disciples to fast. He Himself fasted from food for forty days following His baptism, just before He began His preaching ministry. His disciples apparently did little if any fasting while He was on earth, but He clearly stated that He expected them to fast after He ascended back to heaven (Matthew 9:15). When He taught about fasting, Jesus used phrases such as, *"Whenever* you fast" (Matthew 6:16), and *"You, when* you fast" (6:17). For Jesus, it was not *if*, but *when* you fast. He desires it.

Fasting is simply going without food for a special time of consecration to God. Rather than eating, a person prays and reads the Bible. There were unique occasions in Scripture when people fasted from food and drink (Esther 4:15-17). Jesus said that some demons were so strong they could only be cast out through prayer with fasting (Matthew 17:21). Fasting brings a special anointing of God's power to bless those believers who practice it. It also displays a person's humility and contrition before God (Psalm 35:13).

If you are facing a problem that seems overwhelming, you can strengthen the effectiveness of your prayers through fasting. Almost every person used mightily by God in biblical times and in church history practiced it. God will honor and bless you as you do.

## HOUSEHOLD SALVATION

**Acts 16:31** — _"They said, 'Believe in the Lord Jesus, and you will be saved, you and your household.'"_

Sometimes the most difficult people to evangelize are the members of our own family. Yet they are the very ones we most want to be saved. No one can bear the thought of having a loved one in hell. We all desire the gift of "household salvation."

God conceived the idea of the family, and He longs for every family member to know Him personally. God chose Abraham, _"...that he may command his children and his household after him_ to keep the way of the LORD" (Genesis 18:19). Years later, Joshua made what has become a well-known statement at this point — _"As for me and my house,_ we will serve the LORD" (Joshua 24:15). In the New Testament, when Andrew met Jesus, the first person he brought to Him was his brother, Simon Peter (John 1:41-42). Later, when Jesus delivered a demoniac, He commanded him, _"Go home to your people_ and report _to them_ what great things the Lord has done for you, and how He had mercy on you" (Mark 5:19). When Peter witnessed to Cornelius, a Roman centurion, he and his whole household were saved (Acts 10). Paul and Silas also led Lydia and her household to faith in Christ (Acts 16:14-16). In our text, the Philippian jailer and the members of his household each received Christ as Savior, and they were all baptized together as a family (Acts 16:32-33). Later, every member of Crispus' household was converted to Christ (Acts 18:8), as was the household of Stephanas (1 Corinthians 1:16).

If you have lost loved ones, ask God to convict them (John 16:8), to convert them (Romans 10:1), and to send someone to witness to them. Be prepared to be that person. Do all you can to be sure that your entire household spends eternity in heaven with Jesus.

## JEHOVAH-NISSI: THE LORD OUR BANNER

**Exodus 17:15** — *"Moses built an altar and named it The LORD is My Banner."*

Moses, Israel's aging leader, scanned the battlefield below him from his position on the mountain. The people of Israel had left Egypt and were advancing toward Canaan, the Promised Land. Along the way they found themselves under attack by the people of Amalek. Moses instructed his servant Joshua to lead a group of warriors into the valley to fight against Israel's enemies. Moses stayed on top of the mountain with his hands, and probably the staff of God, lifted toward heaven. As long as his hands were lifted up, Joshua and his troops triumphed. However, when Moses' hands grew weary and he let them down, the Amalekites prevailed. Assessing the situation, Aaron and Hur made Moses sit down on a rock while they each took one of his arms and held it up for him. When they did, Joshua and his armies overwhelmed the Amalekites. Afterwards, Moses built an altar and named it, "Jehovah-Nissi," which means, "The Lord is My Banner."

The Lord is our Banner as well. As we pray and seek His face, He fights for us while we keep silent. No weapon formed against us can prosper, and every tongue that accuses us in judgment, we will condemn (Isaiah 54:17). No evil will befall us, nor will any plague come near our dwelling, for He will give His angels charge concerning us to guard us in all our ways (Psalm 91:10-11). Indeed, we are more than conquerors through Jesus Christ (Romans 8:37). If God is for us, who can be against us (Romans 8:31)?

Are you engaged in a battle? Stand still and let God move. He will fight for you while you keep silent. Go to the hilltop, lift up your hands to Him in prayer, and watch Jesus defeat your enemy in the valley. He is *still* Jehovah-Nissi: The Lord Our Banner!

## GOD'S INDESCRIBABLE GIFT

**2 Corinthians 9:15** — _"Thanks be to God for His indescribable gift!"_

God is generous by nature. The greatest Bible verse of all (John 3:16) tells us that He loved the world so much that He _gave_ us Jesus, who provides regeneration to all who will repent of their sin and trust Him for salvation. Jesus is God's indescribable gift!

**Jesus Provides Forgiveness.** Everyone who believes on the name of the Lord Jesus Christ will be saved and forgiven of sin (Acts 10:43; Romans 10:13). That forgiveness is "through His blood" and "according to the riches of His grace" (Ephesians 1:7). To be forgiven is to receive "redemption" (Colossians 1:14). God graciously pardons the guilt of our iniquities and clears us from the penalty of past transgressions.

**Jesus Provides Freedom.** Once the Lord forgives us, He desires for us to walk in freedom. We are no longer to be slaves of sin because we are servants of Christ (Romans 6:6-18). Whomever Jesus has set free is free indeed (John 8:36). He gave us liberty through salvation, and He wants us to walk in freedom each day (Galatians 5:1).

**Jesus Provides Fullness.** All the fullness of God (His deity) dwells in Jesus (Colossians 1:19; 2:9). All Christians have received "of (Christ's) fullness" (John 1:16). Jesus will continually fill us with Himself through the indwelling Holy Spirit (Ephesians 5:18). Christ's fullness in us is our hope of future glory (Colossians 1:27).

Christ is the greatest gift ever given or received. He is our faithful fountain of forgiveness, freedom, and fullness. No gift compares to Him. He surpasses the value of silver or gold. He is God's "pearl of great price" (Matthew 13:46) whom we must obtain even if it costs us everything! Our blessed Jesus is indeed "God's indescribable gift!"

## OUR HEAVENLY HIDING PLACE

**Psalm 32:7** — *"You are my hiding place; You preserve me from trouble; You surround me with songs of deliverance."*

An airline commercial shows a football official standing midfield at the beginning of the game with the captains. As he searches his pockets, it is obvious that he is stalling for time. He cannot find the coin to toss to decide which team receives the ball. Finally he asks, "Does anyone have change?" A voice quickly injects, "Wanna get away?"

At times, all of us feel the need to "get away." The pressures of life cause us to desire a break. That is why so many people live for the weekend. Others live to "get away" at an athletic club, or perhaps at a nightclub, or bar. But is that what God wants?

David understood that the Lord's presence was his safest "hiding place." For years he fled from King Saul who was jealous of him and wanted to kill him. David hid in caves in the wilderness, constantly moving about as a fugitive. He came to realize that the Lord was his true hiding place. God was protecting him from Saul's wrath. The Lord delivered David from those troubles, and he eventually became Israel's king. The Lord literally surrounded David with joyful songs and shouts of deliverance as the people of Israel celebrated his reign as their king. David trusted the Lord, and He came through!

What difficulty do you face? Jesus wants to be your hiding place. His name is a strong tower into which you can run and be safe (Proverbs 18:10). He will preserve and protect you from every enemy, and help you cope with every problem. He will put a song of victory in your mouth, because in His presence there is fullness of joy. Do you need to "get away?" Do not opt for a worldly form of relaxation. Rather, call on Jesus. He is your hiding place, and He is always as close as the prayerful mention of His name.

## THE PRIORITY OF PRAISE

**Psalm 34:1** — _"I will bless the LORD at all times; His praise shall continually be in my mouth."_

A key to becoming a victorious Christian is learning to praise God. God created us for His pleasure. Praise exalts the name and nature of the Lord. If we are breathing, we ought to be praising Him (Psalm 150:6). King David decided early in life to make praising God a priority. In our text, he shares vital truths that will enhance our worship.

**Praise Must Be Volitional.** "I _will_ bless the LORD." Praise is a choice. David learned to praise God regardless of his circumstances. He worshiped Him even when he did not feel like doing it. Even so, we must not praise God only when we _feel_ like it. We must _choose_ to praise Him. Obedience will then produce the appropriate feelings.

**Praise Must Be Continual.** "At _all times_." David praised God everyday, at all times, in every circumstance. Like Job, despite the bad things that came his way, David exalted God. To be pleasing to God, we too must give preeminence to perpetually praising Him. On the mountaintop or in the valley, we should adore our living Lord.

**Praise Must Be Verbal.** "His praise shall continually be _in my mouth_." David knew that praise in the _heart_ demands expression on the _lips_. True love always results in verbal expression. The redeemed of the LORD must _say_ so! Our sacrifice of praise must involve the fruit of our _lips_. We cannot worship and praise God biblically if our mouths are constantly closed. Our Father wants to _hear_ His children praising Him.

When is the last time you had a mighty release in your spirit as you worshiped God? Do so today! Praise is a choice that must become a lifestyle. It demands verbal expression. Open your heart and mouth, and exalt King Jesus in worship right now!

## KNOWING THE WILL OF GOD

**Romans 12:1-2** — *"Therefore I urge you, brethren, by the mercies of God, to present your bodies a living and holy sacrifice, acceptable to God, which is your spiritual service of worship. And do not be conformed to this world, but be transformed by the renewing of your mind, so that you may prove what the will of God is, that which is good and acceptable and perfect."*

God has a plan for us. He wants us to know it and wants to help us achieve it. Our text gives a pattern, which if followed, will help us know and do His perfect will.

**Step 1 – The Presentation of Our Bodies.** When God saved us, He bought us and made our bodies the temple of His Spirit. We must offer our bodies back to Him as "a living and holy sacrifice." Each bodily part must serve Him (Romans 6:12-14).

**Step 2 – Our Separation from the World.** To know God's will, we must separate from the world. We do not fit in with lost people. We are to "come out from their midst" and live chaste, sanctified lives of purity (2 Corinthians 6:14-7:1). We are part of God's chosen family, and thus aliens and strangers in this world (1 Peter 2:9-11).

**Step 3 – The Transformation of Our Minds.** As we meditate on God's Word, we will renew our minds. The Bible becomes our delight (Psalm 1:2-3). We think on that which is "true, honorable, right, pure, lovely, and of good repute" (Philippians 4:8).

**Step 4 – The Revelation of God's Will.** When we take the first three steps, the fourth follows naturally. We "prove" or discern God's will, which is by nature "good, acceptable (i.e. well-pleasing), and perfect." God discloses His plans *for* us *to* us.

Do you want to know God's will? Offer your body to Him as a living sacrifice, pull away from godless, worldly living, and let Him change your thinking with His Word. Then and only then will He begin to reveal His perfect pattern, purpose, and plan to you.

## GOD BLESS AMERICA

**Psalm 33:12** — *"Blessed is the nation whose God is the LORD, the people whom He has chosen for His own inheritance."*

In 1620, Pilgrims from England sailed across the Atlantic Ocean and established Plymouth Colony in New England. In 1630, another one thousand settlers arrived and soon established Boston under the guidance of the first governor of the colony of Massachusetts Bay, John Winthrop. Over the next decade, the "Great Migration" occurred with an influx of 18,000 Englishmen to the new world. These settlers were primarily "Puritans" who sought to "purify" the Church of England from theological and ecclesiastical corruption. They came seeking freedom of religion. They wanted to distance themselves from the oppressive, hierarchical authorities in the motherland. They educated their children in the ways of Jesus Christ, and spread His Gospel to the non-believers who joined their ranks in the new world. Their work ethic, theological beliefs, emphasis on education, and other admirable qualities are woven irremovably in the warp and woof of American society. America began as a *Christian* nation.

Because of the massive migration and influx of people from all over the world into American society and culture since its founding in 1776, we have become a melting pot of diverse ethnic and religious backgrounds and viewpoints. Consequently, when someone emphasizes our Christian roots, he is typically reprimanded sharply and reminded that America has grown beyond all of "that." Unfortunately, perhaps we have.

Our nation needs to remember the rock from which it was hewn. That Rock is Jesus Christ. Today as we celebrate our nation's birthday, let us pray and ask for Christ's hand of purity, protection, and provision to rest upon us once again. God bless America!

## DEDICATING OUR CHILDREN

**1 Samuel 1:28** — *"'So I have also dedicated him to the LORD; as long as he lives he is dedicated to the LORD.' And he worshiped the LORD there."*

The longer it exists, the more selfish and sinful America becomes. For instance, it is legal to murder an unborn baby through abortion in America, but illegal to crack the egg of an eagle. It is illegal to pass out Bibles in schools, but legal to give condoms to students. As our nation drifts on a sea of moral relativity, parents must rear their children in the ways of Christ, protect them from this world, and dedicate them totally to the Lord.

Hannah was a godly woman living in an ungodly setting centuries ago. She lived in the days of the Judges when there was no king in Israel and everyone did what was right in his own eyes (Judges 21:25). Israel's Judges tried to guide God's people, but they were usually ignored and rejected. The priests were lazy and corrupt. Nevertheless, Hannah prayed for a son. She promised to dedicate him to the Lord, and let him grow up and serve Jehovah in Shiloh under the guidance of Eli the priest. God answered her prayer and gave her a son named Samuel. He became the last of the Judges, and one of the first of the Prophets. God used him to bring spiritual awakening to Israel. He anointed Saul and David as the nation's first two kings. He was a respected man of purity, prayer, piety, and power. Israel went from a state of moral decadence, to one of revival because one woman prayed for a child and dedicated him totally to the Lord!

We need more godly children today, but we will not have them until we have more praying parents. Will you ask the Lord to give you children who will impact this world for Him? "Samuels" only appear when "Hannahs" beseech the Lord and pray.

## TAMING YOUR TEMPER

**James 1:19-20** — _"This you know, my beloved brethren. But everyone must be quick to hear, slow to speak and slow to anger; for the anger of man does not achieve the righteousness of God."_

"Well, _I'll_ just give him a piece of _my_ mind!" Have you ever been offended and retaliated in anger? When that happens, we usually say too much. Our tempers flare with harmful flames that damage others as well as us. How can they be tamed?

**Learn to Listen Quickly.** "Be quick to hear." We must concentrate on _listening_ to others rather than talking harshly to them. Instead of giving them a piece of our mind, we must hear their hearts. They might be experiencing difficult times or suffering from emotional wounds which cause bitterness. When we listen, we open the door for love.

**Learn to Speak Cautiously.** "Be...slow to speak." When I was teaching my son to hunt, I emphasized the need to keep his shotgun's safety lock in the "on" position at all times unless he was about to shoot. Failure to do so could result in death. Likewise, God wants us to keep the safety lock "on" when it comes to our speech. Speaking too quickly is a mark of foolishness (Proverbs 20:3), while controlled speech is a mark of maturity.

**Learn to Anger Slowly.** "Be...slow to anger." We can be angry without sinning (Ephesians 4:26). Jesus was angry when He cleansed the temple of those who had turned it into a den of thieves. But we can only do that when we are angry at sin and not the sinners. We must ask God to remove anger from our hearts because it leads to iniquity.

Our anger does not accomplish God's righteous purposes. His ways are kindness and love, and love never fails. Jesus calmed the raging sea. He can also calm the raging anger in your soul. Let Him fill you with His love today, and begin to tame your temper.

## Born Of The Spirit

**John 3:8** — *"The wind blows where it wishes and you hear the sound of it, but do not know where it comes from and where it is going; so is everyone who is born of the Spirit."*

Wind is interesting. You cannot see it, but you can feel it, breathe it, and see the results of it. Jesus said that the Holy Spirit is like the wind. You cannot see the Spirit, but you can feel Him, "breathe" Him (be filled by Him), and see the results of His work. He is God — co-equal, co-existent, and co-eternal with the Father and Jesus. He saves a person and makes him a Christian. Jesus referred to this as being "born of the Spirit."

**The Spirit Convicts the Lost Person.** The Spirit convicts the non-Christian and convinces him that he is a sinner, that his good deeds ("righteousness") are not enough to get him to heaven, and that he will answer to Jesus in judgment (John 16:8-9). In this way, the Holy Spirit shows the lost person that he is in need of salvation.

**The Spirit Bears Witness to Jesus.** The Holy Spirit points people not to Himself, but to Jesus (John 15:26; 16:14). He convinces the lost person that his sins can be forgiven only through Jesus Christ (John 14:6) and His shed blood (1 Peter 1:18-19).

**The Spirit Saves the Lost Person.** Salvation requires both repentance and faith. The Spirit leads the lost person to repent and return to Christ (Acts 3:19), and then leads him to receive Christ through faith by believing in His name (John 1:12). At that moment, the Spirit transforms the lost person into a Christian.

Has the Spirit ever convicted you of your need for Christ, granted you repentance and faith, and saved you? If not, set your sails today, and allow His gentle breeze to blow into your soul. Only those who have been born of the Spirit will enter the kingdom of heaven.

## THE BAPTISM OF THE SPIRIT

**1 Corinthians 12:13** — _"For by one Spirit we were all baptized into one body, whether Jews or Greeks, whether slaves or free, and we were all made to drink of one Spirit."_

The most powerful force on earth is not electricity, a nuclear bomb, or the military might of any nation. Rather, the most potent force has always been God's Holy Spirit. All Christians have been baptized with His power. Our text explains what that means.

This verse gives the only definition in the Bible of "the baptism of the Holy Spirit." It states that the baptism of the Spirit occurs at our spiritual conversion when we are plunged into the body of Christ by the Spirit Himself. When we repent and trust Jesus to save us and forgive our sins, the Holy Spirit indwells and baptizes us into Christ. Thus, Paul refers to conversion as being "in Christ." The Spirit baptizes "all" Christians into Christ's body. "All" are made to drink of one Spirit. No one is excluded! God saves us through His mercy by "the washing of regeneration and renewing _by the Holy Spirit_" (Titus 3:5). Those who do not have the Spirit are simply not saved (Romans 8:9).

Christian, what must you do to experience "the baptism of the Spirit?" Nothing! The Spirit baptized you into the body of Christ when you were saved. He now indwells you. He has separated you from the world. He is developing His fruit within you (Galatians 5:22-23), and conforming you into Christ's likeness (Romans 8:29). He will fill you (Ephesians 5:18), teach you, comfort you, and empower you each day.

If you are saved, you have been baptized in the Spirit. Let Him control you. Do not grieve Him with sin, quench Him with doubt, or resist Him with pride. Ask the Holy Spirit to fill you today. He will give you more power than you ever dreamed possible!

## THE FILLING OF THE SPIRIT

**Ephesians 5:18** — *"And do not get drunk with wine, for that is dissipation, but be filled with the Spirit."*

God desires for all of His children to walk in the power of the Holy Spirit. Every Christian receives the Spirit at conversion (Romans 8:9, 15-16; Titus 3:5). To be filled with the Spirit is not to receive more of Him. Rather, it is to release His power that is already within us. He is a mighty indwelling river of living water, and He wants out!

The baptism of the Holy Spirit turns lost people into saved people (1 Corinthians 12:13). The filling of the Holy Spirit turns carnal Christians into spiritual ones (Galatians 5:16-17). A Spirit-filled believer walks in power and victory. It is not by chance that Paul warns us to "not get drunk with wine" in this same verse. A person who gets drunk by alcoholic beverages walks, talks, thinks, and acts differently than he does when he is sober. Likewise, a Christian who is filled with (intoxicated by) the Spirit walks, talks, thinks, and acts differently than a carnal, fleshly, self-centered, worldly person.

At the point of conversion, the Spirit baptizes us into Christ. After that, we can be filled with the Spirit many times. Thus, there is one baptism of the Spirit and many fillings. We are filled with the Spirit the same way we are saved — by grace, through faith, in Christ. We simply confess all known sin, and then ask the Lord to fill us (Luke 11:13). We do not wait for any sign. We simply accept His filling by faith.

Are you a Spirit-filled Christian? If not, you can be. God is no respecter of persons. He wants *you* to walk in His plentiful power. He has not left you to fight for yourself alone. Rather, through the power of His indwelling Spirit, He has given you all you need to live as more than a conqueror. Release His mighty River in your life today!

## THE BLOOD OF JESUS

**1 Peter 1:18-19** — _"Knowing that you were not redeemed with perishable things like silver or gold from your futile way of life inherited from your forefathers, but with precious blood, as of a lamb unblemished and spotless, the blood of Christ."_

The religions of this world teach that God grants forgiveness by means of man's good deeds. Christianity, however, teaches that God offers forgiveness of sin through Jesus' substitutionary sacrifice on the cross for the sins of all people (1 John 2:1-2). Without the shedding of His blood there can be no forgiveness (Hebrews 9:22).

**It Is Purchasing Blood.** We are "redeemed" by Jesus' blood. That word is a commercial term that refers to the purchase of something. God bought our forgiveness by paying the price of Jesus' blood. Salvation is free to us, but it cost Jesus His very life.

**It Is Pardoning Blood.** Redemption also involves being pardoned by God. This is a legal concept. Though we are guilty because of sin, Jesus' blood secures our pardon and releases us from sin's penalty, which is death. His blood allows us to go free.

**It Is Precious Blood.** Our salvation could not be secured with perishable items like "silver or gold." These may be valuable currency on earth, but they are useless regarding salvation. Jesus' blood is eternally imperishable, and it _never_ loses its value.

**It Is Perfect Blood.** It is "as of a lamb unblemished and spotless, the blood of Christ." Jesus was free from a sinful nature because He was born of a virgin. Though tempted, He remained sinless (Hebrews 4:15). His blood flowed from a perfect heart.

God wants to take your sin-blackened soul and plunge it into the red blood of Jesus. Only then can He make you "as white as snow" (Isaiah 1:18). The old hymn asks, "Are you washed in the blood?" If not, you will never enter the kingdom of heaven.

## The Discipline Of The Lord

**Proverbs 3:12** — *"For whom the LORD loves He reproves, even as a father corrects the son in whom he delights."*

God is the Father of every Christian. He loves each of His children with an everlasting love (Jeremiah 31:3). He rewards and blesses us when we obey Him, and also disciplines us when we disobey Him. His discipline should neither surprise nor embitter us. He loves us too much to allow us to sin without reproving us.

Disciplining disobedient children is a concept that is foreign to, and often disdained by our society. Children are often allowed to disregard and disrespect parental authority, not to mention that of their teachers at school. Children who are allowed to behave rebelliously without appropriate parental discipline and instruction go on to harm themselves and society as a whole. God is the perfect Parent. He understands the need for disciplining His children. He only seeks our best when He disciplines us for our sins.

The root of the word "discipline" is "disciple." It is different from punishment in that it is a method God uses to teach us that our actions have irrevocable consequences. When we sin by breaking God's laws, He disciplines us appropriately. He thus teaches us the dangers of disobedience and encourages us to walk in righteousness. Divine discipline also proves who God's children really are. He only disciplines His children, not the devil's. Those who sin without being disciplined are not true children of God.

If you are saved and you sin, God will forgive you if you confess your sin and repent (1 John 1:9). But He will still take you to His "woodshed" to discipline you. When He does, do not get upset. Instead, thank Him for loving you so much.

## DEALING WITH DECEIVERS

**2 John 9-11** — _"Anyone who goes too far and does not abide in the teaching of Christ, does not have God; the one who abides in the teaching, he has both the Father and the Son. If anyone comes to you and does not bring this teaching, do not receive him into your house, and do not give him a greeting; for the one who gives him a greeting participates in his evil deeds."_

The doorbell rings. When you open the door, two handsome, neatly dressed, young men face you. Their wholesome appearance is inviting. Their television ads are family-oriented. "Jesus Christ" is in their official title. They must be Christians, right?

Not so fast. Just because they claim to be Christians, talk about family values, and use the name of "Jesus Christ" does not make them His true followers. What do the Mormons really believe? For one thing, they do not believe that Jesus was God who became a man to save sinners through His death on the cross. Rather, they believe that Jesus was first a man who later _became_ a god. They also believe that we can become gods if we do enough of the religious works advocated by Mormon doctrine. Their teachings, especially those concerning Jesus and the afterlife, are so bizarre and non-biblical that it would take many pages to adequately describe them. Simply put, Mormons may be "nice," but they are not true Christians in the New Testament sense.

When someone "goes too far and does not abide in the teaching of Christ," we should "not receive him into (our) house" or even "give him a greeting." Whoever receives him actually "participates in his evil deeds." That sounds serious because it is!

The next time the two young men come to your door, greet them and then say, "Jesus Christ is God in the flesh. He is my only Lord and Savior. I pray that you will know Him in truth." Then close the door, pray for them, and let them be on their way.

## THE CHRISTIAN'S INHERITANCE

**Psalm 16:5** — *"The LORD is the portion of my inheritance and my cup; You support my lot."*

The Lord loves to bless His children just as earthly parents delight in giving good gifts to their children (Matthew 7:11). The greatest blessing the Lord gives to us is Himself, not some other gift. Like David, we must view *God* as our ultimate inheritance.

Salvation is a wonderful gift. Anyone who has the assurance that his sins have been forgiven and his name is written in the Lamb's book of life is blessed. Whoever has received the gift of eternal life has been cleansed by Christ's blood, robed in His righteousness, filled with His Spirit, and is being conformed to His image. Yet, the best blessing is the Savior Himself. The Forgiver is even greater than His forgiveness.

The gift of provision is also a comforting fact for every believer. God supplies our needs according to His riches in glory. He is not limited by economic situations in the world at any given time. The God who provided manna to the children of Israel during their wilderness wanderings will also bless us with food and covering. Yet, provision itself is secondary compared to the greatness of the sovereign Provider.

The gift of heaven will be indescribable. What a day that will be when we walk on streets of gold and live in mansions prepared for us by Christ. Still, the greatest blessing of heaven will be the One who made it for us. Jesus will be the centerpiece and light of the New Jerusalem. We will worship the Person who made heaven, not the place.

As Christians, we should count our blessings and thank God for them. But we must go on to thank the Lord for the greatest gift of all — Himself. The Blesser will always be the greatest blessing. The Giver is still the greatest gift. *He* is our inheritance.

## COMMON PEOPLE

**Mark 12:37b** — *"And the large crowd enjoyed listening to Him."*

Jesus is God in the flesh, and is consequently, the smartest, wisest person ever to live. While He was here, the religious intelligentsia of His day sought to outwit Him in intellectual debates, but to no avail. They had read and studied the Scriptures, but they were no match for Jesus, who because He is God, was both the author and central subject of the Scriptures. They taught about God, but Jesus was God! The Sadducees, Pharisees, and scribes who challenged Jesus in religious and doctrinal debates were uniformly overpowered, outwitted, and outclassed. This uneducated Nazarene rabbi knew more than all of them put together, and they became jealous of His wisdom and His following.

Most of the wealthy, prominent intellectuals of Jesus' day did not follow Him, but the masses of common people did. Our text simply calls them "the large crowd." The King James Version and the New King James Version both rightly render that phrase (Greek *polus oklos*) as "the common people." Those versions also emphasize that they "heard Him gladly." Jesus may have repulsed the theologians, but the prostitutes, tax collectors, fishermen, slaves, and other ordinary citizens were readily drawn to Him.

Today, most Christians are still "common people." Some may possess wealth, prominence, and excessive intellect, but most are just plain people like those of the First Century (1 Corinthians 1:26-31). If you are rich, you can get saved, but because of the strong pull of the things of this world, it will be harder for you than for others (Matthew 19:23-26). Regardless of your social position, you should humble yourself and receive Christ as Savior. Then, like the common people of Jesus' day, you will hear Him gladly.

## Do Not Fear

**Isaiah 41:10** — *"Do not fear, for I am with you; do not anxiously look about you, for I am your God. I will strengthen you, surely I will help you, surely I will uphold you with My righteous right hand."*

Years ago a preacher told me, "There are three hundred and sixty five 'fear nots' in the Bible — one for every day!" Though I have never counted how many times the phrase "fear not" is recorded in Scripture, I do know that God desires for us to walk by faith, not fear. Fear and faith are opposites. God gives the gift of faith (Ephesians 2:8-9), not a spirit of fear (2 Timothy 1:7). Fear comes from our enemy, Satan, to paralyze us.

The book of Isaiah is interesting in that it has sixty-six chapters, just as there are sixty-six books in the Bible. Also, as the thirty-nine books of the Old Testament emphasize the Law and judgment of God against sin, the first thirty-nine chapters of Isaiah focus on God's judgment of Judah as a rebellious nation. But in chapters forty through sixty-six of Isaiah there is a marked change of tone. As the twenty-seven books of the New Testament focus on God's forgiveness and mercy in Christ, the last twenty-seven chapters of Isaiah focus on God's grace that was given to Judah when the people of God repented of their sins. Our text comes from that latter section of grace. In it, God told His people to "fear not" because He would be with them perpetually. He vowed to always be their God who would strengthen, help, and uphold them with His mighty hand.

God will do the same for us. We should not live in fear, but in faith. He will walk with us through any difficulty, helping us every step of the way. Are you afraid? Do not be. God is with you. His right hand will uphold and sustain you. Reach out and in faith, take His hand. He has lovingly given you one more "fear not" to cover today!

## HE MUST INCREASE

**John 3:30** — _"He must increase, but I must decrease."_

John the Baptist listened calmly as some of his disciples told him of their concern. "The one of whom you have testified is also baptizing, and people are turning from you and flocking to Him" (v. 26). How was John to respond? Jesus was indeed gaining in popularity among the multitudes. He was preaching and teaching, healing the sick, and casting out demons. Those who had faithfully followed John were now shifting their loyalty to Jesus. Yet John was not alarmed. Things were as they should be. Jesus was supposed to receive glory and honor. After all, He was the Christ, not John. The events that worried the men were of God's doing. Then John made a marvelous statement: "He (Jesus) must increase, but I must decrease." John knew that this life is not about gaining glory for ourselves. Rather, life's chief goal is to give glory and honor to Jesus Christ.

Every Christian should pray the words from our text. We should ask God to allow Jesus Christ to "increase" in our lives while our fleshly, carnal natures "decrease." Day by day we should desire to grow in grace and become more conformed to Christ's image. His character will transform us. More of the fruit of His Spirit (Galatians 5:22-23) will develop within our lives and be manifest for all to see. "More of Jesus, less of me," should be our daily prayer. As we die to self and allow Christ's life to flow in and through us by the power of His indwelling Holy Spirit, Jesus will increase in our lives.

Allow Jesus to conform you more into His image today. Let your life display His life. Live this day in such a way that He receives all the glory for the good that comes from you (Matthew 5:16). Let Jesus eclipse you. Decrease, so that _He_ will increase.

## WORDS AND MEDITATION

**Psalm 19:14** — *"Let the words of my mouth and the meditation of my heart be acceptable in Your sight, O LORD, my rock and my Redeemer."*

Our words and thoughts are inevitably connected. We speak that which we think, and we think that which we speak. Our thoughts and words are also connected to sinful hearts (Jeremiah 17:9). How then can they ever be acceptable to God?

**Realize the Power of Words.** Words are powerful. Whoever said, "Words can never hurt me," was either a deceiver or deceived. "Death and life are in the power of the tongue" (Proverbs 18:21). Those who speak words of faith, hope, and life will fare better than those who speak negative words of doubt, fear, and death. Our words indicate that which fills our hearts (Luke 6:45). They sound forth from lives prone toward iniquity (Matthew 15:18-20a). Before our words can please God, our hearts must be changed.

**Realize the Power of Thoughts.** Jesus must control our thoughts. Paul said, "We are taking every thought captive to the obedience of Christ" (2 Corinthians 10:5). Because of man's sinfulness, "Every intent of the thoughts of his heart (is) only evil continually" (Genesis 6:5). Our thoughts will please God when our hearts are cleansed.

**Realize the Power of Redemption.** David knew how to have his words and thoughts become acceptable to God. He knew the Lord as his "Redeemer." The Lord continually cleansed his heart and forgave his sins. Thus, both his speech and meditation became pleasing to God. That is how our words and meditation can please God also.

How are your words and thoughts? For them to please God, you must be saved and continually experience Christ's forgiveness and cleansing. What you say and think are as important as what you do. Let Jesus redeem your words and meditation today.

## THE COUNSEL OF THE LORD

**Joshua 9:14** — _"So the men of Israel took some of their provisions, and did not ask for the counsel of the LORD."_

God has a perfect will for each of His children (Romans 12:2). He reveals His will to us as we read the Bible and pray. The Holy Spirit guides us through the insight we receive from God's Word. For every decision we make, there is a personal promise waiting for us in Scripture. Sometimes, what God tells us to do may not "make sense" in human terms. But we must "not lean on our own understanding" (Proverbs 3:5). We must trust God's promises and walk by faith, not by sight (2 Corinthians 5:7). When we walk by what we "think" is best, we become easy targets for Satan's arrows of deceit.

God commanded the people of Israel to kill all the inhabitants of the land of Canaan. They were not to make a peace treaty with any of them because the Canaanites were so wicked. Even the smallest group of them would corrupt God's people with sin. A group of Canaanites known as the Gibeonites devised a deceitful plan to trick Israel. They came to Joshua, Israel's leader, and acted as though they had traveled on a long journey from a distant country outside of Canaan. They had torn wineskins, stale food, and tattered clothes as part of their disguise. They lied to Israel about their identity. Joshua and his fellow Israelites looked at the "evidence" alone without consulting with the Lord for guidance and made a peace treaty only to discover that the "foreigners" were Canaanites! The Gibeonites proved to be a perpetual thorn in Israel's side.

Before you make any decision, consult with the Lord first. Ask Him to give you a promise from His Word, the Bible. Never make hasty decisions based on outward appearances alone. Wait on God, walk by faith, and listen for the counsel of the Lord.

## CONTEND FOR THE FAITH

**Jude 3-4** — *"Beloved, while I was making every effort to write you about our common salvation, I felt the necessity to write to you appealing that you contend earnestly for the faith which was once for all handed down to the saints. For certain persons have crept in unnoticed, those who were long beforehand marked out for this condemnation, ungodly persons who turn the grace of our God into licentiousness and deny our only Master and Lord, Jesus Christ."*

I am a Christian by conversion and a Southern Baptist by conviction. Like most denominations, Southern Baptists had begun to drift into theological liberalism in the mid to late 1900s. Some of our seminaries had embraced the European higher critical method of interpreting Scripture. Many of our preachers were entering seminary with a passion for evangelism, Christ, and Scripture, but were leaving poisoned in their faith. They were told that the Bible has errors, its history is mythological, and its miracles are not real.

In 1979, Adrian Rogers, a biblical inerrantist, was elected President of the Southern Baptist Convention. That began a succession of elections of conservatives. They used their appointive powers to elect trustees who then hired conservative seminary presidents and professors. As a result, Southern Baptists changed their course and turned back to their original roots. That phenomenon has occurred in no other denomination.

Jude warned of such problems in our text. He said that whenever false teachers arise and creep in among Christians, it is time to go to war. Those who believe God's Word must not sit idly by and allow liberalism to take over and win the day. Instead, they must "contend earnestly for the faith" and take back their churches, institutions, and seminaries before it is too late! May God send a similar theological reformation to every denomination today that needs it, so that the biblical faith that has been handed down to us from the Lord Jesus Christ will continue to flourish and prosper!

## REJOICE!

**Psalm 118:24** — *"This is the day which the LORD has made; let us rejoice and be glad in it."*

Christianity is about joy. A joyless follower of Christ should be a contradiction of terms. We have every reason to rejoice. God made us in His image. Jesus died for our sins and was raised from the dead to give us life. The Holy Spirit indwells us and empowers us to live victoriously. When we die, we go to live with Jesus in heaven forever. How much better can things get for someone than that? We should rejoice!

**The Time to Rejoice.** There is a song that says, "Right now is the right time to praise the Lord!" That is what our text means when it says, *"This* is the day...let us rejoice and be glad in *it."* We often allow *today* to be crucified between two thieves called *yesterday* and *tomorrow.* *Now* is the time to rejoice and give praise to God!

**The Reason to Rejoice.** "This is the day *which the LORD has made."* Every day is a gift from God. We must not waste any day He gives to us, because we do not know how many days we will see in the future. Since God made today, we do not have to fear it. He will guide us through it and bless us in it if we seek His will and obey His voice.

**The Command to Rejoice.** Rejoicing is not optional; it is a command! Failure to rejoice indicates ingratitude. God has been gracious and good to us. He expects us to thank and praise Him. We are to "rejoice and be glad." "Be glad" means "to take pleasure in." We must take pleasure in today, knowing that it is a gift from the Lord.

Do not worry about tomorrow (Matthew 6:24) or the events of yesterday (Philippians 3:13-14). Instead, squeeze all you can from every twenty-four hours God gives you. Today is all you have. Do what you do with all your might. And above all, rejoice!

## You Can Run, But You Cannot Hide

**Obadiah 4** — *"'Though you build high like the eagle, though you set your nest among the stars, from there I will bring you down,' declares the LORD."*

One of the few movies I enjoy watching is "It's a Wonderful Life." It is about a man named George Bailey who runs a building and loan business in the small town of Bedford Falls. When eight thousand dollars, a sizeable sum in the 1940s, is inadvertently missing from the company's account, George's archenemy, Mr. Potter, accuses him of embezzlement and swears out a warrant for his arrest. Potter laughs at George's predicament, and yells as he frantically leaves his office, "Go ahead, run. You can't hide in a town the size of Bedford Falls." Indeed, George could run, but he could not hide.

The prophet Obadiah told the ancient nation of Edom the same thing. The Edomites were the direct descendents of Esau, Isaac's wild, rebellious son. From the time he and his twin brother, Jacob, were born, they fought with one another. Jacob was the father of the Israelites. Just as he and Esau had battled one another, so did their descendents. When Israel was coming out of the wilderness after forty years of wandering, the Edomites stubbornly refused to aid them with food, water, or shelter (Numbers 20:14-21). Later, when Israel was invaded by outside forces, Edom openly rejoiced. Obadiah condemned them for their antagonism toward Israel, and told them that God would avenge His people. Although the Edomites tried to hide in the security of their mountains, God knew where they were and He would send appropriate retribution.

Obadiah reminds us not to run rebelliously away from God. Adam and Eve tried (Genesis 3), as did the prodigal son (Luke 15:11f), but to no avail. We must run *to* Him instead. Rebellion is futile. He knows where we are. We can run, but we cannot hide.

## STUMBLING BLOCKS

**Matthew 18:6** — _"But whoever causes one of these little ones who believe in Me to stumble, it would be better for him to have a heavy millstone hung around his neck, and to be drowned in the depth of the sea."_

Jesus loves the little children. When His disciples asked Him who was the greatest in His kingdom, He called a young lad and stood him in their midst. He said that in order to enter God's kingdom, a person must be converted and become like a child. Children do not have to become like adults to be saved, but adults must become childlike!

Within that context, Jesus gave a warning concerning stumbling blocks. He said that God would judge anyone who causes "little ones who believe in (Him) to stumble." "Stumble" (Greek _scandalidzo_, from which we derive our word "scandalize"), means "to cause (someone) to sin, or give up his faith." Jesus said that those who influence a young Christian to turn away from Him would be better off drowning helplessly at sea.

Unfortunately, our world is filled with "stumbling blocks." Producers of ungodly television programs, movies, and music that fill children's minds with all sorts of fearful, wicked, perverted thoughts are "stumbling blocks." Atheistic teachers and professors that belittle the Christian faith of their students are in the same category. Parents who drink alcoholic beverages, look at pornographic literature, use filthy language, or fail to bring up their children in the ways of Jesus Christ are offenses to their children as well.

How are you influencing the younger people in your life? Are you pointing them to heaven or to hell? You must do all that you can to set a godly example before children so that they will want to live for Jesus. Above all, do not cause even one of them to stumble. If you do, God has a millstone pendant that is just the right size for your neck.

## BLESSED ARE THE POOR IN SPIRIT

**Matthew 5:3** — *"Blessed are the poor in spirit, for theirs is the kingdom of heaven."*

The greatest preacher to ever live was Jesus. The greatest sermon He ever preached was the Sermon on the Mount, which is recorded in Matthew 5-7. In that message, Jesus covered many subjects. But at the beginning of the sermon, He gave eight characteristics that should mark a person who desires to be His disciple. These are often called the Beatitudes. The first three have to do with what I call "The Road to Salvation," or what a person should experience spiritually before He becomes a Christian.

Our text says that the first step down the road to salvation is being "poor in spirit." Before we can be converted, we must have a deep sense that we are helpless sinners in need of a Savior. We must be convinced that we are lost before we will ever desire to be saved. There must be a deep awareness and acknowledgement of our sin against the Lord. Like Isaiah who, in a vision, saw God exalted in splendor and holiness, we must fall to our knees and cry out, "Woe is me, for I am ruined! Because I am a man of unclean lips, and I live among a people of unclean lips; for my eyes have seen the King, the LORD of hosts!" (Isaiah 6:5). In short, there must be conviction before there is genuine conversion. We must realize our spiritual bankruptcy before we will grasp our need for what God has done through Christ's death to pay the ransom for our sin debt.

Are you "poor in spirit?" You cannot become a Christian until you reach that spiritual state. Good deeds will never earn your salvation. You are a sinner by nature and choice. You need a Savior. The only One God has ever provided is Jesus. In Him alone "the poor in spirit" receive the eternal, abundant riches of God's glorious grace.

## BLESSED ARE THOSE WHO MOURN

**Matthew 5:4** — _"Blessed are those who mourn, for they shall be comforted."_

The Sermon on the Mount (Matthew 5-7) begins with the eight Beatitudes. These traits should characterize every follower of Jesus Christ. The first three deal with "The Road to Salvation," or what a person must experience before he is saved.

The first Beatitude emphasizes a sinner's _awareness_ of his sin. The second Beatitude takes a person a step further down the road to salvation. In our text, the person escalates in the state of conviction to an actual _brokenness_ over sin. It is possible to be aware of sin without being repentant about it or sorry for it. Before we can be saved, we must realize the depths of the debt we owe to God because of our iniquity. We must come to grips with and be broken over the fact that our sin has offended God.

King David broke at least two of the Ten Commandments when he committed adultery with a woman named Bathsheba and then had her husband killed. The Bible records David's prayer of repentance in Psalm 51. In that classic prayer, David literally weeps and "mourns" over his transgressions against God. He pleads with Him and asks Him to forgive, wash, cleanse, and restore him. Toward the end of the prayer, David says, "The sacrifices of God are _a broken spirit; a broken and contrite heart_, O God, You will not despise" (Psalm 51:17). David was crushed because of his rebellion against God. It was in that state that God poured out His mercy and grace upon the penitent king.

Have you ever mourned before God? Has the fact that your sin has broken His heart ever broken your heart as well? Without heartfelt conviction, there will be no heaven-sent conversion. The path to heaven is watered with the warm, holy tears of repentant sinners.

## Blessed Are The Humble

**Matthew 5:5** — *"Blessed are the gentle, for they shall inherit the earth."*

The first three of the eight Beatitudes given by Jesus in the Sermon on the Mount deal with what a person should experience prior to becoming a Christian. We must first become aware of our sin ("poor in spirit"), and then be broken over our sin ("mourn"). After that, we must humble ourselves because of our sinful condition. The third Beatitude applies at that point. "Gentle" means "meek," or "humble." It paints the picture of a wild animal that has been broken and tamed. God must humble us and make us meek toward Him. We cannot stand arrogantly before Him and demand salvation. Rather, we must kneel in humble, broken contrition and request it in childlike faith.

God requires all of us to "walk humbly with (our) God" (Micah 6:8). Before He will bless and heal us, we must "humble (ourselves) and pray and seek (His) face and turn from (our) wicked ways" (2 Chronicles 7:14). It is not the one who trusts in his own righteousness and views others with contempt that is justified of his sins. Rather it is the one who beats his breast in self-effacing, earnest repentance and acknowledges his iniquity to God. Whoever exalts himself will be humbled with divine punishment. Whoever humbles himself will be exalted and rewarded in heaven (Luke 18:9-14).

Not everyone is ready to be saved, because not everyone has become "poor in spirit." Some have not "mourned" over their sin, nor have they become "gentle, meek, or humble" in God's presence. Whoever remains in his pride will miss the grace and mercy of God in this life and will also experience wrath and punishment in eternity. But the one who humbles himself and accepts Christ as Savior, will be blessed and kept forevermore.

## BLESSED ARE THOSE WHO HUNGER AND THIRST

**Matthew 5:6** — *"Blessed are those who hunger and thirst for righteousness, for they shall be satisfied."*

The Beatitudes reveal a precious pattern that results in a person's conversion to Jesus Christ. The first three share the conditions someone should experience prior to salvation. He must be "poor in spirit," "mourn" over his sin, and he must be "gentle," approaching God in humility and contrition. Those Beatitudes deal with "The Road to Salvation." The fourth Beatitude speaks of what it is like when someone calls on Jesus' name and becomes a Christian. Here we see "The Reception of Salvation."

Jesus used two of the strongest human appetites known to man, "hunger and thirst," to describe how one should seek God's salvation. When a person *hungers* and *thirsts* for Jesus, he is *desperate* for Him. Even as the deer pants for the water brooks, so our soul must pant, yearn, and long for God's Son (Psalm 42:1). We must seek God's "righteousness." Why? Because our so-called "righteousness" is like the filthy bandages of a leper compared to the perfect, holy righteousness of God (Isaiah 64:6). We need the righteousness that comes from "Jesus Christ the righteous" (1 John 2:1). God the Father made Jesus, who knew no sin, to become sin for us on the cross, so that we might become "the righteousness of God in Him" (2 Corinthians 5:21). When He saves us, God imputes the righteousness of Jesus to us. God no longer sees our sin and rebellion. Rather, when He looks at us, He beholds the holy perfection of His sinless, divine Son.

To be saved, we must repent of sin and receive Christ as Lord. At that moment He cleanses us by His blood and clothes us with righteousness. Jesus Christ is our "bread of life" (John 6:35). Take time today to taste and see that He is good (Psalm 34:8).

## BLESSED ARE THE MERCIFUL

**Matthew 5:7** — *"Blessed are the merciful, for they shall receive mercy."*

"The Lord is full of compassion and is merciful" (James 5:11). How tragic it is that God is known as being merciful, forgiving, compassionate, and gracious, but His people are often known as just the opposite — hardhearted, unforgiving, and mean-spirited. Jesus tells us in the final four Beatitudes how a person ought to act after he becomes a Christian. These reveal several of "The Results of Salvation."

The fifth Beatitude insists that Christians should be "merciful." We should be willing to extend the same forgiveness and compassion to our fellow man that Jesus gave to us at salvation. We should not hold grudges or foster bitterness toward others. We must see ourselves as sinners saved by God's grace. Were it not for God's mercy, we would live miserable lives on earth and spend eternity in a Christless hell. When we see someone living in sin, we should humbly say, "There, but for the grace of God, go I!"

The Bible says, "The merciful man does himself good, but the cruel man does himself harm" (Proverbs 11:17). Note in that verse that the antithesis of being "merciful" is being "cruel." We are nothing short of being "cruel" and malicious toward others when we demand that they receive justice from God for their transgressions. We must forgive those who have wronged us and pray for God to bless them with His mercy. It is then, and only then, that His forgiveness and kindness will continue to flow toward us.

One sign that you are saved is that you readily extend God's mercy to those who have failed God and fallen into sin. Rather than casting stones, you desire to lift them up. If we sow the seed of God's mercy, we will reap the harvest of His unmerited grace.

## BLESSED ARE THE PURE IN HEART

**Matthew 5:8** — _"Blessed are the pure in heart, for they shall see God."_

When a person becomes a Christian, the Lord Jesus Christ changes him. Before conversion, his heart is wicked and deceitful (Jeremiah 17:9). Christ makes him a new creation, purging away the old and bringing in the new (2 Corinthians 5:17). As he delights himself in Jesus, God's desires become his desires (Psalm 37:4). He ascends the Lord's holy hill and stands in His presence with cleansed hands and a purified heart (Psalm 24:3-5). He desires to become holy because the Lord is holy (1 Peter 1:14-16). He no longer loves the world or its things that are passing away (1 John 2:15-16).

That is why there is conflict in the heart of every believer who is aggressively growing in grace and in the knowledge of Jesus Christ. As he reads his Bible, prays, witnesses to lost people, fellowships with other believers, worships the Lord in Spirit and truth, and learns the blessing of tithing and giving offerings through his local church, he begins to pull away from the world that once held a lethal grip on him. He no longer thinks, talks, and acts like those around him. He spends his time, energy, and money differently than they do. He dresses differently, because modesty in clothing becomes more important than wearing the latest fashions. He stops going to questionable places such as bars, nightclubs, casinos, fraternity houses, etc., and instead, spends time with his brethren at church and his family. _Everything_ changes. He has become "pure in heart."

This world will grow more wicked as Christ's return draws near (2 Timothy 3:1-5). May all true disciples of Christ separate themselves from its allurements and live holy lives worthy of their Lord (2 Corinthians 6:17). May we be like Jesus — "pure in heart."

## BLESSED ARE THE PEACEMAKERS

**Matthew 5:9** — *"Blessed are the peacemakers, for they shall be called sons of God."*

Jesus Christ is the "Prince of Peace" (Isaiah 9:6). When a person is saved, the Lord gives him His incomprehensible peace (John 14:27). The new believer suddenly has a desire to live at peace with other people. He becomes a "peacemaker," seeking to reconcile others to God by sharing the Gospel with them. He also tries to reconcile people to one another by helping them repair broken, strained relationships.

In local churches, there are both "troublemakers" and "peacemakers." Troublemakers constantly keep problems and conflict stirred up. They have a rebellious spirit, and find it difficult to submit to the God-ordained leadership of the pastor and his staff (Hebrews 13:7, 17). They drive wedges between Christians by means of gossip, slander, and rumors. They also have critical spirits, disapproving of anything they did not think of, or anything they cannot control. If such people refuse to repent after sufficient warnings, they should be expelled from the fellowship (Titus 3:10-11).

Thank the Lord that His peacemakers counterbalance the troublemakers. Peacemakers calm tense situations within the church without compromising biblical principles. They preserve the unity of the Spirit in the bond of peace (Ephesians 4:3). Every deacon and lay leader should ask God to help him have that kind of influence.

Peacemakers are "sons of God" — Troublemakers are "children of the devil." The Lord desires and deserves to have harmony in His house. There is enough fighting and fussing out in the world. That is the devil's way, not the Lord's way! May our churches be heavenly, harmonious havens, and may Jesus grant His blessed "Shalom" to us all!

## BLESSED ARE THE PERSECUTED

**Matthew 5:10-12** — _"Blessed are those who have been persecuted for the sake of righteousness, for theirs is the kingdom of heaven. Blessed are you when people insult you and persecute you, and falsely say all kinds of evil against you because of Me. Rejoice and be glad, for your reward in heaven is great; for in the same way they persecuted the prophets who were before you."_

The final of the four "Results of Salvation" listed in the Beatitudes is that of being persecuted for Christ's sake. If we seek to live godly in Jesus, we _will_ be persecuted (2 Timothy 3:12). Jesus' words help us cope with this unnerving truth.

**The Reality of Being Persecuted.** Jesus said, "Blessed are you _when_ people insult you and persecute you." He said "when," not "if." If we live Spirit-filled, separated, holy, prayerful lives, the devil will see to it that the world harasses us. If the world hated Jesus, it will hate us as well. His servants are not greater than their Master (John 15:18-25).

**The Reaction to Being Persecuted.** Jesus tells us to "rejoice and be glad" when we are persecuted. When the apostles were beaten for preaching about Jesus, they "(rejoiced) that they had been considered worthy to suffer shame for His name" (Acts 5:41).

**The Reward for Being Persecuted.** Persecution is a sign that "(ours) is the kingdom of heaven." We can also rejoice because "(our) reward in heaven is great." Lastly, we can take comfort in knowing that "in the same way they persecuted the prophets who were before (us)." Those "of whom the world was not worthy" (Hebrews 11:38) experienced similar circumstances, as did our Lord. Must they bear it alone?

If you suffer because of foolishness or sin, you should repent, not rejoice. But if you suffer for Christ's sake, you should be glad. He has walked that painful road before you. You must endure your cross for the joy yet to come. Resurrection lies just ahead!

## ONE THING YOU LACK

**Mark 10:21** — *"Looking at him, Jesus felt a love for him and said to him, 'One thing you lack: go and sell all you possess and give to the poor, and you will have treasure in heaven; and come, follow Me.'"*

One day a man came to Jesus and asked the question: "What must I do to be saved?" The man was rich (Mark 10:22), young (Matthew 19:20), and a ruler (Luke 18:18). Yet he lacked fulfillment and purpose in life. Jesus tested his obedience to several of the Ten Commandments. The young man said that he had done a decent job of keeping them since he was a small child. Jesus looked at him and "felt a love for him." Jesus always has a special sense of compassion for genuine seekers of truth. He said, "One thing you lack." Wow! He did not lack a dozen things, nor three or four things, but only one thing! He had made an idol out of his wealth and possessions. Jesus knew that the man could not serve Him and his money, because no one can serve two masters (Matthew 6:24). Jesus told him to give up his possessions and become His disciple. But the young man turned and walked away because he "owned much property" (v. 22). Actually, "he was *owned* by much property." He rejected salvation, freedom, fulfillment, and eternal life in Christ to maintain his earthly wealth. "One thing" sent him to hell!

One thing can keep you out of heaven and send you to a Christless eternity. The man in our text came to the right person (Jesus), asked the right question, but gave the wrong response. What is holding you back from either being saved, or if you are already saved, from living a victorious, abundant life? Whatever it is, it is not worth it. Sell it. Get rid of it. Give it away, and lay up treasure in heaven. Come follow Jesus today. He alone can satisfy your soul. Jesus must become your "one thing" (Luke 10:41-42)!

## WE MUST OBEY GOD

**Acts 5:29** — _"But Peter and the apostles answered, 'We must obey God rather than man.'"_

For many years, the morals of our great nation have been eroding. Bible reading and prayer in public schools were outlawed in America just before I began the third grade. Since then, violence and immorality have sky rocketed. You cannot kick God out of the schools and expect the nation to prosper. What can Christians do about it?

The early believers lived in a day when it was illegal to preach in Jesus' name. They decided to preach and teach in His name anyway. Their ultimate allegiance was to Jesus, not to Rome or their Jewish heritage. When they were told not to speak in His name anymore, the decision was easy to make. They had to obey God rather than man.

Whenever or wherever it becomes illegal to speak about our Lord and Savior, Jesus Christ, we must obey God rather than man. If a child wants to pray at a public school, he should. If students want to stand around a flagpole holding hands while they voice their prayers out loud to God, they should do it. If football players want to kneel midfield after a game and pray, they should do so regardless of who tells them otherwise. We should simply do the right and brave thing, and let the chips fall where they may. If America can no longer tolerate public prayer, then it needs to be prepared and willing to lock all the courageous Christians in jail. If we are forced to suffer for Jesus' sake, we should rejoice that we are being considered worthy to do so (Acts 5:41-42).

Any man, or any man-made law, that defies God must not intimidate Christians. The true Supreme Court has only one Judge — Jesus! We must be completely loyal to Him, for it is to Him we will give an account. We must obey God rather than man.

## ABOUNDING IN HOPE

**Romans 15:13** — *"Now may the God of hope fill you with all joy and peace in believing, so that you will abound in hope by the power of the Holy Spirit."*

God gives hope. When we are overwhelmed by despair, He breathes into us the fresh wind of new dreams and expectations. Hope is the confidence that our future will be brighter than today. We may be weeping now, but joy will come in the morning.

**The Source of Hope.** True hope comes from the Lord, not from mere positive attitudes, or wishful thinking. He can change any circumstance for any person at any time. Nothing is impossible for Him. No problem is too hard for Him to solve. No mountain is too big for Him to move. No situation is too complex for Him to repair. He is still able to work miracles and offer us hope regardless of how bad things may seem.

**The Companions of Hope.** God adds "joy and peace" to hope. "All" means that He gives us *"mega-*joy" and *"super-*peace." He changes our dismay into assurance, celebration, and tranquility of soul. Sadness and worry depart. Joy and peace arrive. We stand on God's promises, trust Him, and receive hope and its delightful companions.

**The Fountain of Hope.** We abound in hope "by the power of the Holy Spirit." The Spirit is an inner artesian well that produces the blessings of God, not the least of which is hope. Although hope is not listed as part of the fruit of the Spirit (Galatians 5:22-23), it is a product of the Spirit just the same. We cannot produce hope; we can only display it. It comes as we abide in Jesus, and allow God's Spirit to fill us from within.

Are you suffocating with a sense of hopelessness? Do you feel discouraged, defeated, and ready to throw in the towel? If so, let God give you His hope, joy, and peace through the indwelling Holy Spirit. Do not give up! There is hope for your future.

## HEAVEN OR HELL?

**Matthew 25:46** — _"These will go away into eternal punishment, but the righteous into eternal life."_

Everyone will spend eternity in either heaven or hell. Jesus said there is a heaven to gain and a hell to shun. The same Bible that speaks of streets of gold also warns of a lake of fire. Scripture describes an eternal abode of light with no need of sun and moon, but also speaks of a place of diabolical darkness. Reincarnation, purgatory, and "soul-sleep," are not biblical concepts. Everyone dies once, faces judgment (Hebrews 9:27), and after that, is either carried to heaven or cast into hell. There, he will spend eternity.

In our text, Jesus spoke of both hell and heaven, in that order. He described hell as "eternal punishment." Jesus did not advocate "soul-annihilation," a false teaching that says that the soul of someone who goes to hell is destroyed, and does not suffer forever. Jesus said that hell is _eternal_ punishment. He also described hell as a "furnace of fire" (Matthew 13:41-42), a place of weeping and agony (Matthew 13:42), and a place of fiery separation (Luke 16:19-31). Those who do not go to hell go to heaven. In our text, Jesus spoke of "eternal life" where the "righteous" spend eternity. Jesus is preparing a mansion for each of God's children in a real place called heaven (John 14:2-3). The redeemed of all the ages will worship and serve God there forever. It is a place void of crying, pain, and death (Revelation 21:4). We will live together in love, joy, and peace forevermore.

Eternal punishment or eternal life awaits you. What you do with Jesus during this lifetime will determine your eternal destination. If you accept Jesus as Savior, you will go to heaven. If you do not, you will go to hell. It is that simple. A million years from now you will still exist somewhere. Will it be in heaven or hell? The choice is up to you.

## GOD'S WAKE UP CALL

**Joel 2:12-14** — "'Yet even now,' declares the LORD, 'Return to Me with all your heart, and with fasting, weeping and mourning; and rend your heart and not your garments.' Now return to the LORD your God, for He is gracious and compassionate, slow to anger, abounding in lovingkindness and relenting of evil. Who knows whether He will not turn and relent and leave a blessing behind Him, even a grain offering and a drink offering for the LORD your God?"

Years ago a young man named Gene Tipps was in a car wreck that left him unconscious. After eight years, he woke up. Describing his lengthy siesta, he said, "It is all very strange. My girlfriend is now married with children. The Vietnam War is over. To everyone else I am twenty-eight, but in my mind I am still twenty!" Just like Mr. Tipps, the Church in America has been slumbering. But God is giving us a wake up call!

**A Gracious Call.** The nation of Judah, to whom Joel preached, was wicked and idolatrous. Yet, God was "gracious and compassionate, slow to anger, abounding in loving-kindness, and relenting of evil." He is also willing to forgive us, *if* we repent.

**A Demanding Call.** God did not *ask* Judah to wake up. He *told* them to do so. How? Through "fasting, weeping and mourning." We must do the same. We have rebelled long enough. God is not *asking* us to wake up. He is *telling* us to do it, or else!

**A Rewarding Call.** God promised to bless Judah if they awakened from their slumber. Likewise, God will bless our nation if we repent and arise. He will restore all that the locusts have eaten (v. 25), and again revive our dead churches.

What America needs is a Jesus-exalting, soul-saving, sin-killing, Holy Ghost-filling, bondage-breaking, devil-whipping, heaven-sent revival! If you are asleep spiritually, wake up! Fast, pray, and repent of your sin. Rise from your rebellious rest, slumbering sinner, and let God use you as a catalyst for spiritual awakening in our day.

## THOSE WHO HAVE NO HOPE

**1 Thessalonians 4:13** — *"But we do not want you to be uni-formed, brethren, about those who are asleep, so that you will not grieve as do the rest who have no hope."*

One by one they filed sadly by the casket. Their normal confident smiles and cocky smirks were replaced by expressions of shock, confusion, grief, and horror. I was performing the funeral service of one of their friends. To my knowledge, they were all non-Christians. Most, if not all of them were partyers, drinkers, and revelers. Normally, they lived for the moment, acting fearless and unconcerned about tomorrow. But now that one of their friends had died, they did not know how to act. Their arrogance paled into anxiety and gave way to a sad silence. Their customary demeanor was little more than a facade. Death had confronted them and exposed their private insecurities. My heart grieved for them. They had been tricked by the devil, caught unexpectedly in his trap of deceit. They were those "who have no hope."

Immediately my mind retrieved vivid memories of the many funerals I had performed for those who knew Christ as Lord and Savior. How differently those guests grieved compared to this group. In the hearts of all the redeemed, there was the reality that the deceased loved one was in a better place. He was absent from his body and present with the Lord (2 Corinthians 5:8). An overarching, triumphant promise sustained every heart: "I am the resurrection and the life; he who believes in Me will live even if he dies" (John 11:25). Unlike non-Christians, their tears were mixed with joy, not sorrow.

As I drove away from the grave, I mourned at their sad condition. I determined afresh to preach the Gospel of Christ to anyone and everyone, as long as I had breath. Why? Because apart from Jesus, we would all be as afraid as those "who have no hope."

## Who Is Like The Lord?

**Nahum 1:3** — *"The LORD is slow to anger and great in power, and the LORD will by no means leave the guilty unpunished. In whirlwind and storm is His way, and clouds are the dust beneath His feet."*

When Jonah preached to the Ninevites, they repented and God forgave their sin. Though they were Gentiles, they were granted the privilege of knowing the true and living God. However, within a hundred years, they turned their backs on Jehovah, and returned to their pagan lifestyles and rituals. As a result, God sent the prophet Nahum to inform them of His coming judgment upon them. In our text, the Lord is described as being "slow to anger." He was gracious to the people of Nineveh and sent salvation to them through Jonah's preaching. He was also very patient with them, allowing them ample time to repent from their backslidden state. But God is also "great in power, and...will by no means leave the guilty unpunished." Not only is He loving, but God is also holy and just. Because of their hardened hearts, He decreed their destruction. The Babylonian army eventually destroyed the city of Nineveh, and it was never again rebuilt.

Who is the Lord? He is a loving, gracious God who forgives rebellious sinners. He is a patient God who allows adequate time for them to repent and turn to Him for help. He is a just God. When people reject His saving overtures, or when they return to their former sins, He "by no means leave(s) the guilty unpunished." God is also majestic — "In whirlwind and storm is His way, and clouds are the dust beneath His feet."

Some people create their own caricature of God, imagining that He is only loving and gracious. But He is also holy and just. He will not leave the guilty unpunished. The God of the Bible blesses repentant sinners, but He also punishes defiant ones in hell.

## Learning From The Hard Times

**Job 42:5** — *"I have heard of You by the hearing of the ear; but now my eye sees You."*

Hard times. Difficulties. Suffering. Sickness. No one in his right mind enjoys thinking about such things. Most people do their best to make their lives more comfortable. But what happens when the bottom falls out? What do you do then?

Job suffered immeasurably. In a matter of hours, he lost everything — his crops, cattle, children, and health. His wife encouraged him to blaspheme God and die. But Job refused to renounce the One who had been so faithful to him. When Job's friends came to visit him, at first they sat with him silently. Eventually, they began to accuse him of harboring unconfessed sin in his life. Job replied, "I've sinned, but not this badly!" God eventually silenced Job's visitors. He then told Job to trust Him even when life did not make sense. Through it all, Job matured in his walk with God. He said, in effect, "Lord, I've heard others talk about how great and kind You are, but now I have experienced it personally. Forgive me for questioning Your love. I repent and surrender to You" (v. 6).

God loved Job's response. He made Job's guests apologize to him. He also restored all that Job had lost twofold. He blessed Job's latter years more than his beginning. Job died a joyful, content, old man. He walked with a wound for the rest of his life, but he gained an intimacy with the Lord that made him a blessing to others. He learned that God was capable of carrying him through even the hardest times of life.

Are you going through a valley? Fear not. You will not always hurt this badly. The sun will shine in your life again. Lift up your heart to Him today in prayer and worship. Your weeping may last for the night, but His joy will come in the morning!

## Rich Toward God

**Luke 12:21** — *"So is the man who stores up treasure for himself, and is not rich toward God."*

Jeff and Sheri Easter sing a song written by Jeff's father and uncles entitled, "Thank You, Lord, for Your Blessings." The brothers were farmers in Georgia when they penned the melody years ago. Many who knew them considered them "poor," but they viewed things differently. The chorus to their simple song says, "There's a roof up above me, I've a good place to sleep; there's food on my table, and shoes on my feet. You gave me Your love, Lord, and a fine family. Thank You, Lord, for Your blessings on me!" Every sensitive Christian can readily identify with these heartfelt words.

What does it matter if you gain the whole world, but you do not know God personally through His Son, Jesus Christ? What do you really gain if you are wealthy by human standards, but you are a pauper toward God? Jesus told of a farmer who enjoyed a great harvest. He decided to save it all for himself instead of sharing some of it with others in need. God called him a "fool" because of his self-centeredness, and punished him by prematurely taking his life. Jesus then quoted our text to warn us of the outcome of a life lived with self in mind, rather than being focused on eternal riches and rewards.

No one can serve two masters. We either lay up treasure for ourselves or seek to be "rich toward God." Life passes so quickly, and the choices we make here are eternal. What we value on earth follows us into eternity. We must set our eyes on things above and seek first His Kingdom. We should read our Bibles, pray, win souls, and be servants. We should attend Bible-believing, Christ-honoring churches, and support them with our tithes and offerings. May we invest our lives wisely, and seek to be "rich toward God."

## ENJOY LIFE

**Ecclesiastes 9:9** — *"Enjoy life with the woman whom you love all the days of your fleeting life which He has given to you under the sun; for this is your reward in life and in your toil in which you have labored under the sun."*

The limousines pull up and the "stars" step out. It is Hollywood's most important annual event — the Academy Awards. As they stroll down the carpeted walkway, the actors and actresses smile and seem to have it all together. But are they really happy? Many of them actually lead miserable lives. Few who work in Tinsel-town maintain happy, life-long marriages. Many are drug addicts, engage in sexual perversion, and suffer from depression. Fame and fortune do not necessarily guarantee an enjoyable life.

The Bible teaches that a loving, life-long marriage between one man and one woman is a primary source of enjoyment and fulfillment in life. King Solomon affirmed this in our text. Solomon reminds us of many modern Hollywood stars. He was a talented, wise man who became foolish. He grew selfish and began to experiment with sin. His sexual lust drove him to marry hundreds of foreign, pagan women who led him away from the Lord. At the end of his miserable life, he realized that there was one thing that could have given him happiness. If only he had focused on one, life-long marriage with the woman he really loved! That sacred relationship would have brought greater joy to him than anything else. Sadly, Solomon died without ever experiencing that.

The common man who loves the Lord and has been married to his sweetheart for many years is much happier than a movie star or a wicked king. This life is fleeting. It passes by quickly. The simple enjoyment of being married to our life-long best friend beats fame and fortune. It always has been one of the best things going under the sun.

## ARISE AND SHINE

**Isaiah 60:1-2** — *"Arise, shine; for your light has come, and the glory of the LORD has risen upon you. For behold, darkness will cover the earth and deep darkness the peoples; but the LORD will rise upon you and His glory will appear upon you."*

"Rise and shine!" That phrase, coming from the mouth of my mother as she awakened us in the morning was not the most welcome or pleasant sound we had ever heard. My brother and I usually did not want to get out of our beds to go to school or to mow yards for extra money on Saturdays. Our eyelids felt as if they each weighed ten pounds as we tried to open them. Both of my parents grew up on farms and they were always early risers. What came naturally for them was very difficult for us!

In our text we read about a time that is coming when Israel will once again become the most prominent nation on earth. After Jesus comes and takes away all the Christians in the Rapture (1 Thessalonians 4:16-17), the earth and its remaining inhabitants will be subjected to a seven-year period of horror, which Jesus called the "Great Tribulation" (Matthew 24:21). "Darkness will cover the earth and deep darkness the peoples." At the end of that horrible time, Christ will come back *with* His Church (Revelation 19:11-19) and will set foot on the Mount of Olives in Jerusalem (Zechariah 14:1f). The Holy City will become the capital of the world and Jesus will reign for a thousand years. He "will rise upon (Israel) and His glory will appear upon (Zion)."

Christians need to awaken *now*! It is time for those who love Jesus to come out of the closet! This wicked world will grow darker spiritually before the Rapture occurs, but in that darkness, our light can shine brighter than ever before. Wake up, child of God. Throw off the covers of sin. Get out of the bed of disobedience and "Arise and shine!"

## I APPEAL TO YOU

**Philemon 8-9** — _"Therefore, though I have enough confidence in Christ to order you to do what is proper, yet for love's sake I rather appeal to you — since I am such a person as Paul, the aged, and now also a prisoner of Christ Jesus."_

Paul was a great leader. He was a learned scholar. He spoke several languages. He received an exclusive education, having studied at the feet of the illustrious Gamaliel (Acts 22:3). He was also a great writer. Under the influence of the Holy Spirit, he penned almost half the New Testament. Paul was a great preacher. Whether reasoning with the Jews in a synagogue, or speaking at the Athenian Areopagus to the Greek Epicurean and Stoic philosophers, he effectively preached the Gospel of Jesus Christ. He was also a missionary. He planted churches throughout the Roman Empire that caused the Church of Jesus Christ to literally conquer the Empire itself. In addition to all these areas of giftedness, Paul was a pacesetting leader. One important leadership trait that he acquired was to appeal persuasively to others rather than forcing his way upon them.

In our text, Paul shows us how to utilize this important trait. A slave named Onesimus had run away from his master, Philemon. While he was a fugitive, Onesimus met Paul. Paul led him to faith in Christ and then wrote Philemon a letter. Paul reminded him that even though he had the apostolic authority to "order" him to take Onesimus back, instead, "for love's sake" he appealed for Philemon to do it willingly.

Like Paul, every great leader understands the wisdom of appealing to others rather than lording over them as a tyrannical dictator. Even Jesus came not to be served but to serve (Mark 10:45). Before you force others to comply, employ the biblical method of appealing to them. It is Christlike, it is effective, and it is a mark of a truly great leader.

## HE WILL REJOICE OVER YOU

**Zephaniah 3:17** — *"The LORD your God is in your midst, a victorious warrior. He will exult over you with joy, He will be quiet in His love, He will rejoice over you with shouts of joy."*

Preaching is a mixture of joy and sadness. The preacher is called to "reprove, rebuke, and exhort with great patience and instruction" (2 Timothy 4:2). The prophet Zephaniah preached both exhortation and condemnation. Judah had been under the malicious rule of Manasseh and Amon. The prophet warned of "The Day of the Lord" that loomed on the horizon, which would be a day of judgment for Judah if she did not repent. The people of God finally turned back to Him under the reign of righteous Josiah. But alas, after Josiah's untimely death, Judah once again rebelled against the Lord.

At the end of his prophecy, Zephaniah promised a better day for God's people. It would be a day of rejoicing and singing. Messiah would rule in the midst of His people as "a victorious warrior." He would remove the arrogant citizens from Jerusalem, and cause His people to serve Him in humility (3:11-12). They would no longer tell lies. They would live free from fear with peaceful conditions and plenty to eat (3:13). This section of prophecy gives a vivid description of the Millennial Reign of Christ. After His return, Jesus will rule in Jerusalem for a thousand years. There will finally be peace on earth. He will "exult over (us) with joy" and "rejoice over (us) with shouts of joy (or, 'joyful singing')." How glorious it will be when the whole earth is filled with His glory!

Does Jesus Christ rejoice because of you? Are you His child through salvation? If so, are you walking obediently with Him? He loves you and longs for you to follow Him wholeheartedly. Submit to Him completely today and He will shout for joy!

## MIGHTY IN THE SCRIPTURES

**Acts 18:24** — _"Now a Jew named Apollos, an Alexandrian by birth, an eloquent man, came to Ephesus; and he was mighty in the Scriptures."_

Biblical illiteracy is common in America. The Bible may still be the best selling book in our nation, but is probably the most ignored book as well. Bibles are not to serve as religious accessories that merely decorate our homes. They are to be opened, read, prayed over, pondered, and above all, obeyed. Even in our churches there seems to be what the prophet Amos called, "A famine...for hearing the words of the LORD" (Amos 8:11). Many modern churches are so "seeker-friendly" and man-centered that they have relegated the plain preaching and teaching of God's Word to the back burner of the worship service. Being "relevant" has become more important than being biblical. The Church needs some folks to rise up and say, "Enough is enough! We are tired of drama, ballet, and self-help speeches! Give us a man of God, full of the Spirit of God, living in the holiness of God, holding the Book of God, saying, 'Hear ye the Word of God!'"

Apollos was that kind of man. He was well educated ("eloquent") and "mighty in the Scriptures." He preached passionately ("fervent in spirit" – v. 25), and boldly (v. 26). He had a teachable spirit, allowing two lay-people, Priscilla and Aquila, to "explain to him the way of God more accurately" (v. 26). His preaching was "powerful" because it came from "the Scriptures" and focused on the fact that "Jesus was the Christ" (v. 28).

Our churches need help. We need zealous leaders who are less "seeker-friendly," and more "Savior-friendly," "Spirit-friendly," "Scripture-friendly," and "soul-friendly." The critical need across our land is for God to raise up bold young men who will "preach the word" (2 Timothy 4:2); men like Apollos who are "mighty in the Scriptures."

## THE LORD BLESS YOU

**Numbers 6:24-26** — *"The LORD bless you, and keep you; the LORD make His face shine on you, and be gracious to you; the LORD lift up His countenance on you, and give you peace."*

God loves to bless His children. He provided this wonderful prayer of blessing to Aaron and the priests of Israel to be used when praying over His people. It can and should be used by Christians today. How should we pray for God to bless us?

**"Bless Us with Your Protection."** "The LORD bless you, and *keep* you." "Keep" (Hebrew *shamar*) means "to watch over, protect." It is actually translated "bodyguard" on one occasion in the Old Testament. God promises to defend and guard us as we walk with Him through this life. He will be our strong shield against the enemy.

**"Bless Us with Your Presence."** "The LORD make His *face* shine on you (and) lift up His *countenance* on you." The greatest blessing for the Jews was for God to look on them favorably. His "face" refers to His presence, which gives us joy (Psalm 16:11).

**"Bless Us with Your Pardon."** "The LORD...be *gracious* to you." Israel was prone to wander rebelliously into sin. Apart from God's grace, none of them would have entered the Promised Land. God's grace saves (Ephesians 2:8-9) and sustains us as well.

**"Bless Us with Your Peace."** "The LORD...give you *peace*." God gave Israel peace when He rescued them from Egypt and from the Canaanites they fought in the Promised Land. He continues to grant peace to His people today. When we pray and walk in faith, He gives us His peace that passes all understanding (Philippians 4:6-7).

The Lord desires to bless you. He has given you this prayer to guide you as you pray. Ask Him to bless you and others with His protection, presence, pardon, and peace. He has been answering this prayer for a long time. He will answer it for you today!

## FOOLS FOR CHRIST

**1 Corinthians 4:10** — _"We are fools for Christ's sake, but you are prudent in Christ; we are weak, but you are strong; you are distinguished, but we are without honor."_

As we drove up to the school I saw them — three teenage boys kneeling in prayer at the foot of the flagpole. My heart was moved. As teachers and other students walked passed them, the boys never looked up. They were lost in the presence of the Holy One. I decided to join them. I parked my truck and walked quietly to their circle. I felt that I was on holy ground. I said, "I'm one of you. May I join you?" They seemed encouraged. As we knelt, I prayed that God would bless and honor them for their commitment, that He would give protection to everyone at the school, and that He would send revival among the student body. I also asked the Lord to send others to join them in prayer. When we finished, I thanked them, and returned to my truck. When I closed the door, I shouted "Hallelujah! Thank you, Lord Jesus, for those fools for Christ!"

Before God can use you, He must kill you. By that I mean you must die to your reputation, and be more concerned about what He thinks than what other people think. Paul told the Christians at Corinth that he was merely a fool "for Christ's sake." Paul's primary goal was to please God. Thus, he feared no man, and desired no man's praise.

If we follow Christ closely, the world will think that we are foolish. Even Jesus' relatives thought He had lost His mind (Mark 3:21). When Paul preached the Gospel, he was called an "idle babbler" (Acts 17:18), "out of his mind," and "mad" (Acts 26:24).

Are you willing to be a fool for Christ? Is your reputation more important to you than obeying and honoring Him? Die to your reputation and bury your glory. Only then can Jesus' glory be birthed in you. Whose fool will you be — the world's, or Christ's?

## LIVE BY THE SPIRIT

**Galatians 5:25** — *"If we live by the Spirit, let us also walk by the Spirit."*

It was a hot summer Saturday and it was time to cut the grass. As I struggled and perspired in the scorching sun, I saw my neighbor mowing with relative ease. When I asked him about it, he said, "My mower is self-propelled." By sunset so was mine!

Many Christians struggle because they rely on their limited, human power to live the Christian life. All the while, they possess a supernatural source of strength — the indwelling Holy Spirit. He has all the power they need to live a victorious life. Instead, many choose to stay defeated, discouraged, and miserable. God wants to change that.

According to John 3:5-8, when we are saved we are "born of the Spirit." At regeneration the Spirit washes and renews us (Titus 3:5). All Christians have already received the Holy Spirit. Those who do not have the Spirit are lost (Romans 8:9). He is the "Spirit of adoption" that assures us that God is our Father (Romans 8:14-16). He baptizes all of us into Christ's body (1 Corinthians 12:13), and makes our physical bodies His temple (1 Corinthians 6:19). The Spirit endows us with gifts for service (1 Corinthians 12:4-7, 11), and assures us of a future home in heaven by sealing us "for the day of redemption" (Ephesians 4:10). If we ask, God will gladly fill us with His Spirit (Ephesians 5:18). As the river of His majestic might is released from within us, He empowers us for victory.

Are you tired of trying to live the Christian life by yourself? Are you weary of the vicious cycle of trying, failing, and feeling defeated? Are you ready to stop relying on your own power? Stop struggling, child of God! Tap into the supernatural, limitless power of the Holy Spirit today. His help is available to all who will ask (Luke 11:13).

## WORSHIP IN THE SPIRIT

**John 4:23-24** — _"But an hour is coming, and now is, when the true worshipers will worship the Father in spirit and truth; for such people the Father seeks to be His worshipers. God is spirit, and those who worship Him must worship in spirit and truth."_

God is good and worthy of praise. The one privilege we have on earth that we will also have in heaven is to worship the Lord. He is surrounded with perpetual, angelic praise (Isaiah 6:1-4), but the worship He prefers comes from those He has redeemed.

**The Requirement of Worship.** Worship is a necessity for a Christian, not an option. Jesus said that a true believer "will worship" (v. 23) and "must worship" (v. 24) God. The Holy Spirit places the desire to worship the Lord in every Christian's heart.

**The Regulations of Worship.** Jesus commands us to worship the Father "in spirit." God is a spiritual being (v. 24) and so is man (1 Thessalonians 5:23). When man praises the Lord, his spirit fellowships intimately with God's Spirit. God and man embrace hearts during worship. We must also worship God "in truth." Our worship must be Bible-based, not tradition-based. Thus, lifting hands, clapping hands, shouting praises, and singing joyfully are just as holy and appropriate for worship as bowing and being quiet in God's presence. Why? Because they are all mentioned in the Bible.

**The Reward of Worship.** "For such people the Father seeks to be His worshipers." The reward for worshiping God is God Himself. He blesses those who worship Him with His presence. God inhabits the praises of His people (Psalm 22:3).

Is praising and worshiping the Lord a priority in your life and in your church? If not, you need to change. God is seeking worshipers. As He searches across this earth, make sure that you are one who attracts His presence. Take time to worship Him today.

## WITNESS IN THE SPIRIT

**Acts 8:29** — *"Then the Spirit said to Philip, 'Go up and join this chariot.'"*

Every Christian is to be a verbal witness for Jesus Christ. All of us are to share compassionately the message of Jesus with lost people in order to persuade them to receive Him as Lord and Savior. Jesus expected His earliest disciples to be witnesses. At the beginning of His ministry, He called them to be "fishers of men" (Matthew 4:19). At the conclusion of His ministry, He was still commissioning them to take the Gospel to the ends of the earth (Matthew 28:18-20). He expects no less from His followers today.

Philip was one of the earliest deacons. He went to Samaria, preached the Gospel, and many were saved. At the height of that successful mission, the Lord instructed Philip to go to a desert road leading to Gaza. There he met a eunuch from Ethiopia who was returning to his country in a chariot. He had been to Jerusalem to learn more about the God of the Jews. The Spirit told Philip to join the man. Philip discovered that he was reading from Isaiah's prophecy concerning the Jewish Messiah. Prompted by the Spirit, Philip opened his mouth, explained the Scripture, and shared Christ with him. The man was saved and baptized beside that dusty road because Philip was led by the Spirit.

We do not have to dread witnessing. God desires for us to learn to flow in the power of His Spirit as we tell others about Jesus (Acts 1:8). Like Philip, the Lord will give us divine appointments to share Christ with the lost. It is our responsibility to do so. Through the indwelling Spirit, we have been given all the power we need for that task.

Ask God to fill you today with His Spirit. Then get ready. God has someone out there waiting to receive Jesus. Who knows? He might even be riding in a chariot.

## WORK IN THE SPIRIT

**Zechariah 4:6** — _"Then he said to me, 'This is the word of the LORD to Zerubbabel saying, "Not by might nor by power, but by My Spirit," says the LORD of hosts.'"_

The Lord's work requires the Lord's power. We cannot accomplish what God desires with fleshly, finite, weak, earthly, human power. We need the strength of the mighty Holy Spirit of God to perform the work He has given us to do on this earth.

Zechariah prophesied during the days when God's people were returning from Babylonian captivity. In 587 B.C. the Babylonian forces destroyed Jerusalem, including Solomon's great Temple. The Jews who survived that massacre were exiled to Babylon where they served as slaves for approximately seventy years. In 539 B.C., Babylon fell to the Persians. The next year, Cyrus, King of Persia, told a Jewish leader named Zerubbabel to return to Jerusalem with a group of Jews to rebuild Solomon's Temple and restore worship there. They faced severe opposition from the local Gentiles who did not want the Temple to be rebuilt. Zerubbabel and God's people soon grew discouraged. It was then that God spoke to them through Zechariah in our text. Their "might" and "power" were insufficient to accomplish the task God had given them. Unless the Lord empowered them in their work, their efforts were in vain (Psalm 127:1). They needed the strength and insight of His Spirit! The people listened to God's voice, and by 515 B.C. the Temple was rebuilt. The worship of Jehovah was restored by the Spirit's power!

The load God has called you to lift requires the muscle of His Spirit. On your own you will fail, but with His power you will succeed. Humble yourself, get clean spiritually, and ask God to fill you with His Spirit. Live in the flow of the Holy Ghost, and you will be absolutely amazed at what _He_ will accomplish through you today!

## WALK IN THE SPIRIT

**Galatians 5:16** — *"But I say, walk by the Spirit, and you will not carry out the desire of the flesh."*

God has a plan for us. His plan, or will, is expressed in His Word, the Bible. There He instructs us about His will. We know to pray (Colossians 4:2), read the Bible (Psalm 1:2-3), fellowship with believers (Hebrews 10:24-25), witness to non-Christians (Acts 1:8), and tithe (Malachi 3:8-10) because the Bible says we should. He also reveals His will about matters not mentioned in Scripture — which college to attend, which house to buy, which person to marry, or which job to take — *if* we learn to walk in the Spirit.

People live/walk either in the Spirit or in the flesh. These two ways of life war with each other in our hearts. The flesh is our selfish nature that seeks independence from God. The Spirit in us desires to please God, but our flesh is weak (Matthew 26:41). To hear from God and walk in His Spirit, we must clear the communication channels. We do that by confessing our sin, dying to self, submitting to God-ordained authority, and surrendering to God's will. We activate the communication lines by immersing ourselves in the Bible, and monitoring what enters our minds. We then receive a promise from God's Word. That "word" will "burn in our hearts" (Luke 24:32). We test it by: (1) making sure it is consistent with other Scriptures, (2) seeing if godly people bear witness with it (Proverbs 15:22), and (3) making sure we have peace in our hearts (Colossians 3:15). If our "word" passes these tests, we stand on the promise and walk in the Spirit.

Nothing is more exciting than learning to walk in God's Spirit. Jesus' sheep hear His voice and follow Him (John 10:27). Ask God to help you learn to hear His voice. How splendid it is to sing, "And He walks with *me* and He talks with *me*," and mean it!

## WAR IN THE SPIRIT

**Ephesians 6:10** — _"Finally, be strong in the Lord and in the strength of His might."_

Christians live in a daily, spiritual battle. Satan and his demons are real, unseen forces that scheme and fight against all believers. The Apostle Paul tells us how we can gain absolute victory by waging war in the spirit world. In our text, he tells us that we have an awesome _power_. We are to be "strong in the Lord and in the strength of His might." The indwelling Holy Spirit enlightens, empowers, and enables us to stand against Satan's attacks. Paul continues by insisting that the Christian's _opponents_ are not people ("flesh and blood"), but Satan and his loyal legions (Ephesians 6:11-12). Satan is a _deceitful_ foe (2 Corinthians 4:4), and he is a _deadly_ foe (1 Peter 5:8). But because of Jesus' vicarious death and bodily resurrection, he is also a _defeated_ foe (Colossians 2:13-15)!

Paul also emphasizes the warrior's _protection_. God gives each believer His "full armor" to stand firm in the battle (Ephesians 6:11, 13). We have the belt of _truth_, the breastplate of _righteousness_, the shoes of _the gospel of peace_, the shield of _faith_, the helmet of _salvation_, the sword of the Spirit, which is _the Word of God_, and the ability to _pray in the Spirit_ (vv. 14-18). We are to "take up" (v. 13) and "put on" (v. 14) this armor daily as we engage the enemy. The main _purpose_ of our warfare is to share the gospel with the lost (vv. 19-20).

Christian, you are in a battle and the stakes are high. Eternal souls literally hang in the balance. Satan is a thief. He desires to steal from you, kill you, and destroy you (John 10:10a). God has given you all the power and protection you need to be victorious. Stand firm. Wage war in the Spirit's strength. Be a good soldier of Christ Jesus (2 Timothy 2:3). Press on and win the fight of faith today (1 Timothy 6:12)!

## TAKING EVERY THOUGHT CAPTIVE

**2 Corinthians 10:5** — *"We are destroying speculations and every lofty thing raised up against the knowledge of God, and we are taking every thought captive to the obedience of Christ."*

"I am having a recurring sinful thought that is driving me crazy," the young man whispered. "What is it?" I asked. With embarrassment, he answered, "I keep hearing: 'You are a homosexual.'" I said, "That is not your thought. Satan is putting that in your mind. You are not a homosexual. God never created anyone as a homosexual or a lesbian. That thought must be taken captive!" We prayed, and God began the process of setting him free.

Every thought we think does not originate with us. Satan attacks our minds. He cannot possess our spirits, but he can harass and oppress us mentally if we allow it. He will put an evil thought in our mind, and then try to convince us that it is ours. He is a liar and cannot tell the truth (John 8:44). If he suggests, "You ought to kill yourself," it is obviously one of his lies. God loves life and would never tell anyone to commit suicide. Satan may give us the thought that we are going to be sick, or have a nervous breakdown. He may suggest that our spouse is being unfaithful to us. He may tell us that we have committed the unpardonable sin and have lost our salvation. What a scoundrel he is!

What can you do? How can you take all thoughts captive to Christ's obedience? (1) Recognize it as *his* thought, *not* yours. (2) Reject it in Jesus' name. That is, refuse to let it lodge in your mind. (3) Replace it with good thoughts from God's Word, the Bible.

Is Satan attacking you or someone you love in the area of thoughts? He is a perverted liar who wants to torment you mentally. Rise up in your authority in Christ! Submit to God, resist the devil, and he will flee. Win the battle for your mind today!

## A LAMENTABLE LIFE

**2 Timothy 4:10** — _"For Demas, having loved this present world, has deserted me."_

When I was in high school I ran track. At one of our meets, there was a young man named Bobby who was a member of our school's two-mile relay squad. On that squad were four young men who each ran a half-mile. Bobby was the anchorman on the team. When their race began, our first three runners were slower than those from the other teams. By the time they finally handed Bobby the baton, our team was in last place. Bobby took the baton and immediately began to sprint. He passed the other runners within the first of his two laps. We were all ecstatic. Bobby was our hero! But then, as Bobby started his second lap, he began to slow down. He had used all of his energy on the first lap. One by one, the other runners began to pass him. He lost his first place spot, and in the end, finished last. He started well, but ended disappointingly.

It is possible to begin the Christian life well and end it poorly. Paul tells of a man named Demas who did just that. Earlier in Demas' life, Paul had referred to him as one of his "fellow workers" (Philemon 24). But by the time Paul wrote our text, Demas had "deserted" him because he "loved this present world." He began well, but ended poorly.

Christians are usually remembered for how they finish their lives, not for how they begin them. Many leaders as well as lay people have started well for Christ only to lose their reputations and ministries because of sin. Jesus called such people "tasteless salt" (Matthew 5:13). If you fail to end well, you will have lived a lamentable life. Your goal should be to cross life's finish line with your eyes on Christ and your reputation in tact. The Christian life is a marathon, not a sprint. Stay faithful to Jesus and finish well!

## A COMMENDABLE LIFE

**2 Timothy 4:11** — *"Only Luke is with me. Pick up Mark and bring him with you, for he is useful to me for service."*

It is amazing to see what people do with their lives. Some who were very popular and talented in their teenage years, end up later in life as dismal failures. Still others, who were not very gifted when they were younger, turn out to be "late bloomers" who experience great success as time progresses. Just as it is possible to start life well and end poorly, it is also possible to begin life as a relative failure and end successfully.

Not long before Paul died, he wrote his second letter to Timothy. In our text, he commended a young man named "Mark" as being "useful...for service." "Mark" was none other than John Mark, who had a less than stellar beginning in the Christian ministry. When Barnabas and Paul went on their first missionary journey, John Mark accompanied them, but grew disillusioned with the work and returned home. When Paul and Barnabas were later contemplating another mission trip, Barnabas suggested that they take John Mark along. Paul vehemently objected, citing John Mark's dismal past performance. Paul and Barnabas separated over the issue, Barnabas taking John Mark, and Paul taking Silas. Apparently, Barnabas mentored John Mark and salvaged his ministry. By the time Paul wrote our text, he affirmed John Mark as one who led a commendable life. Indeed, John Mark went on to write the Gospel of Mark!

If you have sinned and made mistakes, you can still finish your life in victory. God is gracious. He will give you the strength and courage to begin again. If you have failed Him, do not run from Him, run to Him. Repent of your sin, get up, and start again today. God is for you. He will help you. You can end well. Remember John Mark!

## A BALANCED LIFE

**Luke 2:52** — _"And Jesus kept increasing in wisdom and stature, and in favor with God and men."_

As I drove along I noticed a lady in an SUV with a frantic look on her face. In her left hand she held a checkbook. In her right hand she held a pen. Her cell phone was wedged between her left ear and shoulder as she talked and drove. I could not help but wonder, even if she finally balanced her checkbook, was she living a balanced life?

At the age of twelve, Jesus returned with His family from Jerusalem to Nazareth. There He matured until He began His public ministry at the age of thirty. During those eighteen years, Jesus grew in four major areas that represent a truly balanced life.

First, Jesus grew _intellectually_. He "kept increasing in wisdom." Although Jesus was divine, in His humanity He had to learn like we do. He was not born reciting Old Testament Scriptures. Instead, He read, studied, and memorized the biblical text like we should. Jesus also grew _physically_. He grew in "stature." He took care of His body and ate healthily. We should do the same because our bodies are the temples of the Holy Spirit (1 Corinthians 6:19-20). Jesus grew _spiritually_. He increased "in favor with God." We too must "grow in grace" (2 Peter 3:18). Finally, Jesus matured _socially_. He grew "in favor with...men." He loved people and they loved Him. To be like Jesus we must love others as we love ourselves.

A frantic life is indicative of the fact that a person is not balanced. Even as an unbalanced wheel can shake a car and make all its passengers uncomfortable, an unbalanced life can be irritating, unhealthy, and dangerous. Ask God to help you grow in these four important areas and you will live like Jesus, the most balanced person ever!

## SEARCH ME, O GOD

**Psalm 139:23-24** — *"Search me, O God, and know my heart; try me and know my anxious thoughts; and see if there be any hurtful way in me, and lead me in the everlasting way."*

My brother is an amazing person. He has always been brilliant. When we were children, he would sit and read encyclopedias. He scored so high on his A.C.T., my mother thought that I had failed it when she heard my score! He has been very successful in the computer industry, having worked for and excelled with some of the best companies in America. But as smart as he is, he was confronted with a situation that absolutely confounded him. He went in for a routine physical only to learn that, although he had never smoked, he had a tumor on his left lung and a second one in his thymus gland. They were both malignant. He immediately had them removed and subsequently underwent intensive chemotherapy and radiation treatments. One day after Ed's surgery, he said to me, "Steve, it really is amazing. I had two malignant tumors in my body, and I did not have a clue that anything was wrong until I had that check up."

The same thing can happen to us spiritually. We may think that we are doing fine, only to undergo a spiritual checkup and discover that something is wrong in our lives. Our text is a prayer for spiritual examination. Any Christian who desires for God to reveal "any hurtful way" within him should utilize it. Once he confesses and forsakes his hidden sin, Jesus, the Great Physician, will remove it, and make him whole again.

How is your spiritual health? Do not answer that question after having merely examined the outward appearance of your life. Instead, ask the Lord to give you a Holy Spirit CAT scan today. You could be carrying a malignancy of sin and not even know it!

## PRAYING LIKE JESUS

**Hebrews 5:7** — _"In the days of His flesh, He offered up both prayers and supplications with loud crying and tears to the One able to save Him from death, and He was heard because of His piety."_

Jesus was a prayer warrior. In fact, He is the only real prayer expert. Our text reveals several key characteristics of our Lord's prayer life that made it so effective.

Jesus had a _time_ for prayer. He prayed "in the days of His flesh." That is the only time any of us have to pray. In heaven we will commune with God face to face, but until we get there, we must talk with Him through prayer. Jesus' prayers were also _sacrificial_. He "offered up" His prayers. Genuine prayers are costly. That is why God saves our heartfelt prayers as precious incense in golden heavenly bowls (Revelation 5:8). Jesus' prayers had _varied content_. He offered up "both prayers and supplications." We too must lift up different types of prayers such as praise, thanksgiving, confession of sin, prayers for others, and prayers for our own needs. Jesus prayed _passionately_ "with loud crying and tears." He prayed like that in Gethsemane and also on the cross. We must pray fervently with our hearts as well as with our minds. Jesus prayed to _the Father_, "the One able to save Him from death." The Father of Jesus is our Father also. He will help us in our times of need (Hebrews 4:16). Jesus' prayers were _victorious_ in that "He was heard because of His piety." When God hears our prayers, the devil's plans are thwarted, God's kingdom is advanced, and lives are eternally changed for His glory.

How is your prayer life? Allow Jesus to teach you new lessons in prayer. He made prayer a priority while He was on earth. You must also. Draw near to God today and offer up passionate prayers. The more you pray, the more like Jesus you will be.

## ENTHUSIASTIC WORSHIP

**Nehemiah 8:6** — *"Then Ezra blessed the LORD the great God. And all the people answered, 'Amen, Amen!' while lifting up their hands; then they bowed low and worshiped the LORD with their faces to the ground."*

Jesus said that we must worship God "in spirit and truth" (John 4:23-24). As long as God's Spirit and the truth of His Word, the Bible, guide us, God is pleased with our worship. We should worship Him enthusiastically (Greek *ev* and *theos*), which literally means "in God." That is the type of worship described in our text.

**We Should Worship God Verbally.** Ezra "blessed the LORD" vocally and the people responded by saying, "Amen, Amen!" They expressed their praise with words. As a Christian, my praise to God should continually be "in my *mouth*" (Psalm 34:1). The redeemed of the Lord should "*say so*" (Psalm 107:2). God desires to *hear* our worship.

**We Should Worship God Physically.** While the people worshiped, they were "lifting up their hands." Afterwards, "they bowed low." We too can worship the Lord with physical activity. We can "lift up holy hands" (1 Timothy 2:8), "clap (our) hands" (Psalm 47:1), and "bow down...(and) kneel before the LORD our Maker" (Psalm 95:6).

**We Should Worship God Reverently.** The worshipers in our text were reverent in their demeanor. They had respectfully stood when the Scriptures were read (Nehemiah 8:5), and afterward they "bowed low and worshiped the LORD with their faces to the ground." Enthusiasm in worship does not have to degenerate into fanatical emotionalism.

We should worship God both privately (Matthew 6:6) and publicly (Matthew 18:20; Hebrews 10:24-25). Worshiping the living God through His Son, Jesus, is the greatest privilege we have on earth. Enter His presence and give praise to God today!

## THE MIGHTY HAVE FALLEN

**2 Samuel 1:19** — _"Your beauty, O Israel, is slain on your high places! How have the mighty fallen!"_

Earl Tapley was a soul-winner. He made some people, even some preachers, uncomfortable with his evangelistic tactics. He witnessed to everyone he met. Within a few minutes of being in his presence, he was handing you a Gospel tract and asking you about your relationship with Jesus. I once saw him witness to every person in a restaurant as they waited to go through the buffet line. On another occasion, I saw him walking down the halls of the Baptist university I attended, witnessing and handing out tracts during the homecoming festivities. When the Baptist preachers gathered at the associational office every Monday for fellowship, Earl always gave a report of how many he had recently led to Christ. Like Paul, Earl was a "fool for Christ" (1 Corinthians 4:10).

When one of my former deacons faxed Brother Earl's funeral announcement to me, I could not help but think of our text. When I served as pastor in Tennessee, that deacon, Bro. Earl and I, and a few others, prayed almost every Sunday morning in our church's sanctuary, asking the Lord to save people that day. Brother Earl prayed passionately, asking God to convict and convert lost people. Indeed, "How have the mighty fallen!" David wrote that phrase after King Saul and his son Jonathan had been slain by the Philistines on the field of battle at Mount Gilboa. Just as David lamented their deaths, I lamented the death of a great Christian soldier called Brother Earl.

Earl is in heaven now. Though the paper did not say, I know he was in his 90s. "Thank you, Lord, for that great hero of the faith. He was mightier than a millionaire. May I have a passion for souls like he did." Alas, a giant of the faith has fallen!

## HELD BY JESUS

**John 10:28** — *"And I give eternal life to them, and they will never perish; and no one will snatch them out of My hand."*

When I was growing up in Dyersburg, Tennessee, one of my favorite things to do was to go "downtown." I loved the court square with the old men sitting and talking on the bench, and the pigeons walking around under the large shade trees. I enjoyed going to Woolworth's and getting a milkshake. I usually went to the Ben Franklin Store and looked at the latest toys. There, my dad and mom would also buy either a snow cone or a bag of popcorn for me to feast upon. And the Rexall Drug Store had the best comic books in town!

As we went from store to store on the square, we occasionally crossed a busy street. Whenever that happened, my dad or my mom would grab my hand so tightly I thought they were going to squeeze it off! I was not holding on to them. They were holding on to me. Even if they had to drag me across the street, they were not letting go!

That is what Jesus is doing for each of us. When He saves us, He takes us in His omnipotent hand, and holds us securely forevermore. He gives us *"eternal* life" that is guaranteed to last. Once He redeems us, we "will *never* perish." Some Christian songs speak about "holding on to God's hand." The truth of the matter is, we are not "holding on" to Jesus. Rather, Jesus is holding on to us! And no one, not even the devil himself, "will snatch (us) out of (Jesus') hand." That is a comforting promise!

Christian, you are a child of God. You can impair your *fellowship* with Him through sin, but sin can never sever your *relationship* with Him. You are not "holding on" to Christ or your salvation. *He* is holding you! And, even if Jesus has to drag you across the streets of this life, He is going to get you home to heaven, safe and secure!

## LET JUSTICE ROLL DOWN

**Amos 5:24** — *"But let justice roll down like waters and righteous-ness like an ever-flowing stream."*

The bus pulled up in front of the Civil Rights Museum in Montgomery, Alabama. Beside the road was a sketch of Dr. Martin Luther King, Jr. Beneath it was a quote that said, "Let justice roll down like waters." Our tour guide told our group of elementary students and their parents that those words were Dr. King's. I raised my hand and said, "Indeed, Dr. King spoke those words frequently, but he was actually quoting a verse of Scripture." I then quoted our text and included the biblical reference. The guide became noticeably uncomfortable. I suppose he did not want the children to hear from the Bible. Yet, I rejoiced that Dr. King was being memorialized with a brilliant verse of Scripture.

The prophet Amos lived in a day when corruption was the norm for both the kings and the priests in Israel. Hebrew worship had degenerated so much that God said, "I reject your festivals...solemn assemblies...offerings...(and) songs" (Amos 5:21-23). God was tired of the hypocritical charades that were transpiring at the Temple. He demanded more than religious activity. He desired holiness and obedience. He wanted "justice" and "righteousness" to flow down through His people to others in their daily activities. He expected them to be honest in business dealings and compassionate to those in need. Such "justice" was more important than sacrificing lambs on any altar.

We do not please God by merely attending church and going through religious motions. We must be just and righteous in our relationships with others as well. Martin Luther King, Jr. was wise to use these words spoken by God through Amos. May we not only memorialize his words, but also mimic them in our lives each day.

## IF ONE MEMBER SUFFERS

**1 Corinthians 12:26** — *"And if one member suffers, all the members suffer with it; if one member is honored, all the members rejoice with it."*

Her blond hair bounced as she scampered through the den. Our middle daughter, Alli, never walked anywhere when she was little. Suddenly, she let out a bloodcurdling scream. When her mom found her writhing in pain on the floor, she said, "Alli, what happened?" "I bwoke my toe, I bwoke my toe!" she screamed. Donna asked, "Which toe is it?" With tears streaming down her face, she said, "The one that had woast beef!"

When a person injures a part of his body, the entire body suffers from the pain. Even so, when one member of Christ's body suffers, that ache affects all the other members. When a Christian hurts, others should rally around him to bring comfort and healing. We should weep with those who weep, just as we should rejoice with those who rejoice (Romans 12:15). What happens to one believer affects us all.

It is easy to focus on ourselves and not notice others around us who are going through difficult times. Our lives become busy and cluttered with day-to-day activities that cause us to lose sight of the needs of others. We must ask the Lord to give us His eyes of compassion and His heart of mercy to see the hurts and feel the pain of those around us. When we encourage each other, our heavenly Father is delighted. Just like any earthly parent, He loves to see His children minister to one another in authentic love. When we help others, we emulate Jesus. We become His extended hands of mercy.

Pray for someone in need today. Make a phone call or visit. Send a kind note. There are people who need the love that only you can give. Do not let them suffer alone.

## THINKING OF OTHERS

**Philippians 2:3-4** — _"Do nothing from selfishness or empty conceit, but with humility of mind regard one another as more important than yourselves; do not merely look out for your own personal interests, but also for the interests of others."_

An international airport is a busy place filled with people in a hurry. Many of them are upset. Perhaps they missed their flight, lost their luggage, or lost their seat due to over-booking. One day I arrived at the Atlanta airport coming from Tel Aviv via Zurich. I thought I had ample time to make my connecting flight to Dallas. To my surprise, I only had 35 minutes because it was Daylight Savings Time Sunday. By the time I went through customs and rechecked my bags, my flight to Dallas had left. No other flight was available. I had been awake for over 24 hours. I decided to rent a car and drive home to Birmingham, but due to the Master's Golf Tournament, no cars were available. Now I was upset. So I prayed. "Lord, I am out of options. Show me what to do." I looked up and saw an angry lady who had lost her luggage. She was scheduled to make an important presentation the next day and had no clothes for the meeting. Her name was Angela. I said, "Angela, I'm a Baptist preacher. Can I pray for you?" She said, "Please." When I said "Amen," she was crying, yet smiling. She thanked me, and I thanked the Lord for reminding me that I was not the only one with problems.

Guess what else happened? I went back to the counter and was able to rent a car! I drove home and spent the night in my own bed. The next morning I caught a plane to Dallas and made my meeting. Everything turned out fine when I stopped thinking of my problems and started thinking of others. How many "Angelas" out there could use your support today? Look around. Someone is hurting more than you. Will you help them?

## LET YOUR LIGHT SHINE

**Matthew 5:16** — *"Let your light shine before men in such a way that they may see your good works, and glorify your Father who is in heaven."*

God is a God of light. He *is* light, and in Him there is no darkness (i.e. sin) (1 John 1:5). Jesus referred to Himself as "the Light of the world" (John 8:12). He shines brightly against the black backdrop of this dark, sinful world. Jesus also referred to those who follow Him as "the light of the world" (Matthew 5:14). Christ in us gives the light of God's righteousness and holiness. That light must shine forth in a world filled with the darkness of sin. We can either hide the light or let it shine before others. Jesus said that a city set on a hill cannot be hidden (Matthew 5:14). Its light penetrates the night sky for all to see. Likewise people do not light a lamp and then hide it under a basket (Matthew 5:15). It is lit for the purpose of giving light to all who are in the house. In the same way, Christians must boldly let the light of Christ shine forth in all that we do and say. Our good works are meant to bring glory to our "Father who is in heaven."

Are you living a life of light, displaying the light of Jesus to those around you? Do your works penetrate the spiritual darkness of this world, or do you blend in with those who are living in sin? As we approach the coming of Christ, the world will become increasingly darker, engulfed by evil (2 Timothy 3:1-5). In that darkness the light of the Lord Jesus can shine brighter than ever through His holy followers (Isaiah 60:1-3).

We cannot produce the light. We must simply allow the light of Jesus within us to shine forth. Do you remember this song? "This little light of mine, I'm gonna' let it shine. Hide it under a bushel? No! I'm gonna' let it shine. Won't let Satan blow it out; I'm gonna' let it shine." Now there is a song we need to sing in "big church" too!

## ONE THING

**Psalm 27:4** — _"One thing I have asked from the LORD, that I shall seek: that I may dwell in the house of the LORD all the days of my life, to behold the beauty of the LORD and to meditate in His temple."_

Someone once told me that life gets more complicated after you turn eighteen. He was right. The older you get, the more complex life becomes. It grows difficult to stay focused on priorities. David knew his supreme priority and mentioned it in our text.

The "one thing" that was most important to David was to dwell in the Lord's presence, communing with Him. David accomplished much in life. He was a valiant warrior, a great builder, and a successful king. But the "one thing" that consumed him was his love for God. His earthly accomplishments meant little to him compared to being with the Lord, basking in His presence and meditating on His glory. That is probably the reason God called David a man after His own heart (1 Samuel 13:14).

Mary of Bethany knew about that "one thing." When Jesus visited her home, she sat at His feet and listened to His Word. Her sister, Martha, was distracted in the kitchen preparing a meal. She grew angry with Mary for not helping her, and even scolded Jesus for not insisting that Mary do so. Jesus said to her, "Many things bother you, Martha, but only _one thing_ (i.e. loving God) is necessary. Mary has chosen that" (Luke 10:41-42). Paul also knew about the "one thing." He said, _"One thing_ I do" (Philippians 3:13-14). That "one thing" was "knowing Christ" (Philippians 3:8, 10) and loving Him intimately.

What is the _one thing_ that satisfies and gives contentment to a person? David, Mary, and Paul knew. We must sit at Jesus' feet until we know and love Him intimately. Slow down. Simplify your life. Focus on Jesus until He becomes your "one thing."

## THE WAY OF ESCAPE

**1 Corinthians 10:13** — *"No temptation has overtaken you but such as is common to man; and God is faithful, who will not allow you to be tempted beyond what you are able, but with the temptation will provide the way of escape also, so that you will be able to endure it."*

Everyone faces temptation. The devil, the world, and our fleshly natures work collectively to tempt us to break God's laws. Yet, God provides "the way of escape" each time temptations arise. It enables us to experience victory. How can this happen?

**Realize that Temptation Is Universal.** "No temptation has overtaken you but such as is *common* to man." All people, including Jesus, have experienced temptation. Satan will try to make us think that we are the only ones struggling in a certain area. The truth is that others struggle in that same area, and many have experienced victory over it!

**Remember that God Is Faithful.** "God is *faithful*, who will not allow you to be tempted beyond what you are able." God reliably prevents us from being overwhelmed by temptation. His grace and strength increase toward us as our temptations increase in both frequency and intensity. He never leaves or forsakes us.

**Recognize that Escape Is Available.** "With the temptation will provide *the way of escape* also, so that you will be able to endure it." When we are tempted, God supplies "the way of escape." For Joseph it was fleeing (Genesis 39:12). For Jesus it was fasting, praying, and quoting Scripture (Luke 4:1-13). For the disciples it was to "watch and pray" (Matthew 26:41). Whenever we face temptation, we must seek His way of escape.

Are you being enticed to sin? Jesus will not allow you to be tempted beyond your ability to overcome. With each temptation, He faithfully gives the way to victory. Find the way and follow it today. Walk obediently in His way of escape and you *will* triumph!

## JUST SAY THE WORD

**Matthew 8:8** — _"But the centurion said, 'Lord, I am not worthy for You to come under my roof, but just say the word, and my servant will be healed.'"_

God's Word is powerful. With it, He created the entire Universe. When the Old Testament prophets spoke the Word of God, it actually set divine activity into motion. God's Word never returns to Him empty or void. It is a sharp, two-edged sword. When God's children speak it accurately and authoritatively in faith, God's power is unleashed.

One day as Jesus was ministering, a Roman centurion met Him. The centurion's servant was at home, paralyzed and suffering tremendously. Jesus said that He would go to his house and heal him. But the centurion replied, "I am not worthy for you to come to my house, Lord. _Just say the word_ and my servant will be whole." Jesus was amazed at this Gentile's spiritual understanding and faith. He answered, "Go; it shall be done for you as you have believed" (v. 13). The servant was instantly healed, though Jesus never saw or touched him. Jesus simply spoke the Word! Later in chapter 8 of Matthew, Jesus' spoken Word also calmed a raging sea (v. 26) and cast out a legion of deadly demons (v. 32)!

While we cannot "use" God's Word selfishly to attain whatever we desire, we can, nevertheless, learn to appropriate its power and put it to work for His glory. When we do, people's lives will be changed. Mountains will be moved and cast into the sea.

We must avoid speaking negative, fearful, useless words, because death and life are in the power of our tongues (Proverbs 18:20-21). Instead, we must study God's Word, store it in our hearts, and speak it in boldness and faith. Speak God's Word today and watch Him work on your behalf. All heaven will soon break loose in your life!

## SINS OF THE FATHERS

**Exodus 20:5** — *"You shall not worship them or serve them; for I, the LORD your God, am a jealous God, visiting the iniquity of the fathers on the children, on the third and the fourth generations of those who hate Me."*

"He's a chip off the old block." "Like father, like son." Indeed, children often look and act like their parents. But Scripture also teaches that if parents have a sinful stronghold in their lives, it will more than likely be passed on to their descendants.

God told Moses that He would visit the iniquity of the fathers on their children for several generations. Scripture verifies that the parents' sins are often manifested and multiplied in their children's lives. For instance, Abraham lied and told foreigners that his wife, Sarah, was his sister in order to protect himself (Genesis 12:10-20; 20:1-18). His son, Isaac, did the same thing regarding his wife, Rebekah (Genesis 26:6-11). Aaron engaged in idolatry by crafting a golden calf for the people of Israel (Exodus 32:1-35). Likewise, his two sons, Nadab and Abihu, offered "strange fire" at the Lord's altar, and God killed them (Leviticus 10:1-7). David lusted after women and married many wives (1 Chronicles 3:1-9; 14:4-7). His son, Solomon, took that same sin to unprecedented levels by having seven hundred wives and three hundred concubines that turned his heart away from the Lord (1 Kings 11:1-3). King Omri was more wicked than any king before him (1 Kings 16:23-27). Yet his son, Ahab, who succeeded him, surpassed his father in wickedness, and even married Jezebel, the slayer of the prophets (1 Kings 16:28-33).

Whatever sins we refuse to repent of and forsake will become snares to our children. Our sins affect the generations after us. Ask the Lord Jesus to set you free from every sinful stronghold in your life. The legacy you leave your children depends on you.

## HONORING GOD FINANCIALLY

**Proverbs 3:9-10** — _"Honor the LORD from your wealth and from the first of all your produce; so your barns will be filled with plenty and your vats will overflow with new wine."_

The goal of the Christian life is to glorify Jesus Christ. We must do this in every area, including our finances. God does not need our money. The Universe belongs to Him. He owns the cattle on every hill. He even owns the hills! God tells us to give for our sakes, not His. He realizes that we cannot serve Him and money (Matthew 6:24).

Solomon tells us to honor God "from (our) wealth." We must give to Him from "the _first_ of all (our) produce." He deserves our _best_. The Old Testament believers were not allowed to sacrifice defective, maimed, diseased animals as offerings to the Lord (Leviticus 22:20-22). Only the _best_ of their flocks and herds would do. Likewise, we owe God our best financially. We must seek His kingdom first in our giving (Matthew 6:33). We should practice tithing, which means to give at least 10% of our income to our local church's budget in an undesignated fashion (cf. April 4 devotional). We should love God (Mark 12:30) and not money (1 Timothy 6:10), pay our bills on time, avoid too much debt (Proverbs 22:7), learn to be content with what we have (Philippians 4:11-13), live within our means, and give to the poor (Proverbs 19:17). We must lay up for ourselves treasures in heaven and not on this earth, which is passing away. Wherever our treasure (money) goes, there our hearts are sure to follow (Matthew 6:19-21).

Our money matters to God. If we give Him our best, He will bless us abundantly and supply our every need. He gave His best when He sent Jesus to die on the cross. May we honor Him financially with our giving. Abundant blessings await those who do!

## HE IS ABLE

**Numbers 13:31** — *"But the men who had gone up with him said, 'We are not able to go up against the people, for they are too strong for us.'"*

When God reveals His will to His people, He makes sure that it is too difficult for them to accomplish on their own apart from His wisdom and power. He puts His will just beyond our reach to make us depend on Him. It has always been so.

Moses and the people of Israel were commanded by God to appoint a committee of twelve men to investigate the land of Canaan, which the Lord had promised to give them as an inheritance. They had seen Him rescue and deliver them supernaturally from the bondage of Egypt. They had also seen Him provide daily for their needs by feeding them manna and quail. They should have known that He was able to accomplish whatever He wanted in their lives. However, when the twelve were selected and sent, ·they returned and gave a negative report to the people. They said that the land was prosperous and flowing with milk and honey, as the Lord had said, "Nevertheless, (a word they would soon regret) the people of the land are strong, their cities are huge, and we saw giants there (Numbers 13:28)!" Only two of the twelve, Joshua and Caleb, said that God was able to lead them to victory. The people listened to the ten and their evil report. God killed those ten doubters and made His people wander in the wilderness for forty years until that unbelieving generation died. From that group, only Joshua and Caleb were allowed to enter the Promised Land four decades later.

What they said was and is true. *"We are not able."* But God is! His will requires His power. The Christian life is impossible without the Lord's strength and wisdom. Do not limit yourself to what *you* can do. Think of what *He* can do through you. *He* is able!

## THE HIGH COST OF SIN

**Numbers 16:38** — _"As for the censers of these men who have sinned at the cost of their lives, let them be made into hammered sheets for a plating of the altar, since they did present them before the LORD and they are holy; and they shall be for a sign to the sons of Israel."_

Korah and his companions rose up defiantly against Moses, and said, "We have had enough! You are a pathetic leader. We have not entered a land flowing with milk and honey. Instead, we are wandering about aimlessly in this wilderness, suffering from hunger and thirst. You are not the only one to whom God has spoken. _We_ are just as important as you!" Moses told them to assemble the next day before the Lord with censers of incense in their hands. God would choose for Himself who should be the leader of Israel. When Korah and the others assembled before the Lord at the tent of meeting, He told everyone to step away from them. The earth then opened supernaturally and swallowed them! Their censers were used to decorate the Lord's altar and also served as a warning to anyone else who wanted to rebel against the Lord and His leader.

The wages of sin has always been and will always be death (Romans 6:23). When a Christian sins, God disciplines him. If someone sins and does not experience divine discipline, it is a sure sign that he is not a true believer in Christ (Hebrews 12:7-8). The Bible even refers to "a sin leading to death" (1 John 5:16). The fact of the matter is that throughout biblical history, God took the lives of many sinners as He did with Korah.

God is "love" (1 John 4:8), but He is also "light" (1 John 1:5), which means He is holy and just. He "will by no means leave the guilty unpunished" (Exodus 34:7). Some sins usher in God's discipline. But others are so severe they bring about physical death. Whether it is discipline or death, sin always costs. Its pleasure is never worth its price!

## What Time Is It?

**1 Chronicles 12:32** — *"Of the sons of Issachar, men who understood the times, with knowledge of what Israel should do, their chiefs were two hundred; and all their kinsmen were at their command."*

We watched as the towers of the World Trade Center burned and later collapsed into the streets of Manhattan. Thousands were killed. Millions mourned. On that awful day, someone asked me, "What time is it?" Good question. What time is it in America?

**It Is Time to Look Back and Remember.** Today we should remember and pray for those who lost loved ones on September 11, 2001. We should remember the brave civil servants who ran into buildings everyone else was running out of, as well as every volunteer who served in the aftermath. Those people showed us the best of America.

**It Is Time to Look Around and Evaluate.** Will we continue to reject the God of our founding forefathers, the Christian Pilgrims and Puritans? Will we allow radicals to take over our schools, churches, government, courtrooms, media, and entire society? Or, as Christians, will we stand up, speak up, and stop the immoral tide that threatens us?

**It Is Time to Look Up and Believe.** Most of all, today is a day to look up to the God of heaven and trust Him. We walk in faith, not fear. As a nation we must embrace Jesus Christ as the *only* Savior. We must look to Jesus as our sole source of divine help. He could return today! Now is not a time to be dismayed, but to look up and believe!

Do we, like the sons of Issachar, understand the times in which we live? George Washington, once said, "It is the duty of all nations to acknowledge the providence of Almighty God, to obey His will, to be grateful for His benefits, and humbly to implore His protection and favor." Well said, Mr. President. *That* is exactly what time it is!

## PRAYERLESSNESS

**1 Samuel 12:23** — _"Moreover, as for me, far be it from me that I should sin against the LORD by ceasing to pray for you; but I will instruct you in the good and right way."_

How often I have presumptuously rushed into a busy day without first spending time in prayer with my heavenly Father. When that happens, disappointments abound, problems mount, and I am less effective than I could be if I would only commune with Him in prayer. Prayerlessness is perhaps the most insidious form of pride there is. When we fail to pray, we are saying, "Lord, I can handle life on my own today. I really do not need Your help." Such misplaced confidence leads to frustration and failure.

Samuel was the last of the Hebrew judges and one of the first of the prophets. He was dedicated to the Lord as a baby and grew up under Eli, the priest, in the Temple at Shiloh. He became known as a devout man of God, and was well respected throughout Israel. But the people were tired of being led by religious judges. Instead, they wanted to be like the other nations and have a king. Samuel told them that the Lord was their King, but they insisted on having an earthly ruler as well. God told Samuel to anoint Saul as their new king. God then sent a frightening storm with severe lightning. The people cried out in fear to Samuel. His response included the words of our text. He said that even though they were rebellious, he would not "sin against the LORD by ceasing to pray for (them)." He knew that his prayers for them made a difference.

Your prayers make a difference too! That is why Satan fights so relentlessly against your efforts to talk with God. He knows where prayer focuses, God's power falls. Whatever else you do today, make sure you pray. Prayerlessness is a sin you cannot afford to commit. The old saying really is true, "Prayer changes things."

## THE LOVE OF GOD

**Jeremiah 31:3** — *"The LORD appeared to him from afar, saying, 'I have loved you with an everlasting love; therefore I have drawn you with lovingkindness.'"*

Regardless of what happens in life, it is comforting to know that our heavenly Father loves us perfectly. His love is not conditional. Rather, it is given graciously and mercifully even though we do not deserve it and could never earn it.

**God's Love Is Sovereign.** "I have loved you." Before we chose to love God, He loved us first. He initiated the love relationship we enjoy with Him. "In this is love, not that we loved God, but that He loved us and sent His Son to be the propitiation for our sins" (1 John 4:10). He does not force anyone to love Him, for true love cannot be coerced. Rather, God initiates the love relationship, and we must respond willingly.

**God's Love Is Everlasting.** "With an everlasting love." There has never been a time that God did not love you. Before your conversion, while you were still in your sin, God loved you and proved it through Christ's atoning sacrifice for your sins (Romans 5:8). Regardless of what you do, or what happens in your life, God will love you forever.

**God's Love Is Gentle.** "Therefore I have drawn you with lovingkindness." The picture here is that of a mother holding her baby gently to her chest. God loves us tenderly. "He is mindful that we are but dust" (Psalm 103:14). He knows our inherent limitations and our tendency toward sin. Though we deserve eternal punishment in hell, God deals with us affectionately and kindly. He desires to fellowship intimately with us.

God's love is amazing. Thank Him today for loving you in spite of your sin and selfishness. God loved you first. He will love you always. He loves you tenderly. How much does He love you? Consider the cross, and you might begin to understand.

## RECEIVING CHRIST

**John 1:12** — _"But as many as received Him, to them He gave the right to become children of God, even to those who believe in His name."_

Herschel Hobbs, famous Baptist pastor and theologian, once told me that he was saved in a worship service during the singing of an invitational hymn that said, "If you are tired of the load of your sin, let Jesus come into your heart. If you desire a new life to begin, let Jesus come into your heart. Just now, your doubtings give o'er, just now reject Him no more, just now throw open the door, let Jesus come into your heart." Shortly after his conversion, young Herschel told the preacher, "Back there I felt bad, but up here I feel good!" He felt "good" because He had received Christ and had become a child of God.

Salvation is a free gift. We cannot earn it and we do not deserve it. As a gift, it must be received. In our text, John says that those who have "received (Christ)" as Savior are given the "right" (lit. authority) to become "children of God." That privilege and gift of grace is granted to those "who believe in (Jesus') name." Salvation is in His name alone (Acts 4:12). Whoever calls on His name is granted the gift of eternal life (Romans 10:13). God's desire is the salvation of all people (1 Timothy 2:3-4), and He offers salvation to anyone and everyone. But only those who willingly receive His Son become His children. Indeed, Christ seeks to save some who refuse to receive Him (John 1:11). When that happens, He leaves them in their sin. Jesus only goes where He is invited.

Are you "tired of the load of your sin? Let Jesus come into your heart!" God has voted for your salvation. The devil has voted against your salvation. You have the deciding vote! Cast it for Christ today if you have not already done so. If you are saved, rejoice that you are a child of God, and that you became one by _receiving_ Jesus Christ!

## GOD BLESS YOU

**2 Corinthians 13:14** — *"The grace of the Lord Jesus Christ, and the love of God, and the fellowship of the Holy Spirit, be with you all."*

The worst thing a person can say to someone else is, "Go to hell." Hell is a real, eternal place of unimaginable torment and suffering. Regardless of how much someone despises another person, he does not want him to go to hell. On the other hand, the best thing a person can say to someone is, "God bless you." The writings of the Apostle Paul are filled with blessings. One of them tells us exactly what "God bless you" means.

**Be Blessed with the Love of God.** "The love of God...be with you all." God loves everyone (John 3:16), both Christians and non-Christians. He loves the people on earth, all who are in heaven, and even those who, having rejected Him, are in hell. No one is outside the parameters of His love. "God bless you" means, "God loves you."

**Be Blessed with the Grace of Jesus.** "The grace of the Lord Jesus Christ...be with you all." Though God loves everyone, He only extends His grace to Christians. His saving grace is given to those who repent of their sins and trust Jesus (Ephesians 2:8-9). No one in hell has known God's saving grace. It is reserved for the redeemed.

**Be Blessed with the Fellowship of the Holy Spirit.** "The fellowship of the Holy Spirit, be with you all." All are blessed with God's love, and Christians are blessed with Christ's grace, but only obedient Christians are blessed with the fellowship of the Holy Spirit. Worldly, rebellious believers miss out on the wonderful Spirit-filled life.

"God bless you" is a mouthful. It means, "May the Father bless you with His love, may the Son bless you with His grace, and may the Spirit bless you with His fellowship." May God's love, grace, and presence be given to you abundantly today.

## A GODLY HOME: A SUBMISSIVE WIFE

**Colossians 3:18** — _"Wives, be subject to your husbands, as is fitting in the Lord."_

There is nothing more precious and fulfilling than a godly home. God blesses every home that is aligned with Scripture. Husbands and wives each have specific roles in the family. A godly home includes a wife who submits to her husband as to the Lord.

Men are not better than women, nor are husbands supposed to "lord it over" their wives. The husband is not Tarzan, and the woman is not Jane. However, the husband is God's ordained leader for the family. A wife must recognize his God-given authority and submit to him as to the Lord (Ephesians 5:22-24). Some teach that husbands and wives are to be "mutually submissive." That phrase is a contradiction in terms. If both husband and wife are mutually subject to one another, then there is no distinct leader. But Scripture clearly declares that the husband is the leader or head of the woman (1 Corinthians 11:3). As Adrian Rogers has well said, "Anything with no head is dead, and anything with two heads is a freak." When a husband leads out of love and service, and the wife submits and respects his leadership, the Lord blesses the marriage and the entire family.

This concept contradicts the teachings of modern feminists. Our society promotes a spirit of independence, selfishness, and rebellion. It despises God's rule as well as His ordained channels of authority. Rebellion is the sin of Satan, and is akin to witchcraft (1 Samuel 15:23). The Bible states clearly that a wife should submit to her husband.

Wife, do not be a rebel. Do not belittle your husband. Do not nag him or run him down. Rather, pray for your husband, respect him, encourage him, and as long as he does not try to lead you into sin, submit to him. God will honor you with a godly home.

## A GODLY HOME: A LOVING HUSBAND

**Colossians 3:19** — *"Husbands, love your wives and do not be embittered against them."*

A man went to his doctor because he was feeling tired. His doctor said that his symptoms were stress related. "You need some exercise," said the physician. "Try running ten miles a day for two weeks, and then report back to me." At the end of the two weeks, the man phoned his doctor who asked, "How are you feeling?" The man replied, "Much better. Thanks for your help." "How is your wife?" the doctor asked. The man answered, "How should I know? She's one hundred and forty miles *that* way!"

Husbands (and wives) may wish they could run away from the problems in their marriages, but God has another plan. He tells us how to have a godly home in Colossians 3:18-21. An integral part of any godly home is a loving husband.

Husband, you are commanded by God to love your wife like Jesus Christ loved the Church and gave Himself for it on the cross (Ephesians 5:25). You are to sacrificially put her needs above your own. You are to love her with the kind of love described in 1 Corinthians 13. You are not to be selfish, easily angered, rude, or moody. You are to meet her needs like you would those of your own body. You are to live with her in an understanding, compassionate manner, granting her honor as a fellow heir of the grace of life (1 Peter 3:7). A godly wife will have no problem submitting to a husband like that.

Husband, do not treat your wife like a second-class citizen or a doormat. She is not your slave. She is your sister in Christ. Treat her with respect, honor, and care. Be a gentleman and practice the Golden Rule. Love her as you want to be loved, and lead her as you would want to be led. Christ is your example. Just love her like He loves you.

## A GODLY HOME: OBEDIENT CHILDREN

**Colossians 3:20** — _"Children, be obedient to your parents in all things, for this is well-pleasing to the Lord."_

God expects children to honor and obey their parents. The fifth of the Ten Commandments deals with this subject (Exodus 20:12). As long as their parents do not tell them to do something sinful, children living at home should respectfully obey them.

Christians should submit to God's ordained channels of authority. Whether it is divine authority (Exodus 20:1-3), civil authority (Romans 13:1-7), pastoral authority (Hebrews 13:7, 17), a husband's authority (1 Corinthians 11:3), or parental authority (Ephesians 6:2), we must submit in order to enjoy God's blessings and protection.

Children living at home are to obey their parents as well as honor them. Obedience must be learned. It is not natural to our fallen, sinful natures. As a boy growing up in Nazareth, Jesus obeyed Joseph and Mary (Luke 2:51-52). Children who obey their parents are imitating Christ. A married child is not obligated to obey his parents because he is supposed to "leave" his parents and "cleave" to his new spouse (Genesis 2:24). Likewise, single adults not living in their parents' home are not obligated to obey their parents. Jesus did not (Matthew 12:46-50). Yet all children are commanded to respect and honor their parents. This Jesus always did. Also, grown children should care for their needy parents to prevent them from being a burden to the church (1 Timothy 5:3-4, 8). Jesus did this while dying on the cross (John 19:26-27).

If you honor and obey your parents, God will bless you (Deuteronomy 5:16). If you do not, He will curse you (Leviticus 20:9; Deuteronomy 27:16; Proverbs 30:17). A godly home has obedient, respectful children. They are "well-pleasing to the Lord."

## A GODLY HOME: ENCOURAGING PARENTS

**Colossians 3:21** — *"Fathers, do not exasperate your children, so that they will not lose heart."*

Parenting is a daunting task. As James Dobson wisely says, it "is not for cowards!" Most parents wish that their children came with an instruction manual. Each child is different, but Scripture does give guidelines on how to be a godly parent.

**Parents Should *Love* Their Children.** They must not "exasperate" or provoke them to anger (Ephesians 6:4). Children will not always agree with their parents, but parents can still be positive, encouraging, and gentle while being firm and in charge. Parents need to bring their children up without putting them down. Gary Chapman says that they can love them with kind words, time, loving touch, gifts, and acts of service.

**Parents Should *Train* Their Children.** They are to bring them up in the "discipline" (training) of the Lord (Ephesians 6:4). Parents do this effectively by demonstrating appropriate behavior and setting good examples. If a child is trained in the ways of Christ, he will likely continue to follow Christ in later years (Proverbs 22:6).

**Parents Should *Teach* Their Children.** They should teach them the Word of God (Deuteronomy 6:6-7). Parents should dialogue with their children, listening as well as talking. They should affirm and correct them when appropriate. Spanking is a viable teaching method (Proverbs 13:24; 19:18; 22:15; 23:13-14; 29:15), but should be administered only when a child willfully defies parental authority, and never for mere childish behavior.

A godly home must have encouraging parents. Parents should look to their heavenly Father as the perfect example of what a parent is supposed to be. If we love, train, and teach our children the way God does, He will help us build a godly home.

## GOD WILL TAKE CARE OF YOU

**Isaiah 46:4** — _"Even to your old age I will be the same, and even to your graying years I will bear you! I have done it, and I will carry you; and I will bear you and I will deliver you."_

My mother is a strong person. She grew up on a farm in Lauderdale County in West Tennessee. Her parents were hard workers and so were their children. They took care of cows, chopped and picked cotton, tended a vegetable garden, and did all sorts of farm work. My mother's first full time job was at a cotton gin when she was sixteen years old. She worked throughout her life. Some of her jobs included: being a salesperson at Sears, working on an assembly line at the Sylvania plant, and serving as the Welcome Wagon hostess in our home town. When my brother was ready to enter college, a banker encouraged her to start a janitorial service, and he offered his bank as her first place to clean. She accepted his advice, and began her own business, which she continued to operate for thirty years. When she finally retired, she was in her 70s and over fifty people were on her payroll. She was not only able to send us to college, but God also blessed her financially beyond anything she ever could have dreamed.

When dad became sick with Alzheimer's, she cared for him until she no longer could. He lived the last years of his life in a nursing home. Though she now lives by herself, she says, "I'm not alone. The Lord is with me." She has had her knees replaced, breast cancer, and a stroke, but God has faithfully cared for her "in her graying years."

God will take care of you. He is always faithful (Lamentations 3:22-23). He will provide for you from the cradle to the grave. Fear not. The God who cared for you as a child will continue to do so until you cross over Jordan and step into the land of Beulah.

## BE PATIENT

**Numbers 21:4** — *"Then they set out from Mount Hor by the way of the Red Sea, to go around the land of Edom; and the people became impatient because of the journey."*

Dottie Rambo wrote a children's song that said, "Be patient, be patient, don't be in such a hurry. When you get impatient it only leads to worry. Remember, remember, the Lord is patient too. Just think of all the times that others had to wait on you!"

Impatience is dangerous. If left unchecked, it often leads to rebellion, disobedience, and disaster. The people of Israel were wandering in the desert as a result of refusing to enter the Promised Land. Their food was manna, which they detested. They were weary of wandering in the hot sun. They yearned to return to Egypt, believing it would be better to be slaves there than to be free in the desert. They grew "impatient." The King James Version says they were "much discouraged." Their impatience caused them to "(speak) against God and Moses" (v. 5). God disciplined them by sending poisonous serpents among them. After many perished, the people repented and God removed the plague. But not before their impatience proved lethal.

Impatience is indeed deadly. Abraham's lack of patience resulted in the birth of rebellious Ishmael when God desired to give him righteous Isaac. Saul's impatience led him to sacrifice sheep rather than to wait for Samuel. As a result, Saul lost his mind and his kingdom.

Have you become impatient with God and the way He is leading you? Consider how patient He has been with you. You must learn to be patient as well. Learn to wait on the Lord. His timing is ideal and His plan is perfect. Do not take matters into your own hands. Let God have His way. He will come through if you will just be patient.

## GOD'S MANIFEST PRESENCE

**Matthew 18:20** — *"For where two or three have gathered together in My name, I am there in their midst."*

God is everywhere. Theologians refer to Him as being "omnipresent" because there is no place where He is not. If we could ascend to the highest part of the heavens above us, or if we could descend to the lowest depths of the earth or any ocean, He would be there (Psalm 139:7-9). God's omnipresence is a reality, but the Bible also refers to what some call His "manifest presence." In the Old Testament, "the glory of the Lord" would fill the temple and the priests would be unable to enter God's house because the sense of His presence was so overwhelming (1 Kings 8:11). In the New Testament, the Lord filled the upper room where the disciples were praying on the day of Pentecost (Acts 2:1f). Later, He filled the place where some disciples were praying, and the room itself began to shake as God filled each of them afresh with His Spirit so they could witness with boldness (Acts 4:31). God's manifest presence was and is awe-inspiring!

Jesus gave us a promise that if only two or three would gather together "in (His) name," He would be in our midst. That refers to God's manifest presence. It does not take a huge crowd to attract the Lord. He is searching for people who will worship Him "in spirit and truth" (John 4:23-24). As long as we hunger for Him and gather simply to glorify Him, He promises to show up in power.

Our churches desperately need God's presence. Worship services must not be designed to attract people. Rather, they should attract God. *He* will attract the people. His presence brings full joy and eternal pleasures (Psalm 16:11). Why are you waiting? Find a Christian, call on Jesus' name, and ask Him to come to you in power and glory!

## CALL TO ME

**Jeremiah 33:3** — *"Call to Me and I will answer you, and I will tell you great and mighty things, which you do not know."*

The secret for living as a victorious Christian is to make prayer the priority of your life. No activity is more important than prayer. It is the heartbeat of our fellowship with God. Yet, prayer seems to be the most neglected of all Christian disciplines. Satan fights it more than any other activity. He knows that when we pray, God always moves!

God spoke a wonderful promise to Jeremiah at a time when the prophet was imprisoned. The Lord told Jeremiah that he should call to Him in prayer in order to learn precisely how He would deal with His people in Judah in the coming years. These were matters that no one else knew about except the Lord Himself. Yet He desired to reveal His plans to Jeremiah. The Lord told the prophet that the prerequisite for receiving divine revelation was for him to pray and ask Him to disclose His future plans to him. When Jeremiah called to God in prayer, the Lord gave him an amazing revelation ("great and mighty things") of which Jeremiah would have never dreamed. Even though He would soon cause the Babylonians to defeat and destroy His people in Jerusalem and Judah due to their sinful idolatry, He would afterwards be gracious to them and allow them to return to the Promised Land. He promised to discipline, but also to restore His people. Jeremiah would never have known that had he not taken the time to pray.

God will share "great and mighty things which (we) do not know" with us also if we will spend time with Him in prayer. Are you calling regularly on God? Is prayer an integral part of your daily life? It must become *the* priority of every day. God wants to reveal some amazing things to you. He is only waiting on you to give Him a call.

## REFINER'S FIRE

**Job 23:10** — _"But He knows the way I take; when He has tried me, I shall come forth as gold."_

Every person who becomes a Christian enters his new life in Christ with a great deal of spiritual dross. To be sure, his sins are forgiven, but there are selfish patterns of behavior and sinful tendencies that have been deeply imbedded and ingrained into the warp and woof of his personality. God makes every believer in Christ "a new creation" (2 Corinthians 5:17). He also immediately begins to conform every believer to the image of His Son, Jesus Christ. As one elderly preacher wisely said, "When we get saved, God takes us out of Egypt. After that, God begins to take Egypt out of us!"

One way God refines and purifies us is through times of testing. Job was a godly man. In fact, God Himself said that Job was the most righteous man on the face of the earth at the time he was living (Job 1:8; 2:3). Yet God tested him with severe trials. In our text, Job said, "He (God) has _tried_ me." The word "tried" (Hebrew _bachan_) means "to examine, prove, or test." It carries with it the idea of a developmental process during which a person is made morally pure and spiritually strong. Just like fire is used to refine metals by purging away their impurities and dross, God uses the fire of trials to eliminate sinful tendencies in our lives that are not consistent with Christ's character.

Are you going through a difficult time? It could be an attack from the devil. But, as in Job's case, it could also be a time of divine purging. An old hymn says, "When through fiery trials thy pathway shall lie, My grace, all sufficient, shall be thy supply; the flame shall not hurt thee; I only design thy dross to consume, and thy gold to refine!" When the flames of trials get hot, remember the outcome — you shall come forth as gold!

## STRAYING SHEEP

**Isaiah 53:6** — *"All of us like sheep have gone astray, each of us has turned to his own way; but the LORD has caused the iniquity of us all to fall on Him."*

I once surprised my wife on her birthday by taking her to Atlanta for a special "getaway." I planned a dinner and a time of shopping at a mall. The next day as we were checking out of our hotel, I heard a commotion behind us at the front desk. Some parents were shouting at their son as he was attempting to run down the escalator that was going up. I looked at my wife and said, "Honey, I guess everyone likes to go the wrong way!"

Our text says that "each of us," enjoys doing his own thing. We do not naturally desire to please God. Rather, we are selfish sinners by nature. All of us inherit a sinful nature that was passed down to us from the first man, Adam (Romans 5:12). We were all "brought forth (i.e. born) in iniquity" (Psalm 51:5). Jesus referred to all people as "being evil" (Matthew 7:11). The Apostle Paul described all of us as being "by nature children of wrath" (Ephesians 2:3). We are sinners by nature who become sinners by choice. We have all "like sheep gone astray." Every person throughout history "has turned to his own way." We are, as an old hymn says, "Prone to wander, Lord, (we) feel it, prone to leave the God (we) love." We simply enjoy going the wrong way.

But our text also provides good news. God the Father "caused the iniquity of us all to fall on Him." He made Jesus, who never sinned, to "be sin" for us on the cross (2 Corinthians 5:21). His atoning sacrifice paid our sin debt so that we can be forgiven!

All of us enjoy our "own way," but Jesus died for our sins so that we could begin to live for God and not ourselves. If you are sick and tired of wandering away from God, come to Christ. With Him as your Good Shepherd, you will never need to stray again.

## SUCH WERE SOME OF YOU

**1 Corinthians 6:11** — _"Such were some of you; but you were washed, but you were sanctified, but you were justified in the name of the Lord Jesus Christ and in the Spirit of our God."_

I shudder to think what I would have become had it not been for Christ. I do not look down on lost sinners because I know that apart from the grace of God I could have lived a life of rebellion against Him. Jesus has made all the difference for me!

The Corinthian church was made up of people who had committed virtually every sin mentioned in God's Book. Immediately prior to our text, Paul warned that those who are lost habitually practice sins such as fornication, idolatry, adultery, homosexuality, stealing, and getting drunk. He warned that such people, apart from salvation, "will not inherit the kingdom of God" (1 Corinthians 6:9-10). But then Paul made an interesting comment when he said in our text, "Such were some of you." Some of the Christians at Corinth had been immoral before coming to Christ. Others were thieves, drunkards, or idol worshipers. But in Christ, they had each been "washed...sanctified...(and) justified." They had called on "the name of the Lord Jesus Christ" (Romans 10:13) and He had cleansed and filled them with "the Spirit of God."

Jesus can do that for anyone. Do you practice homosexual behavior? Christ can set you free. Are you a thief? Christ can make you honest. Are you a drunkard or addicted to drugs? Jesus can make you sober.

Child of God, were it not for God's grace in salvation, there is no telling where or what you would be. Christ has washed you in His blood, sanctified and set you apart for Himself, and justified you from the guilt of your sin. Praise Him today that although you may not be what you ought to be, at least, by His mercy, you are not what you used to be!

## WHERE IS JESUS?

**Luke 2:43** — *"And as they were returning, after spending the full number of days, the boy Jesus stayed behind in Jerusalem. But His parents were unaware of it."*

The caravan of Jewish pilgrims slowly progressed as it made its way out of Jerusalem following the sacred festivities of the Passover Feast. As Joseph and Mary journeyed, they realized that it had been hours since they had seen or heard from their twelve-year-old son, Jesus. They checked with those around them, but no one else had seen Him either. His absence initiated a frantic, three-day search by his beleaguered parents. Finally, they found Him in the Temple with the Jewish religious leaders. He was listening, asking profound questions, and astonishing everyone with His insightful answers to their theological inquiries. His upset parents asked, "Son, where have you been? Why have you treated us like this?" He calmly replied, "Why were you looking for Me? Did you not know I had to be about My Father's business (Luke 2:49)?"

All of us have spent days that were void of Jesus' manifest presence. We presumptuously enter those days without first spending time with the Lord in His Word, and in prayer and worship. We discover that not only are those days unproductive and unfulfilling, but they are also frustrating. The only thing we can do is to retrace our steps and search for Jesus. He is never hard to find. He is exactly where we left Him — in that empty prayer closet, that unread Bible, that unwritten tithe check, or that neglected Bible Study class. We rediscover His presence when we focus on our Father's business.

You do not have to spend this day without Jesus. Before you touch the television, work out, eat breakfast, read the paper, or leave your house, spend some quality time with Him. He will walk with you all day long, if you will seek Him early in the morning.

## THE GRASS WITHERS

**Isaiah 40:7-8** — _"The grass withers, the flower fades, when the breath of the LORD blows upon it; surely the people are grass. The grass withers, the flower fades, but the word of our God stands forever."_

As I watched the statue of Saddam Hussein being torn down and desecrated by the liberated Iraqi people, I felt a sense of satisfaction in my soul. For thirty years a demonized despot who had tortured and butchered all who opposed him had ruled Iraq. When his statue was toppled in the central square of Baghdad, I thought of our text. People are like grass and flowers. They grow and bloom and we sometimes think they will last forever. But eventually, all people, even dictators, wither and fade away.

One of the reasons I am convinced that atheistic evolution is a lie is because it proposes the idea that everything gets progressively better with age. Anyone who owns a mirror and lives a long time knows better! Even the most beautiful people on earth, the "flowers" among us, eventually grow old, wrinkled, and gray. Someone has wisely said that we can and should exercise physically, but it is akin to the person who had the futile job of rearranging the deck furniture on the Titanic — it is all eventually going down!

What lasts? The Word of God! It is eternal because it comes from an eternal God. Long after the Hitlers and Husseins of this world have vanished and become dust, someone somewhere will be holding an open Bible and preaching the saving Gospel of Jesus Christ. As long as the earth exists, God's Word will be prevalent on it. The Bible will outlast all its critics. It is settled "forever" on earth and in heaven (Psalm 119:89).

Today, instead of looking at a _daily_ paper, or a book of the _month_, read the Book of the _Ages_ — the Bible. After all of us have faded and withered, it will continue to stand!

## ARE YOU KNOWN IN HEAVEN?

**John 10:27** — *"My sheep hear My voice, and I know them, and they follow Me."*

Do you know God? Some might consider that to be an awkward question. Nevertheless, it is a valid and very important question. The Apostle Paul said that one of his chief goals on earth was to "know Him (Jesus) and the power of His resurrection, and the fellowship of His sufferings" (Philippians 3:10). Paul knew the Lord personally.

But an equally valid and important question is, "Does God know you?" In our text, Jesus gives three characteristics of any true Christian. First, as one of Christ's "sheep," a Christian will "hear (His) voice." The Holy Spirit within the believer will speak to him primarily through Scripture, and also through inner promptings from the Spirit Himself (Acts 16:6-7). Second, Jesus' followers will be marked by the fact that *He* "know(s) them." They will not only know Him, but they will be known by Him as well! Third, a true Christian will be obvious because he desires to "follow (Jesus)" obediently.

The second of these three characteristics is fundamentally important. It is not enough for someone to say that he knows Christ in salvation. Christ Himself must also acknowledge that person as one of His own. Jesus warned that "many" would claim to be His children on the final day of judgment in heaven, only to hear these dreadful words: "I never knew you; depart from Me, you who practice lawlessness" (Matthew 7:23).

I know of the President of the United States, but he does not know me. Even so, many people know about Jesus, but they do not know Him personally, nor does He know them as their Savior and Lord. When God looks down on this vast earth, does He say regarding you, "That one is Mine!"? Are you known in heaven? Think on that today.

## ARE YOU KNOWN IN HELL?

**Acts 19:15** — _"And the evil spirit answered and said to them, 'I recognize Jesus, and I know about Paul, but who are you?'"_

When the demons get together for their strategy meetings, do they ever bring up your name? In the previous devotional thought, we considered the importance of being known in heaven. Those who have been born again by the Spirit of God, are known by God in eternal salvation. But not every Christian makes news in hell. That is, not every Christian is considered a formidable threat to the strategy of Satan. Are you?

The Apostle Paul was. In his day, a group of Jewish men were traveling about, attempting to exorcise demons from individuals who were possessed. In the process, they were trying to evoke the name of Jesus in their rituals. There were seven of them, all brothers, the sons of a man named Sceva, a Jewish chief priest. One day they encountered a demonized man who called their bluff. When they pompously began to try to cast out the demon, they said, "We adjure you by Jesus whom Paul preaches" (v. 13). The demon's reply is recorded in our text. The demoniac jumped the seven men and "subdued them." That means he beat the living daylights out of them! They left the house "naked and wounded" (v. 16). Jesus does not allow His name to be "used."

Do the demons know who you are? Do you have a reputation in hell as being a true disciple of Jesus Christ? Do evil spirits know you as a prayer warrior who regularly sabotages their plans? Must they fight you relentlessly because you are constantly sharing the Gospel of Christ with lost people? Have you inflicted them with blows from the sword of His Spirit, which is the Word of God? How significant it is to be known in heaven. But oh that we might live in such a way that we are also known in hell!

## GOD'S ALTERNATIVE TO ANXIETY

**Philippians 4:6-7** — *"Be anxious for nothing, but in everything by prayer and supplication with thanksgiving let your requests be made known to God. And the peace of God, which surpasses all comprehension, will guard your hearts and your minds in Christ Jesus."*

Sleepless nights. Nail-biting. Nervous stomachs. All of these are signs of obsessive worrying. Anxiety is a nagging nemesis that our society seemingly loves to hate. It is a deadly killer that can produce physical disease and death. It also produces a spiritual problem. It leads to fear, which is the opponent of faith. Anxiety is caused by our unwillingness to trust God. When we choose to worry rather than put our faith in Him, we sin. How can we combat worry? Is there an alternative to anxiety?

In our text we are told that when we are tempted to be anxious, we ought to pray instead. We are to worry about *nothing* and pray about *everything*. We are to say "No!" to worry, and take our problems to the Lord in prayer. We are to do so earnestly ("supplication") and with gratitude ("with thanksgiving"). God has taken care of us in the past, and He will do so in the future. When we take our burdens and requests to Him in prayer, He envelopes us with His perfect, divine peace that defies human comprehension. That peace guards and protects both our emotions ("hearts") and our thoughts ("minds") in Christ Jesus. We begin to walk in peace, joy, hope, and complete confidence in God. Those around us see our victorious tranquility and long to have it.

A popular song says glibly, "Don't worry, be happy." But God has a better alternative to worry — prayer! There is nothing so "big" that we should worry about it, and there is nothing so "small" that we should not pray about it. Worry changes nothing, but prayer changes everything. May prayer become our first choice, not our last resort.

## THORNS IN THE SPIRIT

**Mark 4:18-19** — _"And others are the ones on whom seed was sown among the thorns; these are the ones who have heard the word, but the worries of the world, and the deceitfulness of riches, and the desires for other things enter in and choke the word, and it becomes unfruitful."_

Jesus was an effective communicator. He made complex issues understandable. One technique He used was the telling of parables. These earthly stories conveyed strong spiritual lessons. His most famous parable was about a sower who sowed seed on four types of soil — hard, shallow, thorn-infested, and good. The seed represented God's Word, and the soils, the hearts of men. Regarding the thorn-infested soil, Jesus mentioned three "thorns" that choke the seed of God's Word and make it unfruitful. What are they?

**The Worries of the World.** Things that cause unbelievers to worry should not concern us. What we will eat, drink, or wear must not be our focus. God knows that we need all these things. He will provide them for us if we will seek first His kingdom.

**The Deceitfulness of Riches.** Money is not moral or immoral. Rather, it is morally neutral. Money is not the root of all evil, but the _love_ of money is (1 Timothy 6:10). Money is a good servant but a wretched master. We cannot serve it and God.

**The Desires for Other Things.** Here is the thorn of covetousness, which violates the Tenth Commandment (Exodus 20:17). We must not covet, or jealously desire what others have. The lust of the flesh, the lust of the eyes, and the pride of life will consume and conquer us if we do not learn to become content with what we already possess.

How is your heart's soil? Are these "thorns in the spirit" present? If so, ask God to pull them up by the roots, and to turn your heart into good soil. His Spirit's fruit will be manifested instead of these lethal thorns, and the seed of His Word will flourish!

## THE CHURCH OF ICHABOD

**Jeremiah 5:30-31** — *"An appalling and horrible thing has happened in the land: the prophets prophesy falsely, and the priests rule on their own authority; and my people love it so! But what will you do at the end of it?"*

Once there was a boy named "Ichabod." His name meant "no glory." On the day of his birth, his family died, and the Ark of the Covenant was captured. "Ichabod" served as a daily reminder that God's glory had departed from Israel. Jeremiah described what it was like when God's glory departed. Notice the members of "The Church of Ichabod":

**Mr. Perverse Proclamation.** "The prophets prophesy falsely." In Jeremiah's day, most of the preachers were false prophets. Today, there are still liberal preachers who proclaim to their listeners what they want to hear rather than the Word of God.

**Mr. Ailing Administration.** "The priests rule on their own authority." The priests in Jeremiah's day stressed their traditions over God's laws. Today when churches are run like a secular business instead of a Scriptural ministry, God's glory departs.

**Mr. Carnal Congregation.** "And My people love it so." Jeremiah's contemporaries desired leaders who would wink at their sin. Today some church members disdain genuine men of God as their pastors, and prefer hypocritical hirelings.

**Mr. Embarrassing Evaluation.** "But what will you do at the end of it?" God eventually judged the leaders and people of Jeremiah's day and sent them into exile. Likewise, Jesus, will reprimand The Church of Ichabod at His Judgment Seat.

How is your church? Does it have the touch of God's glory, or is "Ichabod" stamped across it? May God's glory return to every Bible-preaching congregation in our land, and may He graciously spare us from becoming like "The Church of Ichabod."

## REWARDS OF RESTORATION

**Mark 5:15** — *"They came to Jesus and observed the man who had been demon-possessed sitting down, clothed and in his right mind, the very man who had had the 'legion'; and they became frightened."*

Jesus stepped out of a boat into a graveyard. He met a demonized man named "Legion" who had a vast army of evil spirits within him. Day and night they tormented him. He ran naked all over the countryside, screaming and gashing himself with stones. But when Jesus arrived, the demons were cast out, and the demoniac rested at Jesus' feet "sitting down, clothed and in his right mind." Here we see the "Rewards of Restoration."

**Rest.** He was "sitting down." This is a picture of peaceful rest. The man who was crazy had now become calm. Jesus will also give us rest. We too can sit serenely at His feet. He will lead us beside still waters and give rest to our weary, sin-sick souls.

**Righteousness.** He was "clothed." Apparently, Jesus gave him His outer garment. Just as the Father clothed the guilty pair in Eden's Garden (Genesis 3), Jesus restored this man by clothing his nakedness. Likewise, Jesus will clothe us with His righteousness and cover our spiritual nakedness if we repent and trust Him in salvation.

**Right Thinking.** He was "in his right mind." When Jesus restored the man, he could think clearly again. He received "the mind of Christ" (1 Corinthians 2:16). His mind had been renewed (Romans 12:2). Jesus can also take our thoughts captive to Himself (2 Corinthians 10:5), and help us think on that which is good (Philippians 4:8).

We may not have a literal "Legion" harassing us, but all of us need the restoration that Jesus alone can give. We need His rest, righteousness, and right thinking. If we will fall humbly at Jesus' feet today, He will restore us and make us completely whole.

## ENEMIES OF REVIVAL

**Psalm 85:6** — *"Will You not Yourself revive us again, that Your people may rejoice in You?"*

The Church was born on the Day of Pentecost in an atmosphere of revival (Acts 2). There were no buildings or budgets, yet through God's power, they turned their world upside down for Christ. Before revival can come, several enemies must be overcome.

**Traditionalism.** This enemy of revival prefers the religious customs of man over the teachings of Scripture. "We've never done it that way" becomes more authoritative than "the Bible says." God's ways must supercede our tradition if awakening is to come.

**Formalism.** When we sing in Latin, preach in Greek, and play operatic music, revival is delayed. Formalists equate reverence with silence. A corpse is silent, but not because it is being reverent. *Deity* must be valued above our *dignity* if revival is to come.

**Fanaticism.** God wants revival fire. Satan wants wild fire. Revival attracts sign-seekers and thrill-chasers. People who bark like dogs, laugh uncontrollably, and see gold dust and angel feathers should not blame it on God. Such extremism must be avoided.

**Liberalism.** This is a ditch on the *left*. It questions the accuracy and authority of Scripture, trying to lift up fallen humanity without lifting up the standard of God's Word.

**Legalism.** Here is a ditch on the *right*. This enemy adds religious traditions to the teachings of Scripture. It tries to hold up God's Word without lifting up the fallen.

If we want to see spiritual awakening in our churches today, we must stand against these deadly "Enemies of Revival." Only Christ can set us free from such ungodly tendencies and send real renewal to His people. When He does, His power and presence will be openly manifested, and we will once again rejoice and glory in Him!

## PRACTICE WHAT YOU PREACH

**Ezra 7:10** — *"For Ezra had set his heart to study the law of the LORD and to practice it, and to teach His statutes and ordinances in Israel."*

"Do as I say, not as I do." Has anyone ever said that to you? It is the motto of a hypocrite. That person has the audacity to try to tie a burden on you that he is personally unwilling to bear. How can we make sure we "practice what we preach?"

**We Must Study God's Word.** Ezra lived in a day when God's people were returning to Jerusalem from Babylonian captivity. A few decades earlier, Zerubbabel had rebuilt the Temple and reestablished corporate worship. Now Ezra was returning to bring back the teaching of God's Word. Before he could teach it, he had to study it. In the same manner, you and I must become students of God's Word. We cannot share what we do not know. Like Apollos, we must become "mighty in the Scriptures" (Acts 18:24). We do this by reading it, hearing it, studying it, memorizing it, and meditating on it daily.

**We Must Practice God's Word.** Ezra practiced what he learned in Scripture. We too must be both hearers and doers of God's Word (James 1:22). We must analyze it and apply it. If application does not follow interpretation, the result is contradiction.

**We Must Teach God's Word.** Like Ezra, we should share God's Word with others after we study it and put it into practice. We are to teach it to lost people so they can be saved, and also to believers so they can grow and mature in their walk with Christ.

Are you practicing what you preach? Is your Christian walk consistent with your talk? If not, begin to focus your heart on God's Word, the Bible. Seek it, obey it, and communicate it to others. People are not looking for someone who is perfect, but they are looking for someone who is real. Be a consistent Christian today.

## PRIORITIES FOR EVERY PASTOR

**Acts 6:4** — *"But we will devote ourselves to prayer and to the ministry of the word."*

What are the priorities of a pastor? The apostles of the First Century served as the pastors of the Church at Jerusalem. A problem among the church's widows threatened to distract them, but they remained faithful to their three ministerial priorities.

**A Pastor Must Intercede.** "We will devote ourselves to prayer." These men had prayed for ten days before Pentecost, Peter had preached only a few minutes, and three thousand were saved! They were men of prayer. Prayer ushers in the power of God. It cultivates the soil of the human heart making it receptive to the seed of God's Word.

**A Pastor Must Feed.** "We will devote ourselves to...the ministry of the word." These early pastors loved God's Word. They studied it, obeyed it, taught it, and preached it. Today's pastor should also be mighty in the Scriptures and be able to preach. The message preached is still God's primary tool for saving the lost and maturing the saved.

**A Pastor Must Lead.** When the Jerusalem Church faced its crisis, the pastors (apostles) led their members to do the right thing. Seven laymen, the first deacons, were selected to take care of the matter. The pastors led, the people followed, and the church advanced! That is God's pattern. Jesus is the Chief Shepherd, and the pastor and his staff are the leaders. The pastor is not to be a dictator, but a humble overseer who leads.

A pastor will have many responsibilities, but he must focus on these three emphases of ministry. If the congregation will allow him to do so, the church will grow both spiritually and numerically. Pray today that your pastor will intercede, feed, and lead, and pray that the members of your congregation will encourage him in these areas.

## THE BELIEVER'S AUTHORITY

**Luke 10:19** — *"Behold, I have given you authority to tread on serpents and scorpions, and over all the power of the enemy, and nothing will injure you."*

One day as I was driving, I saw two cars that had been damaged in a wreck. A policeman had begun to direct traffic while the area was being cleared. I watched him perform his duties with confidence and skill. He kept traffic flowing steadily. When people tried to slow down to look at the accident, he quickly blew his whistle and waved them on. The drivers promptly obeyed his order. How did that one man command so much respect? The answer is simple — authority. He was authorized by the city government to enforce laws and to give orders that would help benefit society. He was not using physical strength to move that traffic. He was simply using his authority.

Christians have been deputized with authority over demonic spirits. Jesus told the early disciples that He had given them authority to tread spiritually over the power of demonic "serpents and scorpions" they faced as they went about preaching the Gospel and healing the sick. They had authority "over all the power of the enemy." No demon could harm them as long as they were walking obediently with Him. The New Testament describes many instances when Jesus' disciples took authority over demons, bound them, and cast them out of people. That same authority is still available to every believer today.

Has the devil attacked you, someone you love, your family, or your church? Man your battle stations! Christ has deputized you with authority over all the power of the enemy. As a soldier of the cross you are to engage in spiritual warfare. Go to your prayer closet, submit completely to the Lord, and then stand up, resist the devil and watch him flee! Satan may be a roaring lion, but he is afraid of the Lion of Judah — King Jesus!

## TASTELESS SALT

**Matthew 5:13** — *"You are the salt of the earth; but if the salt has become tasteless, how can it be made salty again? It is no longer good for anything, except to be thrown out and trampled under foot by men."*

God has called every Christian to make a powerful, positive, and penetrating impact upon society. We are to be "the salt of the earth," adding spiritual flavor to the settings around us, and also preserving righteousness in a world that gravitates toward spiritual rottenness. We do this primarily by sharing the Gospel of Jesus Christ with non-Christians. We are to take the liberating message of Christ to those who do not know Him in order to persuade them to turn from sin and accept Jesus as their Savior and Lord.

Satan, our archenemy, will wholeheartedly attempt to stop or at least impede such evangelization. One of his primary tactics is to set traps of temptation for God's children. If Satan can successfully tempt a Christian to fall into gross sin, he can tarnish that believer's testimony and also bring reproach on the name of Christ. Lost people are turned off to the Gospel message when they hear of a Christian who has fallen. That Christian becomes tasteless salt. He remains saved, but both his reputation and Christ's work are rejected ("thrown out") and ridiculed ("trampled underfoot") by men.

It is a serious matter to be a follower of Jesus Christ. We must seek to hate sin, love righteousness, and live holy lives. We must ask the Lord to help us to be holy, and try not to commit any sin that would bring shame on the name of Christ (Psalm 69:6).

Are you toying with sin, taking Satan's temptations lightly? Sin is serious and its consequences are costly. God has a plan for your life, but so does the devil. Do not be ignorant of his wicked schemes against you. Do not let him reduce you to tasteless salt.

## NOT ASHAMED OF THE GOSPEL

**Romans 1:16** — *"For I am not ashamed of the gospel, for it is the power of God for salvation to everyone who believes, to the Jew first and also to the Greek."*

Every Christian is called by God to be a verbal witness for the Lord Jesus Christ. We are all commanded to go and tell others that Jesus saves. We are to persuasively evangelize the lost and win souls for Christ. We cannot obey God with a zipped lip.

Paul was a soul-winner. Everywhere he went he told others about how Jesus had saved Him, and how they could find forgiveness and eternal life in Him. When Paul wrote the Christians in Rome, he began his letter by telling them how much he had longed to see them. He wanted to establish and strengthen them in their walk with Christ (Romans 1:11). He also wanted to encourage them and be encouraged by their faith (v. 12). However, Paul's chief desire was to "obtain some fruit among (them) also, even as among the rest of the Gentiles" (v. 13). That is, Paul yearned to go to Rome to share the Gospel and win lost people to Christ. He felt a sense of indebtedness to all non-Christians (v. 14). He paid that debt by sharing Christ with them (v. 15). In our text, Paul said that the reason he emphasized proclaiming the Gospel was because he was "not ashamed" of it. He knew that the Gospel was "the power of God for salvation to everyone who believes." The Good News of Jesus is powerful enough to forgive any sin and change any life. It reveals how God miraculously makes a sinful person righteous in God's sight through faith in Christ (v. 17). Paul's entire being was devoted to sharing the Gospel with others.

Winning souls is not the pastor's job alone. We all must tell others about Jesus. He was not ashamed of us on the cross. We must not be ashamed of Him. The Gospel is "Good News." May we open our mouths and share it with lost people today!

## OUR FIERY TONGUES

**James 3:6** — *"And the tongue is a fire, the very world of iniquity; the tongue is set among our members as that which defiles the entire body, and sets on fire the course of our life, and is set on fire by hell."*

A young family sat next to us as we ate breakfast at a restaurant. The parents had become frustrated with their three preschool children who were crying, making noise, and disturbing the other customers. To me, their children were beautiful. I longingly remembered the days when our four children were small enough to sit in high chairs at restaurants with us. In an attempt to cheer them up, I said to the parents, "Your children are beautiful and precious. They will grow up quickly, and you will miss them when they are gone." The mother then said something that broke my heart. "*I* won't miss them!" she quipped. "I'll be *glad* when they are gone!" Sadly, the children heard her. Though she had spoken in jest (hopefully), her words were deplorable. Her fiery tongue had assailed their little hearts and ears. It was too late. The damage, unfortunately, was done.

Our speech can either build people up or tear them down. We can either lift others or level them with our tongues. Unwholesome words do hurt! James warned that although the tongue is little, it is like a tiny fire that destroys a huge forest (James 3:5). Our text says that it is "the very world of iniquity." The tongue's problem is that it is attached to the human heart, which according to Jesus, is sinful (Matthew 15:18-20). No wonder people who are incessant talkers inevitably engage in sin (Proverbs 10:19).

An ungodly tongue is emotionally and spiritually poisonous, causing great damage to others (James 3:8). Jesus alone is capable of keeping it under control. Beware! A hellish fire smolders behind your lips, ready to wreak inestimable havoc.

## A HOUSE DIVIDED

**Mark 3:25** — *"If a house is divided against itself, that house will not be able to stand."*

America is divided. On the left are the liberals, many of whom are atheists, refusing to acknowledge the existence of God. Many of them are also humanistic, believing that man is in charge of his own destiny. Socialism and communism originated from such philosophies. These people have a defined, aggressive, comprehensive agenda for this nation. They persistently promote their radical program, seeking to rid our nation of any reference to God in public life, and any common standard of morality. They stress relativism, diversity, and tolerance (with the exception of the Christian viewpoint).

On the right are conservatives, most of whom adhere to the Gospel of Jesus Christ. They are Bible-believers. They are pro-family. They believe that marriage is a lifelong commitment between one man and one woman. They believe that homosexuality is perversion. They are also pro-life. They disagree with pro-abortionists because they believe that an unborn baby's right to life supercedes the expectant mother's right to choose an abortion. They think that "under God" should remain in the Pledge of Allegiance, prayer in public places such as schools, civic functions, and athletic events is desirable, and that the posting of the Ten Commandments in a courthouse is legitimate.

"Division" is an interesting word. "Di" means "two." Thus, the word means, "two visions." America is divided because two groups with two visions are vying for control. Which side are you on? Before you decide, consider this: "Righteousness exalts a nation, but sin is a disgrace to any people" (Proverbs 14:34). Christian Pilgrims, not atheistic fanatics, founded America, and only Christ can unite this "house" once again.

## SING A NEW SONG

**Psalm 96:1** — *"Sing to the LORD a new song; sing to the LORD, all the earth."*

As I stood on the pew between my father and mother, I belted out the words to the old hymns of the faith. "Rock of Ages," "What a Friend We Have in Jesus," "There Is a Fountain Filled with Blood" — it does not get any better than that! As the organ and piano played the sacred melodies, I learned early in life that worship involves joyful singing.

The Lord put a hymnal in the middle of the Bible called the Book of Psalms. The words of those Hebrew hymns are included, but the musical accompaniments are not. It is as if the Lord deliberately left out the musical scores so that each new generation could write its own. Thus, the message remains constant while the music changes and adapts.

Each generation is to sing a "new song" to the Lord. Sadly, some people feel that their style of music is the only type that God accepts in worship. Such a narrow-minded view is unfortunate and often causes "worship wars" that divide local churches. Instead of defending our favorite type of music, we should embrace God's love for musical variety. If a song is based on biblical truth, the musical style should not be a stumbling block. Some enjoy classical songs. Others prefer folk style, or southern Gospel, or even a more rhythmic beat. Many worship best with the older hymns. Others like the newer praise songs. In my opinion, a blend of various styles of music is preferable.

Every "old" song used to be "new." All of us should be willing to sing new songs that focus on Christ. The personal preferences of any individual or group should not dictate the styles of songs used in public worship. Some might say, "You can't teach an old dog new tricks." But we are not dogs; we are Christians, and we can sing a new song.

## THE RIGHTEOUSNESS OF GOD

**2 Corinthians 5:21** — _"He made Him who knew no sin to be sin on our behalf, so that we might become the righteousness of God in Him."_

What happened on the cross? While it would be impossible to appropriately describe the full ramifications of Christ's death, at least one thing is certain. Because of the cross, we are not only forgiven, but we also become "the righteousness of God."

Jesus was sinless. He was born of a virgin which allowed Him to be free from inheriting a sinful nature at birth as all other men have received (Romans 5:12). While He was on earth, Jesus was tempted in all ways like we are. Yet He never yielded to a single temptation with which the devil enticed Him (Luke 4:1-13; Hebrews 4:15). Because Jesus was free from sin, He owed no sin debt. But the good news of the Gospel is that Jesus paid our sin debt, which we could never pay! Our text says that God the Father "made Him (Jesus) who knew no sin to be sin on our behalf." Jesus bore our sins on the cross. When He did, the sky above turned black as the iniquity of all mankind was placed upon Him (Isaiah 53:6). On the cross, God punished the sin that He had placed on His Son, leaving Jesus to suffer as an atoning sacrifice for all mankind. Jesus, quoting from Psalm 22:1, cried out, "My God, My God, why have You forsaken Me?" Indeed, Jesus was forsaken of God so that we would never have to be God-forsaken!

One of the most amazing results of Jesus' sacrificial death is that when we put our faith in Him, we become "the righteousness of God." We are no longer sinners on the way to hell. We become saints covered in Christ's blood, clothed in His righteousness.

The next time Satan condemns you as an unworthy sinner, just remind him and yourself who you really are. God says you are "the righteousness of God in (Christ)!"

## THE BOOK OF GOD

**Joshua 1:8** — *"This book of the law shall not depart from your mouth, but you shall meditate on it day and night, so that you may be careful to do according to all that is written in it; for then you will make your way prosperous, and then you will have success."*

God has written a best-seller. It is absolutely unique. Without question, it is the greatest book ever. A person can be well read in every field of knowledge known to man, but if he ignores God's book, he will remain ignorant. God's book is the Bible.

Joshua was standing at the threshold of a daunting challenge. Moses, the great leader of the Jews, had died (1:2). Joshua had been chosen by the Lord to take Moses' place and to lead the children of Israel across the Jordan River into Canaan, the Promised Land. That land was filled with giants, fortified cities, well-armed soldiers, and ruthless pagans. Yet God had promised to give His children victory if they would fight for His glory and obey His commands. He ordered Joshua, the leader, to immerse himself in the "book of the law," which consisted of the first five books of our present Bible. Moses had written it during the years of wandering in the wilderness. God told Joshua to keep its words always on his tongue, and also to think about its teachings day and night. He was also to obey its commands promptly and precisely. If Joshua would honor God's Word, God would cause him to become "prosperous" and enjoy remarkable "success."

God's promise to Joshua is still applicable. We must immerse our hearts and minds in God's inerrant, infallible, eternal Word. It will be a lamp to give us guidance (Psalm 119:105), a sword to defend us (Ephesians 6:17), and milk (1 Peter 2:2) as well as solid food (Hebrews 5:12-14) to nourish us. The greatest book you will ever read is God's book, the Bible. Study it, believe it, obey it, and share it with someone else today.

## GOD'S BOTTOM LINE

**Ecclesiastes 12:13-14** — *"The conclusion, when all has been heard, is: fear God and keep His commandments, because this applies to every person. For God will bring every act to judgment, everything which is hidden, whether it is good or evil."*

I am a pragmatist. I have an aversion to excessive chitchat. I have a hard time enjoying a joke because I am anxious to hear the punch line. I do not really want to know how a clock works; just tell me what time it is. Please, just give me the bottom line!

Did you know that God Himself has a bottom line? Solomon mentions it in our text. Solomon was the third king of Israel. His father, David, who reigned as king before him, had been a great warrior. Solomon was a builder. God often sends a warrior to prepare the way for a builder in His kingdom. Solomon tried to find fulfillment in life in his many endeavors. The Book of Ecclesiastes describes his frantic and futile search for happiness. He married hundreds of women, but they could not fill the void in his heart. He built great buildings and cities, yet he remained frustrated. He read books and acquired knowledge until he became, other than Christ Himself, the wisest man ever to live. However, in all his accomplishments and pursuits, Solomon discovered that a selfish life is a wasted, miserable life. Thus, in our text he wrote, "the conclusion (i.e., the bottom line) is: fear God and keep His commandments" which are applicable "to every person." If we fail at these two points, life will indeed be worthless!

What about you? Have you rightly revered God by receiving His only begotten Son, Jesus, as your Lord and Savior? Do you study His Word and obey His commands? You may succeed in every other aspect of life, but if you fail in these areas, your life will have been in vain. "Fear God and keep His commandments." *That* is God's bottom line!

## Your Sin Will Find You Out

**Numbers 32:23** — *"But if you will not do so, behold, you have sinned against the LORD, and be sure your sin will find you out."*

When I was young, a friend of mine caught a catfish. A group of us decided that it would be fun to throw it into the swimming pool of our fifth grade math teacher. We plotted our attack, and stealthily maneuvered our bicycles behind her privacy fence. I then lobbed the hapless fish into the water, and away we went, peddling faster than ever before. When we arrived at my house three blocks away, we breathed a sigh of relief, certain that our caper had gone undetected. But to our chagrin, into my driveway came our math teacher — and she was not a happy camper. She made us go back to her house, dive into her pool, catch the fish, and remove it. After my dad was finished with me, I never had a desire to go "fish chunking" again! Without a doubt, my sin found me out.

Some Jews who had journeyed with Moses from Egypt decided that God's inheritance of land for them lay on the eastern side of the Jordan River, rather than on the western side in Canaan. Moses accused them of being traitors who were abandoning their brethren in their time of need. They, however, assured Moses that they fully intended to cross the Jordan and fight. But after the conquest, they would rejoin their wives and little ones on the eastern side of the River. Moses agreed, but warned them in our text that if they did not fulfill their promise, their sin would certainly find them out.

Sin has a payment, and its wages always involve a form of death (Romans 6:23). We reap *what* we sow, *more than* we sow, and *after* we sow. No one ever gets away with sin. It finds a way to catch up with its perpetrator. Beware. A seemingly small sin today can produce colossal consequences later on. "Be sure your sin *will* find you out."

## MAKING UP FOR LOST TIME

**Joel 2:25** — *"Then I will make up to you for the years that the swarming locust has eaten, the creeping locust, the stripping locust and the gnawing locust, My great army which I sent among you."*

One of my favorite hymns says, "Years I spent in vanity and pride, caring not my Lord was crucified, knowing not it was for me He died at Calvary!" William R. Newell wrote those words in 1895. They give a timeless description of the way many Christians feel. Before they repented and came home to God in salvation, they, in the words of another great hymn, "wasted many precious years," and their hearts are filled with regret.

Joel preached to the nation of Judah six hundred years before the birth of Christ. During his lifetime, a devastating swarm of locusts came upon the land and literally devoured everything that was green and growing. The plague left God's people in shock and in a state of economic disaster. Joel told the people that the Lord had allowed the locusts to come upon their crops because of their sin. Yet he held out the hope and assurance that if they would return to the Lord and keep His commandments, He would miraculously "make up to (them)" for the devastating damage the locusts had inflicted.

Have you lived a life of regret? Are you plagued by haunting memories of wasted years spent in rebellion against God? Has Satan told you that your life is worthless and wasted, and you might as well end it all? Not so fast! God deserves to have the final say in your life. If you repent, He will forgive you and He will make up to you for the sinful years you have wasted. It is never too late to start doing right.

Do not waste another day. Let go of your past. Give it to God. There is hope for your future. God's plans for you are wonderful. Jesus loves you dearly and He is ready to help you make up for lost time!

## A CHOSEN PEOPLE

**1 Peter 2:9** — *"But you are A CHOSEN RACE, A royal PRIEST-HOOD, A HOLY NATION, A PEOPLE FOR God's OWN POSSESSION, so that you may proclaim the excellencies of Him who has called you out of darkness into His marvelous light."*

In the Old Testament, God selected Abraham to be the father of His chosen people, the Jews. Abraham's descendants through Isaac and Jacob (Israel) are still precious to the Lord in our day. Though most Jews have rejected Jesus as their Messiah (John 1:11), the day will come, after a sufficient number of Gentiles are saved, when many of them will indeed embrace Jesus as their Messiah and Lord (Romans 11:25-26).

Today, Christians are the primary chosen people of God. In this age of grace, we are God's "chosen race...royal priesthood...holy nation...(and) people for (His) own possession." We are chosen in Christ. That is, Christ is God's exclusive way to salvation. There is no other name under heaven by which a person, Jew or Gentile, can be saved (Acts 4:12). Thus, all who are saved in Christ are part of God's chosen people.

Once we accept Jesus as Lord and Savior, it becomes our privilege to "proclaim the excellencies of Him who has called (us) out of darkness into His marvelous light." We are to faithfully and fervently share the saving Gospel of Jesus to the Jew first and also to the Gentiles (Romans 1:16). Every believer has become a new creation in Jesus. The former things have passed away, and new things have come! We are to turn our backs on the old, sinful, fleshly way of life, and walk in holiness and purity (1 Peter 1:14-16).

Christian, you belong to God. You are to live a separated, holy life. You are to share the Gospel of Christ with lost people. God has called you out of darkness. You do not belong to this world. Live today as a royal, chosen ambassador of King Jesus.

## No Shortage

**Mark 6:41-42** — _"And He took the five loaves and the two fish, and looking up toward heaven, He blessed the food and broke the loaves and He kept giving them to the disciples to set before them; and He divided up the two fish among them all. They all ate and were satisfied."_

Bill struggled to hold back the tears as he shared about a mission trip he and some of our church members had taken to Ecuador. They went to a remote area and found people who were both materially poor and unaware of the Gospel of Christ. Many had never even worn a pair of shoes. Our team set up benches in a meeting place in each village and invited the Ecuadorians to come inside. They would sit as our people washed their feet. Each of them was then given a new pair of shoes. Our members would share the Gospel with them at that point. Not surprisingly, hundreds gave their hearts to Christ.

Bill then told me about something quite unusual that God did on that trip. One day as they came into a village, they noticed that they had run out of shoes in several specific sizes. However, when the people began to file in, someone exclaimed, "There is an extra bag here full of shoes that are the exact sizes we need! Where did they come from?" No one had an answer. The shoes had appeared out of nowhere. They thought that it was a random coincidence until the same thing happened again the next day in another village. When it happened a third time a few days later, they knew that it was miraculous, divine provision. Three bags of new American shoes, exactly the right sizes! God taught them that as long as they were doing His will, He would supply their needs.

Whether it involves feeding thousands, or giving shoes to the poor, God provides for His children. If we will give of ourselves and focus on others, the Lord will grant abundant, and at times, miraculous provision. With Jesus, there is absolutely no shortage.

## No Other Gods

**Exodus 20:1-3** — *"Then God spoke all these words, saying, 'I am the LORD your God, who brought you out of the land of Egypt, out of the house of slavery. You shall have no other gods before Me.'"*

Who does God think He is, and why should we listen to Him? Does He have the right to tell us how we should live? Indeed He does! He reigns over the Universe, and according to the first of the Ten Commandments, He allows no other gods before Him.

**Our Revealing God.** "Then God *spoke*." God has spoken to mankind through creation (Romans 1:20), the presence of a moral conscience within each person (Romans 2:14-16), and Holy Scripture (2 Timothy 3:16). His supreme revelation to man is through His Son, Jesus Christ (Hebrews 1:1-4), who is God in the flesh (Colossians 2:9).

**Our Personal God.** "I am the LORD *your* God." God is not distant, separated, or aloof from those He has created. He fashioned us for the purpose of having fellowship with Him. He wants to walk with us, talk with us, and assure us that we are His own!

**Our Delivering God.** "Who *brought you out* of the land of Egypt, *out of the house of slavery*." God delivered Israel from Egyptian bondage. Likewise, He saved and delivered us from being slaves to sin so that we could walk in freedom (Galatians 5:1).

**Our Jealous God.** Because of who He is and all He has done for us, God says we must have *"no other gods* before (Him)." We should exalt Him above everything and everyone else. God is jealous (Exodus 34:14). He deserves and demands all the glory!

God tolerates no other gods before Him! He has revealed Himself to us, enabled us to know Him personally, and set us free from sin. No wonder He is "jealous." He fervently refuses to allow anyone or anything to take His place as the Lord of our lives!

## MAKE NO IDOLS

**Exodus 20:4-6** — *"You shall not make for yourself an idol, or any likeness of what is in heaven above or on the earth beneath or in the water under the earth. You shall not worship them or serve them; for I, the LORD your God, am a jealous God, visiting the iniquities of the fathers on the children, on the third and the fourth generations of those who hate Me, but showing lovingkindness to thousands, to those who love Me and keep My commandments."*

"You are what you eat." That may be true, but another more important maxim is, "You become like whatever you worship." Worship things and you become materialistic. Worship pleasure and you become hedonistic. Worship self and you become egotistical. Worship sex and you become animalistic. Worship Christ and you become like Him.

God commanded the people of Israel to worship Him only, and to avoid idols, or graven images. "You shall not make *for yourself* an idol." Idols are self-centered. They are for the worshiper, not for the Lord. God then said, "You shall not *worship* them." Idols are earthly objects that are treated as divine. God added, "You shall not...*serve* them." Idols hold mastery over those who worship them. The reason Israel was not to worship idols was because God described Himself as "a *jealous* God." He refused to share His glory with carved or fashioned, man-made images. He vowed to punish such idolatry by "visiting the iniquity of the fathers on the children." Idolatrous parents commit spiritual harlotry against God (Hosea 4:12). They pass on to their children a predisposition to commit the same sins. But God promised to bless those who would "love (Him) and keep (His) commandments," by "showing lovingkindness to thousands."

God is jealous for our devotion and obedience. He demands absolute loyalty from us and expects us to revere *Him*, the Creator, and not what He has created or what we have fashioned. Idolatry is blatant spiritual adultery. May all of us be *faithful* to Jesus!

## HOLY IS HIS NAME

**Exodus 20:7** — *"You shall not take the name of the LORD your God in vain, for the LORD will not leave him unpunished who takes His name in vain."*

God is holy. Day and night, from eternity past to eternity future, angels circle His throne in heaven and cry out, "Holy, holy, holy is the Lord!" (Isaiah 6:1-5; Revelation 4:8). Satan, however, loves to disparage and blaspheme God's name. For instance, many modern movies and television programs, as well as most forms of secular music, ridicule and misuse God's name, especially the name of His holy, only begotten Son, Jesus. Hollywood never uses the names "Buddha," "Allah," or "Krishna" in any type of slang or cursing because none of them is the true and living God. It is Jesus' name that generates animosity and resentment among the heathen on earth and the evil forces in the spirit world. Jesus is God in the flesh and Satan trembles at His name. Likewise, demons are helplessly expelled by His name. Eternal salvation is available exclusively in His name. No wonder Satan and this wicked world take His glorious name in vain!

Do you misuse the name of the Lord? Do you curse using His name? Do you flippantly and disrespectfully say "God" this, or "Jesus" that? Beware! God promises "not (to) leave him unpunished who takes His name in vain." His name is holy (Psalm 111:9). His name brings provision (Genesis 22:14). His name causes us to be triumphant (1 Samuel 17:45). His name can bring healing (Acts 3:6, 16; 4:10). His name is exalted (Psalm 8:1). His name brings us salvation (Matthew 1:21; Acts 4:12; Romans 10:13).

God's name is to be revered, respected, rightfully used in worship, and never used carelessly. God gave us His name for blessing Him, not for cursing our fellow man. Let Jesus' holy name be on your lips today as you praise Him and share Him with others.

## REMEMBER THE SABBATH

**Exodus 20:8** — *"Remember the sabbath day, to keep it holy."*

God does not intend for anyone to work twelve hours a day, seven days a week. There is a general principle in both the Old and New Testaments that at least one day of the week should be devoted especially to the Lord for rest and worship. For the Jews it was and still is Saturday (actually sunset on Friday through sunset on Saturday). For Christians it is Sunday, the first day of the week, because that is the day Jesus was raised from the dead. But even those who are forced to work on Sunday should have one day devoted especially to the Lord. Why? What does God have in mind for that day?

It provides *rest*. All of us need to relax, refresh, and refuel at least one day a week. And we should not feel guilty for doing so! God ceased from His creative activity after working six days (Genesis 2:1-3). We should too. It is a time for *reflection*. We can evaluate the activities of the past week, take time to think about how God has blessed us (Psalm 103:1-2), and meditate on the truth of God's Word, the Bible. Thirdly, our Sabbath is a day for *relationships*. We should spend time with our local church family (Hebrews 10:24-25), our earthly family, and our close Christian friends. It is a time for *reverence*. We should gather in Jesus' name and corporately worship God with other believers (Matthew 18:20). Finally, our Sabbath day is a time for *recommitment*. We should forget past failures, face the future, and refocus on Jesus.

Machines, farm animals, athletes, and soldiers all need rest. So do *Christians*! Everyone needs at least one day a week for relaxation and worship. You cannot afford to neglect this principle. Take time this week to remember His Day and to keep it holy.

## HONOR YOUR FATHER AND MOTHER

**Exodus 20:12** — *"Honor your father and your mother, that your days may be prolonged in the land which the LORD your God gives you."*

The basic building block of any society is the family. The Bible defines a family as one man married to one woman for life. Most couples will experience the blessing of children (Psalm 127:3-5). God commands those children to obey and honor their parents.

The word "honor" (from Hebrew *kabad*) means "to glory in; to respect." It carries with it the idea of holding a person in high esteem with sincere admiration. That is how God expects us to relate to our parents. When a child is young and living at home with His parents, the Bible says that he is to honor them by submitting to them and by obeying them. The Apostle Paul says that children should obey their parents, "in the Lord, for this is right" (Ephesians 6:1). A rebellious child is a sinful child. His parents should discipline him for his own good (Proverbs 22:15; 23:13). On the other hand, a child who respects and obeys his parents pleases the Lord. An obedient child will be prone to revere and obey the Lord even as he did his parents. When Jesus grew up in the home of Joseph and Mary, "He continued in subjection to them" (Luke 2:51). His obedience is an example for all children. After a child grows older and moves away from home, he is not obligated to obey his parents, but he is still to honor them. He must be willing to provide care for his aging parents just as Jesus did while He was on the cross (John 19:26-27). God will bless respectful children with long life (Ephesians 6:2-3).

If your parents are living, honor them. Talk kindly to them, and listen to them. If you are living at home, obey them. If not, you must still hold them in high esteem. How you treat them is a reflection of how much you respect the God who gave them to you.

## YOU SHALL NOT MURDER

**Exodus 20:13** — *"You shall not murder."*

Life is a sacred gift from God. After God created Adam and Eve, He commanded them to be fruitful and multiply. From that time forward, the womb became a hallowed place where the Lord Himself would not only cause conception, but also fashion the inward parts of humans as He pleased. Thus we are "fearfully and wonderfully made" (Psalm 139:14). We are not mere animals, as atheistic evolution espouses. Rather, we are the apex and crowning zenith of God's creative activity. We are the only aspect of creation made "in the image of God" (Genesis 1:27). Only human beings possess the God-given capacity to know and worship Him intimately and personally.

After Adam and Eve committed the first sin and ate of the forbidden fruit in the Garden of Eden, their sons, Cain and Abel, later presented offerings before the Lord. Because Abel gave God his best and Cain gave God a token offering, the Lord accepted Abel's sacrifice and rejected Cain's. Cain's jealousy and resentment led to anger, which led to the first murder. God punished Cain by making him "a vagrant and a wanderer on the earth" (Genesis 4:12). Eventually, God made murder a capital offense, saying, "Whoever sheds man's blood, by man his blood shall be shed, for in the image of God He made man" (Genesis 9:6). Innocent life, like that of an unborn baby, is sacred, while those guilty of murder are worthy of death. The punishment must fit the crime.

Thank the Lord today for the gift of life. Thank Him also for the unique way He made you. He created you in His image. Respect the life He has given to others. Murder is an abomination in God's eyes and should be in ours as well. Why? God is pro-life!

## You Shall Not Commit Adultery

**Exodus 20:14** — *"You shall not commit adultery."*

"For better or worse, for richer or poorer, in sickness and in health, to love and to cherish until death parts us." Most married couples have made vows such as these to each other. Marriage is serious business. It is not to be entered into frivolously. God intends for it to last forever. God does not hate divorced people, but He does hate divorce (Malachi 2:16). Divorce does inestimable damage to the husband and wife, as well as to their children. When two people marry, they cease to be two. Rather, they become "one flesh" (Genesis 2:24). Consequently, divorce does not produce two whole individuals. Instead, two broken halves are the result. That is why Jesus said, "What therefore God has joined together, let no man separate" (Matthew 19:6). "No man" includes judges, as well as lawyers seeking profit from the turmoil of troubled marriages.

As sacred as marriage is, Jesus said that there is at least one justifiable ground for divorce, and that is "unchastity" (Matthew 5:32), or "immorality" (lit. "fornication," Matthew 19:9). Divorce for any other reason is sin, according to Scripture. If people divorce for reasons other than immorality and remarry, Jesus said that they are committing adultery (Matthew 5:32; 19:9; Mark 10:11-12). I once heard a married man, who loved to stare at women, say, "Just because I've already ordered doesn't mean I can't still look at the menu!" Predictably, in time he had an affair and left his wife.

If you are married, love your spouse. If you have been unfaithful, repent and ask God to forgive you. If you are single, love Jesus and wait for His timing. Adultery is a serious sin that leads "to the chambers of death" (Proverbs 7:27). Avoid it at all costs.

## YOU SHALL NOT STEAL

**Exodus 20:15** — _"You shall not steal."_

My parents were hard workers. They both grew up on farms. They both began earning their own living when they were teenagers. After serving in World War II, dad went to work with the Illinois Central Railroad. He worked on a section gang before being promoted to a foreman's position and eventually became a track supervisor. He was responsible for the construction and repair of all of his company's railroad track in West Tennessee. Mom had various jobs before she began a janitorial business, which she had for thirty years. When she retired at age 72, she employed over fifty people. Our parents taught my brother and me the importance of working hard and doing a quality job. Consequently, I have always been employed and I have never had to "back-peddle" when I take my paycheck. I learned early in life that God is pleased when we work diligently.

The sixth commandment prohibits stealing because it is the exact opposite of hard work. When someone steals, he takes a shortcut to obtain something that God may not have ever wanted him to have. If God did want him to have it, He intended for him to work for it instead of taking it illegitimately. Stealing takes various forms. A person steals when he does not report all of his income on his tax returns. When he leaves work early, he is stealing from his company. Christians steal from God when they fail to give ten percent of their income back to Him through their local church (Malachi 3:8-10).

While most people would never consider robbing a bank or a convenience store, many of them steal in various ways. Ask the Lord to reveal to you if you are being a thief in some area. God blesses workers, not crooks. Do your work as unto the Lord.

## You Shall Not Bear False Witness

**Exodus 20:16** — *"You shall not bear false witness against your neighbor."*

W. A. Criswell, longtime pastor of First Baptist Church, Dallas, once described his home state of Texas in a sermon by saying, "It's some place where I come from; where every molehill is a mountain, every dry creek is a river, every hole in the ground is an oil well, and every man is a liar! That's Texas!" God does not want any of us to be liars. He wants us to refrain from giving false testimony about anyone else. That is what the ninth of the Ten Commandments is all about — telling the truth!

**God Is a God of Truth.** God the Father is a God of truth (Numbers 23:19), as is His Son, Jesus (John 1:14), as is the Holy Spirit (John 14:16-17). It is impossible for God to lie. If we desire to be like God, we must walk in the truth.

**The Bible Is a Book of Truth.** God's judgments in Scripture are true (Psalm 19:9). Likewise His commandments are true (Psalm 119:151). Jesus asked His Father to sanctify His disciples in truth, and then He added, "Your Word is truth" (John 17:17)!

**Satan Is the Enemy of Truth.** The devil lies and is the father of lies (John 8:44). He does not promote, possess, pronounce, or propagate truth. Thus, he hates the Gospel.

**Jesus Is the Way of Truth.** Jesus claimed to be truth incarnate (John 14:6). He told Pilate that He came to earth to impart truth to those who have been deceived (John 18:37). His truth shatters chains of deceit and liberates the captives (John 8:31-36).

If you want to obey and please God, you must forsake all forms of dishonesty and begin to walk in truth. God honors those who refuse to bear false witness against others. If we will embrace the truth that comes from Jesus Christ, His truth will set us free!

## YOU SHALL NOT COVET

**Exodus 20:17** — _"You shall not covet your neighbor's house; you shall not covet your neighbor's wife or his male servant or his female servant or his ox or his donkey or anything that belongs to your neighbor."_

The most comprehensive of the Ten Commandments is the final one. Each of the other commandments relates to it in some way. Covetousness is greed. It promotes other sins such as idolatry, working seven days a week, adultery, stealing, and lying. When selfishness dictates our actions, we covet and lust after that which is not rightfully ours.

This commandment is very pointed in its application. For instance, it tells us not to covet someone else's "house." How many wars have been fought over land disputes? How many married couples have straddled themselves with too much debt because they foolishly purchased a house they could not afford? This commandment also tells us not to covet another person's spouse. Too many good marriages have gone bad and ended tragically in divorce because individuals failed to appreciate the God-given partners they had, and instead lusted madly after someone else with whom they worked or knew otherwise. This commandment also warns us not to covet someone else's "servant...ox or...donkey." These were the holdings of a rich person in Moses' day. Likewise, we must not covet the butlers, maids, cars, planes, or "toys" of wealthy people in our day.

God's cure for covetousness is contentment (Hebrews 13:5). Contentment is not natural. It must be cultivated (Philippians 4:11). We must learn to be content with the basics, such as "food and covering" (1 Timothy 6:8). We are not rich when we have what we want. Rather, we are rich when we want what we have. Content people are happy people. Covetous people are miserable people. What kind of person are you?

## WITCHES AND WIZARDS

**Deuteronomy 18:10-11** — *"There shall not be found among you anyone who makes his son or his daughter pass through the fire, one who uses divination, one who practices witchcraft, or one who interprets omens, or a sorcerer, or one who casts a spell, or a medium, or a spiritist, or one who calls up the dead."*

As my wife and I walked into the restaurant, I noticed that our hostess was reading a book entitled, "How to Become a Witch." I said, "If you knew Jesus, you would not need that book." She replied, "What's wrong with it? Why wouldn't anyone want to be a witch?" Sadly, her attitude is indicative of the times in which we live.

Before God brought His people into the Promised Land, He warned them against the occultic practices of the Canaanites. They worshiped demonic idols to whom they actually sacrificed their children, a horrendous practice that many of the Israelites eventually emulated (Psalm 106:36-38). The Canaanites also participated in sorcery and witchcraft. Some were "mediums" that claimed to be channels of communication between the spirits of dead people and those who were alive who wished to speak with them. The Canaanites cast spells and curses, much like the voodoo practices of our day. God told His people to avoid such evil activities, which He condemned as capital offenses (Leviticus 20:27). But alas, the Israelites ultimately went "whoring" after the demon idols, and brought the fury of God's wrath down upon themselves (Hosea 9:1f).

America has developed a dangerous and unhealthy appetite for the same type of occultic practices that caused Israel to fall. There is nothing new about the "New Age" movement. It is simply a resurrection of ancient Canaanite idolatry, witchcraft, and wizardry. Today is Halloween, an important day to avoid such paganism. We do not honor demons. Rather, we revere Him before whom the demons tremble — Jesus Christ!

## THE SHADOW OF HIS WINGS

**Psalm 57:1** — *"Be gracious to me, O God, be gracious to me, for my soul takes refuge in You; and in the shadow of Your wings I will take refuge until destruction passes by."*

Trials are a part of life for everyone, even Christians. Following Jesus does not exempt us from facing times of trouble and distress. David referred to his trials as "destruction." The manner in which he faced trials gives us excellent advice for today.

**Cry to God in Prayer.** When David met with calamities, he prayed with passion ("O God") and in faith ("my soul takes refuge in You"). He asked God to be gracious. He knew that as his prayers went up, God's power would come down. We must pray in our times of difficulty. Prayerlessness is pride. It says, "God, I do not need you." Oh, but we do need Him! We must bombard heaven with prayer if we want to see victory.

**Take Refuge in God's Presence.** After David prayed, he entered into the refuge of the Lord's presence, "the shadow of (His) wings." That same place of protection and peace is available to us. The Lord will protect us from the attacks of the evil one, as well as from the attacks of man. While others are fearful and falling, we will boldly stand.

**Realize the Calamity Will Pass.** David discovered that trials do not last forever. Sooner or later, "destruction passes by." Though King Saul tried to murder David, all of Israel would one day hail him as their new king. David's weeping lasted for a night, but his joy came in the morning. Child of God, your time of trial will one day end as well.

Trials come and go. God gives us grace to experience victory in the midst of them. Rest in perfect safety until the danger has passed. Do not panic or fear. The storm may rage, but the Savior will rescue. Be at peace. Jesus *will* defeat your "destruction."

## A New Beginning

**Isaiah 43:18-19** — *"Do not call to mind the former things, or ponder things of the past. Behold, I will do something new, now it will spring forth; will you not be aware of it? I will even make a roadway in the wilderness, rivers in the desert."*

God loves new beginnings. He gives hope to the hopeless, and makes a way when there seems to be no way. In Isaiah's day, Judah was facing tough times. The nation was about to be plundered by a foreign army and exiled into captivity. God's people would be disciplined for their idolatry. But after the discipline, He promised hope for their future, a fresh start. How can we find a new beginning in our lives today?

**We Must Put the Past Behind Us.** When the Jewish people sinned, God disciplined them. But afterwards they did not have to dwell on the "former things." Neither do we! God will discipline *us* if we sin (Proverbs 3:11-12), but if we genuinely repent, He will forgive us and wipe away the "former things" into the depths of the sea (Micah 7:19). He does not make us drag the ball and chain of our past forever.

**We Must Trust God's Path Before Us.** "Behold, I will do something new, now it will spring forth; will you not be aware of it? I will even make a roadway in the wilderness, rivers in the desert." God promised Judah that He would create a new path and provide for them in the future, even in the wilderness. That is what He desires to do for us as well. He will make our paths straight and prosperous in the midst of seemingly barren circumstances. We can trust God's new path. He walks before us as our shield.

Have you sinned? Come home to Jesus. Repent humbly and honestly, accepting His divine discipline. Then give your past to Him and embark on His new path. Your new beginning is only a prayer of repentance away. Press forward today in Jesus' name.

## EVANGELIZING THE WORLD

**Matthew 28:18-20** — _"And Jesus came up and spoke to them, saying, 'All authority has been given to Me in heaven and on earth. Go therefore and make disciples of all the nations, baptizing them in the name of the Father and the Son and the Holy Spirit, teaching them to observe all that I commanded you; and lo, I am with you always, even to the end of the age.'"_

"Any religion is as good as the next. All religions lead to the same God." Such thoughts pervade our culture. Should Christians persuasively share the Gospel of Christ and try to convert non-Christians to Him? What did Jesus tell us to do?

**The Authority of World Evangelization.** Jesus said that His Father gave Him "all authority." Based on that authority, He commands His disciples to communicate the Gospel with all non-believers around the world. We are authorized to be global witnesses for Him. We have the right to share Christ with anyone, anyplace, anytime.

**The Assignment of World Evangelization.** Jesus expects His followers to: (1) make disciples, (2) baptize disciples, and (3) teach disciples. We must witness to the lost, win them to Christ, baptize them in water, get them involved with a group of believers, and then teach them the truths of Scripture so they will mature spiritually.

**The Assurance of World Evangelization.** Jesus assures us that He will be with us wherever we go if we will obey Him in evangelism. He blesses us with His manifest presence as we witness. He will always accompany those who are busily sharing His Gospel with others. Jesus still comes to seek and to save that which is lost.

Are you actively involved in evangelizing the world for Jesus? He has authorized and commanded you to do so. He will bless your obedience and go with you as you share. Jesus is calling. The world is eagerly waiting. Will you obey His voice?

## APPROPRIATE AMBITIONS

**1 Thessalonians 4:11** — *"And make it your ambition to lead a quiet life and attend to your own business and work with your hands, just as we commanded you."*

People sacrifice their health, families, and spiritual growth to climb ladders of success. Such selfish ambition leads to "disorder and every evil thing" (James 3:16). Paul suggested three appropriate ambitions that Christians of all ages should seek.

**Lead a Quiet Life.** The Greek word for "quiet" means, "still, tranquil, rested." It refers to a life of inner calmness. Paul was busy and suffered many hardships. Nevertheless, he learned to possess true personal tranquility (Philippians 4:7). Jesus also had great inner peace (Mark 4:38). He gives us that same quietness of soul as well (Matthew 11:28-30).

**Tend to Your Own Business.** Christians are to focus on taking care of their own concerns without running the lives of others. There is something very Christlike about not nosing around in the affairs of other people. We will have our hands full if we focus on keeping ourselves straight. Each of us needs to mind his own business.

**Work with Your Hands.** God wants people to work if they are physically able to do so. The Bible rebukes lazy people, or "sluggards" (Proverbs 6:6-11). Before Adam sinned, God told him to go to work (Genesis 2:15). Early Christians who would not work were not allowed to eat (2 Thessalonians 3:10). Work is a God-pleasing ambition.

Do you want to have goals that truly please God? If so, lead a quiet life, mind your own business, and work with your hands. These honorable objectives will keep you out of trouble, help make you productive, and cause you to be pleasing to your heavenly Father. A life spent on selfish objectives and worldly endeavors is a life wasted. May you embrace and practice these God-pleasing, Christ-centered ambitions instead.

## ALL THINGS WORK TOGETHER

**Romans 8:28** — _"And we know that God causes all things to work together for good to those who love God, to those who are called according to His purpose."_

The little boy sat on the floor at his grandmother's feet staring curiously at the bottom of the tapestry she was sewing. From his vantage point, the whole thing was a mess. There were different colored threads hanging down in what seemed to be a chaotic, random creation with no apparent pattern. Eventually he said, "Grandmother, whatever it is you are sewing doesn't look too good from down here." The wise, elderly seamstress smiled as she continued her work. She replied, "Child it may not look good from down there, but after awhile you will get to see how beautiful it is from up here."

Is that not the way our lives are as Christians? Sometimes life on earth seems so disordered, frenzied, and confused. There seems to be no overarching purpose or meaning to the various events that come our way. At least that is how it appears to us. But God has a different angle and view of our lives. He sees things from His providential perspective. He knows that He will take all the fabric and thread of the various events that come our way, and like a master weaver, He will weave it all together to create a beautiful tapestry. He is so wise and powerful that He is able to take the good, along with the bad, and blend it together into a wonderful work of art. It is all a work of His grace.

Whether you are suffering or walking in victory and joy inexpressible, God will take both your affliction and elation to effect His will for you. If Jesus is your Lord, God will cause _all things_, both good and bad, to work together for your good. The old hymn is still true: "He whose heart is kind beyond all measure gives unto each day what He deems best — lovingly, its part of pain and pleasure, mingling toil with peace and rest."

## BEHOLD MY PAIN

**Lamentations 1:18** — *"The LORD is righteous; for I have rebelled against His command; hear now, all peoples, and behold my pain; my virgins and my young men have gone into captivity."*

Someone has said that a wise man learns from his mistakes but an even wiser man learns from the mistakes of others. Indeed if you have seen someone else err and suffer unpleasant consequences as a result, it makes no sense for you to make the same mistake.

Jeremiah lived in a time when the people of Judah and Jerusalem were suffering for their past sins of idolatry and rebellion against the Lord. The Lord had allowed the cruel Babylonian army to invade the Promised Land and destroy their homes, places of business, and even the elaborate Temple built four centuries earlier by King Solomon. God's people had been raped, tortured, impaled, and butchered. The young women ("virgins") and young men had been taken as prisoners into captivity in distant Babylon. Jerusalem lay in ruins. Why? Because "the LORD (who) is righteous" would not let His people sin without paying the unavoidable penalty — death! Afterward, the prophet cried out on behalf of the nation to anyone who would listen, "Behold my pain!" It was a sorrowful wail, as well as a solemn warning to anyone who might be tempted to yield to sin without seriously contemplating the inevitable result of death.

How are you being tempted to sin? Stop! Behold the pain of those who have disobeyed the Lord. He never allows the guilty to go unpunished, nor does He ever let His children sin without disciplining them. Regardless of what Satan is using to entice you, realize that the price you will pay will far surpass any joy you experience. Learn from the mistakes of others. Hear the cry of Judah through Jeremiah: "Behold my pain!"

## THE DIVINE SON OF GOD

**John 1:1** — _"In the beginning was the Word, and the Word was with God, and the Word was God."_

Who was Jesus? Some say He was a teacher of radical religion. Others say He was merely an itinerate Jewish rabbi who mistakenly believed Himself to be the Messiah. Others say He was the greatest person ever to live. Who was He? Better yet, who _is_ He?

Jesus is the divine Son of God. When the Apostle John wrote his Gospel, He began by referring to the deity of Jesus Christ. He described Jesus as "the Word" (Greek _logos_). God has revealed Himself to man in specific ways, including _creation_ (Romans 1:20), the human _conscience_ (Romans 2:14-15), and _the canon of Scripture_ (2 Timothy 3:16). Yet God's ultimate revelation of Himself is in His only begotten Son, _Jesus Christ_. He is "the radiance of (the Father's) glory and the exact representation of His nature" (Hebrews 1:3) and the agent through whom the Father created the Universe (John 1:3, Colossians 1:16). In Him "all the fullness of Deity dwells in bodily form" (Colossians 2:9). He is God in the flesh, the perfect God-man — 100% God and 100% man. He is coequal and coeternal with the Father (John 10:30). Jesus is both the _Son_ of God, and _God_ the Son. He could perform mighty miracles such as walking on water and commanding the wind to stop blowing because He had created them. He could cast out demons, heal the sick, and raise the dead because He was Lord over the devil, disease, and death. He is the same yesterday, today, and forever (Hebrews 13:8).

A wonderful Savior is Jesus our Lord! He is God in the flesh, exalted in heaven, and adored by angels and saints. We should worship and serve Him with all our hearts. He is King of kings, Lord of lords, and deity in humanity — Jesus, the divine Son of God!

## THE VIRGIN-BORN SON OF GOD

**Matthew 1:23** — *"'BEHOLD, THE VIRGIN SHALL BE WITH CHILD AND SHALL BEAR A SON, AND THEY SHALL CALL HIS NAME IMMANUEL,' which translated means, 'GOD WITH US.'"*

Christianity is different than any other religion. World religions like Islam, Buddhism, Taoism, and others teach men how to earn favor with their gods through religious activity and "good" behavior. Christianity is unique. The true God knows that sinful man is incapable of meriting salvation through works. The good news is that no one needs to try. In Christ, God has provided eternal salvation. How did it happen?

In order for Jesus to become a human and retain His deity, He had to experience a special birth. Therefore, when Jesus stepped onto this earth, He did so through the womb of a virgin. All people are born with a sinful nature that they inherit from Adam (Romans 5:12). We are "brought forth in iniquity" (Psalm 51:5) and are "by nature children of wrath" (Ephesians 2:3). Our very "being" is "evil" (Matthew 7:11). As an old hymn states, we are "prone to wander." We have an innate propensity toward selfishness. Thus, Jesus could not be born of the seed of Adam or He too would have inherited a sinful nature. He was born, not of Adam's seed, but of woman's seed (Genesis 3:15), free from a nature of sin, so He could die vicariously for the sins of man.

The first person to question Jesus' virginal birth was the virgin (Luke 1:34). What seemed a biological impossibility to Mary was a theological necessity for God. He performed it by His Spirit. Joseph "kept her a virgin" until after Jesus' birth (Matthew 1:25). This is no optional doctrine. Without it, there is no salvation. We should be thankful for the miracle of Jesus' virginal birth. After all, how else could God have been born?

## THE SINLESS SON OF GOD

**Hebrews 4:15** — *"For we do not have a high priest who cannot sympathize with our weaknesses, but One who has been tempted in all things as we are, yet without sin."*

We sat in the car, and I listened as the teenage boy poured out his heart to the Lord in fervent prayer. I was his youth pastor. He was struggling with a temptation that is common for teenage boys. At the end of his prayer, He made an insightful statement. He said, "Please, Lord Jesus, help me. You know what I am going through. You were seventeen once!" That young man had grasped one of the greatest truths of the Bible. Jesus understood him because He too had been tempted, "yet without sin."

Jesus understands our struggles with temptation because He Himself was enticed to sin. After the Holy Spirit anointed Him with power (Acts 10:38) at His baptism, Jesus went into the wilderness. There He fasted and was tempted by Satan for forty days with "every temptation" (Luke 4:13). Satan tried to persuade Jesus to sin throughout His earthly ministry. Jesus experienced all the tactics of temptation used by the devil. Thus, He understands the temptations we face, and He is able and willing to lead us to victory.

Although Jesus was "tempted," we must remember that He was "without sin." He alone is the Righteous One (1 John 2:1) who knew no sin (2 Corinthians 5:21). He was born of a virgin and thus free from a sinful nature. Likewise, each time Jesus was tempted, He chose to walk in perfect obedience to the Father's will. He is our sinless high priest as well as our sympathetic high priest, and He expects us to walk in holiness.

Are you struggling with temptation today? Jesus cares and knows what you are going through. He was tempted, yet without sin. He will help you overcome as well. Call on Him. He will give you victory. He understands — He was seventeen once.

## THE SACRIFICIAL SON OF GOD

**1 John 2:2** — *"And He Himself is the propitiation for our sins; and not for ours only, but also for those of the whole world."*

Jesus died vicariously for sinners. He was actually born to die. Across the manger of Bethlehem lay the shadow of Calvary's cross. God sent His Son, Jesus Christ, to reconcile fallen man back to Himself through His death. He was God's redemptive grain of wheat that fell into the earth and died to bear much fruit (John 12:24).

**Jesus' Death Was Sacrificial.** Jesus was a literal offering. Every Jewish sacrifice in the Old Testament was a prophetic picture of His atoning death. The Passover Lamb was especially an image of Jesus' sacrificial death. He shed His blood as a "propitiation," (KJV, NAS) or "atoning sacrifice" (NIV) to pay the penalty for our sins.

**Jesus' Death Was Substitutionary.** The wages of sin is death (Romans 6:23). Since Jesus never sinned, nor was He born with a sinful nature, He did not deserve to die. Yet He died in the place of all guilty sinners. As an old chorus says, "He paid a debt He did not owe; I owed a debt I could not pay!" He was bruised, crushed, and crucified for our transgressions. God laid all our iniquities on Jesus and judged them (Isaiah 53:4-6).

**Jesus' Death Was Universal.** Our text says that Jesus died for the sins of "the whole world." He did not just die for a select few. Rather, Jesus paid the sin-debt for all people of all time. Consequently, we can walk up to anyone in the world, look them in the eyes and say, "Jesus died for you," and know that we are speaking the absolute truth.

At the heart of the Gospel (Good News) of Jesus Christ is an old rugged cross, stained with His blood. That cross is man's only source of redemption. Today, thank God for Jesus' death. His atoning sacrifice still gives salvation to all who will believe.

## The Resurrected Son Of God

**Matthew 28:6** — _"He is not here, for He has risen, just as He said. Come, see the place where He was lying."_

Jesus is alive. We serve a living Savior. If His bones are still in Jerusalem, there is no hope of salvation for anyone in the world. But His body is not there. He is alive. His resurrection is the Bible's greatest miracle and history's most important fact.

**Jesus Rose Bodily from the Dead.** When the Christians came to Jesus' tomb, His body was missing. It had not been stolen, as the Jewish leaders asserted. Rather, God had raised Jesus from the grave. The Father predestined His Son's death, but He also prevented Jesus' body from undergoing death's decay (Psalm 16:10; Acts 2:27). It was not merely Jesus' influence that came out of that tomb; it was His actual body!

**Jesus Rose Victoriously from the Dead.** When Jesus walked out of the tomb, death and the grave lost their "sting" (1 Corinthians15:54-57). He came forth with the keys of death and hell in His hands (Revelation 1:18). The grave could not hold Him. Death could not harm Him. The stone could not hold back the Light of the World!

**Jesus Rose Eternally from the Dead.** Others had been raised from the dead besides Jesus. Elijah and Elisha saw people raised from the dead. Jesus brought back to life Jairus' daughter, the widow's son at Nain, and Lazarus of Bethany. But all of those people died again. Jesus, however, came forth "alive _forevermore_" (Revelation 1:18).

The greatest fact of history is the resurrection of Jesus Christ. He died for our sins and was raised for our justification (Romans 4:25). Because He lives, we can face tomorrow. His resurrection guarantees our resurrection at the Rapture. Rejoice and be glad today, child of God. Death can never harm you. Jesus Christ is risen indeed!

## THE ASCENDED SON OF GOD

**Acts 1:9** — *"And after He had said these things, He was lifted up while they were looking on, and a cloud received Him out of their sight."*

The disciples gathered on top of the Mount of Olives as Jesus spoke His final words before departing back to heaven. He had accomplished His mission of conquering sin, Satan, and death, by dying sacrificially and rising from the dead. Following His resurrection, Jesus appeared to His disciples over a period of forty days (Acts 1:3). In His final words to them, He emphasized the power of the Holy Spirit they were about to receive, which would enable them to take His Gospel "to the remotest part of the earth" (Acts 1:8). Having said that, He ascended into the heavens.

When Jesus returned to heaven, at least three significant events took place. First, He entered and led captive "a host of captives," (Ephesians 4:8). Having disarmed Satan and all the fallen, rebellious angels that followed him, Jesus "made a public display of them," showing that they were forever defeated (Colossians 2:14-15). Secondly, Jesus entered the heavenly Holy of holies. There, as the eternal high priest, He offered the sacrifice of His blood on the mercy seat as the atoning sacrifice for man's sins (Hebrews 9:11-12). Consequently, man does not need a pope, priest, or preacher to enter God's presence. Jesus is the sole Mediator between God and mankind (1 Timothy 2:5). Thirdly, Jesus sat down at the Father's right hand (Hebrews 1:3; 8:1-2). He now reigns there while His enemies daily become a footstool beneath His feet (Psalm 110:1).

Jesus' ascension was an awesome event. He returned to heaven as the Ruling Regent. Angels now adore Him as Lord of the Universe. One day, every knee shall bow before Him. He is forever high and lifted up. "All hail!" to the ascended King Jesus!

## THE HEAVEN-PREPARING SON OF GOD

**John 14:1-3** — *"Do not let your heart be troubled; believe in God, believe also in Me. In My Father's house are many dwelling places; if it were not so, I would have told you; for I go to prepare a place for you. If I go and prepare a place for you, I will come again and receive you to Myself, that where I am, there you may be also."*

Heaven. The realm of the redeemed. The celestial city of the saints who worship at the feet of their Savior, King Jesus. God allows Christians to join Him in heaven after their brief life on earth. In our text, Jesus shared three glorious truths about heaven.

**Heaven Is Encouraging to the Soul.** "Let not your hearts be troubled." Jesus' disciples were upset because He was about to die. In their grief, He comforted them by speaking about heaven. As a pastor, I have ministered to those whose loved ones have died. They do not care about the stock market, athletic events, or daily headlines. The only thing that gives them hope is to know that their loved one is with Christ in heaven.

**Heaven Is Erected for the Saints.** "I go to prepare a place for you." Jesus went back to His "Father's House" to build "dwelling places" (KJV — "mansions") for us. Nazareth's carpenter is also heaven's architect and builder. God created the Universe in six days. Imagine the beauty of heaven since He has been working on it all these years!

**Heaven Is Entered through the Savior.** When Thomas told Jesus that he did not know how to get to heaven, Jesus answered, "I am the way...no one comes to the Father but through Me" (v. 6). Jesus is not *one* way to heaven, nor is He the *best* way. Jesus is the *only* way to heaven! No one will ever go to heaven apart from faith in Him.

This world is not our final destination. Christians are on their way to a real place prepared by Jesus called heaven. Only if you are saved, will you be there. May Jesus fill your heart today with His eternal life so that heaven will be your home by and by.

## THE INTERCEDING SON OF GOD

**Hebrews 7:25** — *"Therefore He is able also to save forever those who draw near to God through Him, since He always lives to make intercession for them."*

Jesus prayed. While on earth, our Lord spent multiple hours in prayer with the Father. He arose early each morning and prayed (Mark 1:35). He often slipped away into the wilderness and prayed (Luke 5:16). At times, He prayed all night (Luke 6:12). Prior to His arrest, He prayed fervently in Gethsemane (Luke 22:39-46). He prayed graciously (Luke 23:34) and passionately (Mark 15:33-34) while on the cross. In His resurrected state, Jesus would not even eat a morsel of bread before He prayed over it (Luke 24:30). According to our text, Jesus continues to pray today. He is with the Father right now making intercession for every believer. Christian, you are going to be victorious because the Son of God is praying specifically for you!

Just as prayer was a priority for Jesus, it should be the priority of every Christian as well. God's power is poured out on those who pray. He blesses praying Christians more than those who do not pray. God does some things only if and when His people intercede. It is a fact — prayer changes things! The early Christians understood that. Though they had no buildings, budgets, denominational organizations, or television ministries, they turned their world upside down with the Gospel. How? They prayed and operated with the power and anointing of the Holy Spirit. Prayer made the difference!

Jesus prayed and continues to do so. We should too! God's house should be a house of prayer, not merely a house of fellowship, singing, preaching, or business. The most powerful rooms on earth are our prayer closets. Find a quiet place today and commune intimately with Jesus. You will never be more like Him than when you pray!

## The Returning Son Of God

**Revelation 22:20** — *"He who testifies to these things says, 'Yes, I am coming quickly.' Amen. Come, Lord Jesus."*

Jesus is coming back. Before He returns, evil will be rampant (2 Timothy 3:1-5). He will remove all Christians from earth in the Rapture (1 Thessalonians 4:16-17). There will come a time of unique suffering called the "Great Tribulation" (Matthew 24:21). After that, Jesus will return and defeat Antichrist at Armageddon (Revelation 19:11-21). Jesus will then touch down on the Mount of Olives (Zechariah 14:1-9), and will rule the earth from Jerusalem for a thousand years (Revelation 20:1-6). The Final Judgment will then occur (Revelation 20:7-15), followed by the destruction of the earth and the heavens. A new heaven and earth, along with the New Jerusalem will appear. There the saints will live forever (Revelation 21-22). His return is the apex of all these end-time events.

**Every Eye Shall See Him**. Though only Christians will see Jesus at the Rapture, everyone on earth will see Him at His return (Revelation 1:7). Those who rejected Him as Savior will mourn because He is coming to judge them, not to save them.

**Every Knee Shall Bow Before Him**. On that day every knee shall bow respectfully before Jesus. Overcome by His splendor, they will fall at His feet and pay homage (Philippians 2:10).

**Every Tongue Shall Confess Him As Lord**. Though wicked men curse His name today, they will bless His name on that day. All will call Him Lord and Master, even though their confessions at that time will not alter their eternal destinies (Philippians 2:11).

Are you ready for the end of time? If the Rapture occurred, would you be taken up or left behind to suffer through the Great Tribulation? God inaugurated history. He will consummate it as well. He promised to come quickly. "Amen. Come Lord Jesus."

## THE SAVING SON OF GOD

**Acts 4:12** — *"And there is salvation in no one else; for there is no other name under heaven that has been given among men by which we must be saved."*

Jesus came to earth to seek and to save the lost (Luke 19:10). Man was alienated hopelessly in sin. Christ came to reconcile man to God so that the fellowship God originally intended could again be possible. What does the Bible say about salvation?

**Salvation Is by Grace Alone.** The Old Testament Jewish concept of attaining salvation involved the strict observance of a long list of commandments, as well as the legalistic performance of religious rituals. But the Gospel of Christ declares that God saves by grace. Salvation is God's gift that we cannot earn and that we do not deserve (Titus 3:5).

**Salvation Is through Faith Alone.** God's grace can only be accessed through our faith (Romans 5:1; Ephesians 2:8-9). We must believe the facts of the Gospel, trust the grace of God that is offered in Christ, and wholly commit our lives to His lordship. That is the essence of saving faith. Without faith, we cannot please Him (Hebrews 11:6).

**Salvation Is in Christ Alone.** The apostles were adamant about the fact that salvation was to be found only in Jesus Christ. Observing Jewish rituals, sacrificing animals, and keeping meticulous commandments could never wash away sins. Only Jesus Christ can save a person. He is the only way to God and heaven (John 14:6).

Has Jesus saved you? If you will reach out to Him with the hand of faith, He will reach down to you with His hand of grace. When man's faith and God's grace unite, salvation is the inevitable result. Jesus is the sole Mediator between God and all people (1 Timothy 2:5). If you are lost, be saved today. If you are saved, share the good news of the Gospel with others. Tell them God has only one way to salvation — Jesus Christ!

## The Blessing Of The Lord

**Proverbs 10:22** — _"It is the blessing of the LORD that makes rich, and He adds no sorrow to it."_

Most people think that being rich is desirable. Yet Jesus warned that riches often hinder a person spiritually. One day He said to His disciples, "It is easier for a camel to go through the eye of a needle than for a rich man to enter the kingdom of God" (Luke 18:25). Just because a person is rich does not necessarily mean he is blessed. God's blessings are what make us truly rich. What are some of His greatest blessings?

**The Blessing of Christ.** The greatest of all God's blessings is His Son, Jesus Christ. That is the message of John 3:16: "For God so loved the world, that _He gave His only begotten Son._" Jesus is indeed God's "indescribable gift" (2 Corinthians 9:15).

**The Blessing of Salvation.** Salvation is "the gift of God" (Ephesians 2:8-9). When we receive Jesus as our Savior (John 1:12), He gives us eternal life (John 6:47). We know for certain that He is our Redeemer and we are His children (1 John 5:13).

**The Blessing of the Bible.** God has written a precious love letter to His children to teach, guide, inspire, counsel, and disciple us. The Bible is a lamp for our feet and a light for our path (Psalm 119:105). It equips us for _every_ good work (2 Timothy 3:17).

**The Blessing of Heaven.** Jesus has gone back to heaven to prepare an eternal dwelling place for all of His people. He will come for us and take us home in due time (John 14:1-6). After this life, we will dwell eternally in a land that is fairer than day!

These are just some of the gifts God has given to us. There are many more. Earthly treasures are not necessarily blessings. They can become idols. The fact of the matter is, we are not blessed because we are rich; we are rich because we are blessed!

## God's Unlimited Power

**Numbers 11:23** — *"The LORD said to Moses, 'Is the LORD's power limited? Now you shall see whether My word will come true for you or not.'"*

One of my favorite songs says, "What a mighty God we serve; what a mighty God we serve! Angels bow before Him, heaven and earth adore Him; what a mighty God we serve!" Indeed, with men, some things are impossible, but not with God. All things are possible with Him (Matthew 19:26; Mark 9:23; 10:27; 14:36). His power is unlimited.

Moses and the people of Israel were traveling in the wilderness on their way to the Promised Land. The "rabble" (foreigners) became greedy and began causing dissension among the people by complaining that they had no meat to eat. They reminded everyone of the good food they enjoyed while they were still slaves in Egypt. They also grumbled about the manna that God was giving them daily, saying that its taste was so disdainful it had caused them to loose their appetites. God told Moses that in addition to manna, He would send them quail to eat. The Lord said that He would give them meat for an entire month until it became loathsome to them. Moses said to the Lord, in effect, "There are 600,000 men in our midst, yet You say that they all shall eat meat for a month! How!?!" God responded with the words of our text. He caused a great wind to blow and sent an abundance of quail from the sea. God did it His way, with His power, so that He would receive all the glory. Nothing is impossible for Him.

Are you facing a problem that seems insurmountable? God can handle it! Cast your cares upon Him, for He cares for you (1 Peter 5:7). He is the same yesterday, today, and forever (Hebrews 13:8). Speak to that mountain and watch Him move it (Matthew 17:20; 21:21). His power is available, more than adequate, and absolutely unlimited.

## A CHRISTIAN'S SPEECH

**Colossians 4:6** — *"Let your speech always be with grace, as though seasoned with salt, so that you will know how you should respond to each person."*

One of the primary ways people will know you are a Christian is through your speech. Jesus taught that whatever comes out of your mouth issues forth from your heart (Matthew 15:18). If your heart is full of sin, you will speak evil words. If your heart is full of Jesus, you will speak godly words. What kind of speech should a Christian have?

**Gracious Speech.** "Let your speech always be *with grace.*" God saves people "by grace" (Ephesians 2:8). No one is good enough to be saved. Rather, God mercifully bestows the gift of eternal life upon us when we repent of our sins and trust Christ to save us. Once we have experienced God's grace, we should extend it to others. One way to do that is to be gracious to them in our speech. We should speak to them as Jesus would.

**Salty Speech.** "As though *seasoned with salt.*" Christians are "the salt of the earth" (Matthew 5:13). We are responsible for sharing the Gospel. Thus, our speech should be intentionally evangelistic. We must open our mouths and talk with others about coming to Jesus. Our speech should be salty enough to make them thirst for Him!

**Wise Speech.** "So that *you will know how you should respond* to each person." As we witness, we must ask God to fill our hearts and mouths with His words. No two people are alike; therefore no two witnessing interviews are alike. We must customize our evangelistic presentations without compromising the essential message of the Gospel.

How is your speech? Is it gracious, salty, and wise? Are you a verbal witness for Jesus? If not, why? When is the last time you shared Christ with a lost person? God has given you a mouth to praise His name and to proclaim His Word. Be sure to do so today.

## THAT I MAY KNOW HIM

**Philippians 3:10** — *"That I may know Him and the power of His resurrection and the fellowship of His sufferings, being conformed to His death."*

Do you know Christ? Are you certain that you are saved? If today were the last day you would spend on earth, would you enjoy the rest of eternity in heaven with Him? If you do know Jesus Christ as your Lord and Savior, *how well* do you know Him?

**Do You Know Christ in the Power of His Resurrection?** Paul knew Christ in salvation, yet he longed to know Him more completely. He wanted to experience the power and victory in Christ that are available to every Christian. When others look at you, do they see the workings of a supernatural God? Or is your Christianity easily explained as the result of human effort? Is God's power manifested in your life or not?

**Do You Know Christ in the Fellowship of His Sufferings?** When Paul wrote our text, he was imprisoned (Philippians 1:13-14). He suffered greatly for the sake of Christ (2 Corinthians 11:23-28). Yet in those times of hardship, he came to know Christ more intimately. Are you willing to know Christ more closely through "sufferings?"

**Do You Know Christ by Being Conformed to His Death?** Paul knew that in order to be truly alive in Christ, he had to die to self. Christians cannot know and obey the Lord as they should unless they take up their crosses every day and follow Him (Luke 9:23). Thus, Paul said, "I die daily" (1 Corinthians 15:31). There can be no resurrection unless there is a death. You must first die to self if you want to experience abundant life.

Regardless of how well you know the Lord, there is always the need to know Him more fully. Though you will never plumb the depths of His personality and presence, your constant goal should be to know Him better. How intimately do you know Jesus?

## PRAYING FOR YOUR CHILDREN

**Isaiah 54:13** — _"All your sons will be taught of the LORD; and the well-being of your sons will be great."_

Children are a gift from the Lord. Though our society often selfishly views children as a burden, God sees them as a blessing. The Bible says that married couples that have many children are especially blessed (Psalm 127:3-5). That concept is poles apart from modern thinking, but it is correct because it comes from the very heart of God.

My wife and I have been blessed with four precious children. They have unique temperaments and talents. We have had to customize our parenting skills and adapt our approaches to each child. Parents must "train up a child in _the way he should go_" (Proverbs 22:6). They may live in the same house, eat the same food, breathe the same air, and be exposed to similar experiences, but they are delightfully different!

Despite the differences in children, there is at least one thing they all need, and that is the prayers of their parent(s). Donna and I have found that our prayers for our children are most effective when we pray Scripture verses for them. Our text is one of our favorites. We pray that "All (our children) will be taught of the Lord." We ask the Lord to teach them through His indwelling Spirit and His inspired Word. We also ask Him to allow "the well-being of (our children) to be great." We ask Him to bless them with peace, prosperity, and favor. We want them to be _godly_, and not merely "good."

If you have children, pray! The devil is out to destroy their lives. God has placed parents as spiritual shields to protect their offspring from the enemy's attacks. Dad and mom, enter the battle. Go to your knees, lift up your voices, stand on God's Word, and intercede for your children. They need your prayers today. You must not let them down!

## GOD'S BEAUTY QUEEN

**Proverbs 31:30** — *"Charm is deceitful and beauty is vain, but a woman who fears the LORD, she shall be praised."*

As she walked across the stage in front of the crowd, I smiled and wondered at how quickly time had passed. Our oldest daughter, Lindsey, was in a beauty pageant, and she was stunning! Though she looked like a grown woman, my mind reminisced of earlier years when she still played with Barbie dolls, and had fun "playing dress up" with her friends. At the end of the pageant, when they placed the crown on Lindsey's head, it became obvious that others recognized her beauty as well. We were grateful and proud.

God has beauty queens. He measures beauty differently than the world does. In God's eyes, beauty is within a person's heart. A godly woman who loves Jesus and "fears the Lord" is a beauty queen in God's sight. She cultivates "the hidden person of the heart, with the imperishable quality of a gentle and quiet spirit, which is precious in the sight of God" (1 Peter 3:4). Man looks at the outward appearance, but the Lord looks at the heart. Outer beauty may be a blessing, but it will not last. Time and circumstances diminish its glory. Inner beauty, however, increases and intensifies through the years.

To possess true beauty, we must trust Jesus as our Savior, and then cultivate our spiritual lives through Bible intake, prayer, worship, witnessing, and fellowship. Then, when we see Jesus, He will crown us with His righteousness (2 Timothy 4:8).

God has many godly women who revere Him and possess a Christlike spirit. Regardless of their outward appearance, they are the most beautiful women on earth. God Himself will honor and crown them one day. They are all first-place winners in His pageant. He is their proud Father, and all of them are *His* precious beauty queens!

## FIXING YOUR EYES ON JESUS

**Hebrews 12:2** — _"Fixing our eyes on Jesus, the author and perfecter of faith, who for the joy set before Him endured the cross, despising the shame, and has sat down at the right hand of the throne of God."_

"Just keep looking and you will see it, dad." My son was looking at a picture in a novelty shop that looked like a chaotic confusion of colors to me. Yet, as I continued to gaze into the print, sure enough, images began to emerge. At first I could not see them, but after I looked for a while, there really were dinosaurs galore in all of that disorder.

Sometimes life seems to be little more than a frenzied mess. The clouds of trouble hide the light of God's presence, and we loose sight of all that He is doing in our lives. Like driving in the fog, we can barely see far enough ahead to make progress. Those are the times that we need to focus our attention on the Lord. As our text says, we need to "(Fix) our eyes on Jesus, the author and perfecter of our faith." At first, we may not see Him. But if we continue to cast our gaze toward Him instead of our problems, suddenly He appears in grace and glory. He manifests His presence and power and completely changes our perspective. He replaces fear with peace, hope, and assurance.

Jesus victoriously endured the cross by gazing in faith at the promised glory of His resurrection and ascension to the Father's side. We too can endure hardships "for the joy set before (us)" if we focus our attention on the Lord rather than on our problems. When we look at the waves of circumstances, we sink; but when we fix our eyes on Jesus, we can walk on turbulent waters (Matthew 14:29-31).

Today may you believe and sing the hymn that lovingly says, "Turn your eyes upon Jesus, look full in His wonderful face, and the things of earth will grow strangely dim in the light of His glory and grace!"

## SUBMITTING TO THE GOVERNING AUTHORITIES

**Romans 13:1** — *"Every person is to be in subjection to the governing authorities. For there is no authority except from God, and those which exist are established by God."*

God established the concept of government. He places a premium on law and order rather than societal confusion. When there is no governmental authority, and people try to co-exist without a common code of morality, everyone does what is right in his own eyes (Judges 21:25). Social anarchy is the inevitable result when that occurs.

That is why Christians need to be good citizens. A child of God has a dual citizenship. He is a member of both a spiritual kingdom and a physical one as well. His primary allegiance is to God, but he also owes allegiance to his earthly country. Christians should respect governmental leaders. We are to "Render to (them) what is due them: tax to whom tax is due; custom to whom custom; fear to whom fear; honor to whom honor" (Romans 13:7). Christians should always be absolutely above reproach in paying their taxes. We should also be obedient in other areas such as obeying the speed limit when we drive. No Christian should have a radar detector in his car. The reason a person breaks the speed limit is because he is being defiant against governmental authority. He believes that the law applies to others but not to him. You may say, "Now preacher, everyone drives a little fast." I no longer do. I used to, but the Lord convicted me years ago through this text that speeding is nothing less than a form of rebellion.

The only exception to obeying governmental authorities is when man's law contradicts God's Law. If the government tells you to do something that is against the clear teachings of Scripture, then like the apostles, you "must obey God rather than man" (Acts 5:29). Otherwise, God expects you to submit to them and obey the law of the land.

## Under Construction

**Philippians 1:6** — *"For I am confident of this very thing, that He who began a good work in you will perfect it until the day of Christ Jesus."*

The church where I serve as pastor has been blessed with both spiritual and numerical growth. We have had to build new buildings to accommodate the number of people who attend our Bible study classes and worship services. Each time we enter a building project, I grow impatient with how slowly the construction progresses. Sometimes it seems that our facilities will never be finished. Our contractors often have to remind me that our buildings are still "under construction." There is more to come.

That is the way it is with Christians. The day we meet Jesus in salvation, He begins to change us into the believers He desires for us to become. We make progress, but sometimes the process of discipleship is slow. We often grow impatient and desire to develop more quickly. But God is not always in a hurry as we are. He desires to produce "oaks of righteousness" (Isaiah 61:3), not overnight mushrooms. Despite the pains-taking and tedious process of maturing in Christlikeness, we have the Lord's promise in our text that God always finishes what He starts. Like Paul, we too can be "confident of this very thing, that (the Lord) who began a good work in (us) will perfect it." That is, the God who saved us is the same God who will help us "grow in grace" (2 Peter 3:18). We will continue to grow until we at last see Jesus face-to-face in heaven.

Have you become impatient with your progress as a disciple of Christ? Does it seem that you are taking one step forward and two steps backward? Relax. God is not finished with you yet. The end of a project is better than its beginning (Ecclesiastes 7:8). Do not be discouraged. Remind yourself today that you are still "under construction."

## THE SHEPHERD AND HIS SHEEP

**1 Peter 2:25** — *"For you were continually straying like sheep, but now you have returned to the Shepherd and Guardian of your souls."*

If you are a Christian, you are one of God's beloved sheep, and He is your Shepherd (Psalm 23:1). He takes care of those who are part of His flock. He provides for them, protects them, and guides them. Jesus referred to Himself as "the Good Shepherd" (John 10:11-14). He knows those who are His own, but He also seeks to add new sheep to His fold. He came to seek and to save the sheep that are lost (Luke 19:10).

**Sheep Tend to Stray.** "For you were continually straying like sheep." Before a person meets Christ in salvation, he lives a selfish, sinful life. He enjoys going astray and turning to his own way (Isaiah 53:6a). The reason for this is simple. We are all sinners by nature and by choice. We have a natural inclination to go astray spiritually.

**Sheep Can Return.** "But now you have returned." When the Lord convicts a person of his sin, he can then repent and return to God in salvation (Acts 3:19). Unless a person repents of sin, he cannot be saved (Luke 13:3, 5). We must first repent, and then believe in Christ alone to save us (Mark 1:14-15). Repentance precedes regeneration.

**The Shepherd Receives Sinners.** "To the Shepherd and Guardian of your souls." Jesus, the Shepherd, never refuses to receive a repentant sinner into His flock (John 6:37). Regardless of how sinful and rebellious you have been, come to Christ and He will forgive you. He wants to be the "Shepherd and Guardian" of your eternal soul!

An old hymn says, "I've wandered far away from God, now I'm coming home! The paths of sin too long I've trod; Lord, I'm coming home!" Have you strayed from God? Repent and come home. He longs to take you in as one of His precious sheep.

## THE FIRE OF FELLOWSHIP

**Hebrews 10:24-25** — _"And let us consider how to stimulate one another to love and good deeds, not forsaking our own assembling together, as is the habit of some, but encouraging one another; and all the more as you see the day drawing near."_

When I graduated from college, my roommates gave a charcoal grill to me. I kept their gift for several years. I cooked many times on it, but I always dreaded the process required to light the fire. First, you had to stack the charcoal in a neat pile. Next you had to drench that pile in lighter fluid. Then you had to light it, fan it, and blow on it until the charcoal was good and hot. I noticed something that would happen almost every time I went through that wearisome procedure. Inevitably, a few of the pieces of charcoal would fall away from the burning pile. When they did, the fire in them would go out and they would grow cold. They were no longer useful because they fell away from the fire.

Christians are like that. Sometimes believers turn their back on the local church and Christian fellowship. Perhaps they get their feelings hurt at church. On occasion, they simply get out of the habit of attending Sunday School and weekly worship. Maybe they purchase a lake house and start to spend their weekends in recreation, even on the Lord's Day. Regardless of why they avoid Christian fellowship, the result is always the same. They become hard and cold toward the things of God, and they lose the fire of the Holy Spirit's anointing. They do not lose their salvation, but they do lose the _joy_ of it!

Every Christian needs to be active in a local church. He should meet regularly with other believers to worship the Lord. A believer needs a pastor, a place to give his tithes and offerings, a place to minister, and Christian friends to love and to serve alongside. Is your heart cold? Perhaps you need to fan the fire of Christian fellowship.

## You Were Unwilling

**Matthew 23:37** — *"Jerusalem, Jerusalem, who kills the prophets and stones those who are sent to her! How often I wanted to gather your children together, the way a hen gathers her chicks under her wings, and you were unwilling."*

Can man say "No" to God? The answer to that question is, "Yes." Is God's perfect will always accomplished? The answer to that question is, "No." Some people believe and teach that God coerces specific people to be saved. They say that grace is "irresistible." They believe that God's foreknowledge is synonymous with His predetermined will. That, in my opinion, is a false assumption. God knows everything that is going to happen in the future, but that does not mean that He wills for all future events to occur. If that were the case, God would be guilty of foreordaining temptation and sin. God never tempts people to sin, nor is it His will for them to sin (James 1:13-15).

People who believe that God causes everything to happen, even sin, are fatalists, not biblicists. Sin comes from man, not God. Man, who is created in God's image, is endowed with the freedom of choice. He therefore can, and often does, resist God's will and saving grace. In our text, Jesus cried out to the Jewish people of His day, lamenting their rejection of His gracious overtures of salvation. He wanted to save them, but they "were unwilling." They resisted and rejected His grace. People can do the same today.

Jesus came to save His people, the Jews, but most of them *"did not receive Him"* (John 1:11). Christ never forces anyone to be saved. He offers salvation to them, but if they resist and reject it, He allows them to suffer the consequences. Forced love (i.e. rape) is a sin. God convicts people, but never coerces them. Have you resisted God's grace? God will allow you to do so, but you will be held accountable for your choice.

## THE SIMPLICITY OF SALVATION

**Romans 6:23** — _"For the wages of sin is death, but the free gift of God is eternal life in Christ Jesus our Lord."_

Salvation is simple. In fact, it is so uncomplicated that a child can understand and accept it. Jesus never said that children had to become like adults in their thinking before they could be saved, but He did say that adults had to become childlike (Mark 10:15). What must a person understand to be born again? What are the essentials for salvation?

**The Need for Salvation.** "The wages of sin is death." Before a person can be converted to Christ, the Holy Spirit must convict him of his sinfulness before God (John 16:8). All people have sinned and fall short of God's standard of righteousness (Romans 3:23). The "wages" or payment of our sin is spiritual "death" and separation from God.

**The Gift of Salvation.** "But the free gift of God is eternal life." Man is a sinner and cannot earn his own salvation. The best that man can do is no better than "a filthy garment" before God because He is utterly holy (Isaiah 64:6). Thus, God must _give_ man salvation. Eternal life is not a trophy to be won, but a present to be received (John 1:12).

**The Way to Salvation.** "In Christ Jesus our Lord." God has only one way for man to be saved, and that is through His only begotten Son, Jesus Christ. He is "the way, and the truth, and the life; no one comes to the Father but through (Him)" (John 14:6). Jesus is not the _best_ way to God; He is the _only_ way to God. There is only one God, and only one way to know Him — through salvation in Christ Jesus, His Son (1 Timothy 2:5).

Whoever you are, God wants to save you (1 Timothy 2:3-4). He does not desire for anyone to perish, but wants everyone to come to repentance (2 Peter 3:9). All you must do is repent of sin and by faith receive Christ. Even a child can understand that!

## THE UNSEEN LORD

**1 Peter 1:8** — *"And though you have not seen Him, you love Him, and though you do not see Him now, but believe in Him, you greatly rejoice with joy inexpressible and full of glory."*

We serve a God we have never seen. Jesus, God's Son, was obviously seen while He was on earth, but no one has ever beheld God the Father "at any time" (John 1:18; 1 John 4:12). In our text, Peter addressed people who came to faith in Christ after He had ascended back to heaven. Like them, though we have never seen Jesus, we know Him!

**We Love the Unseen Lord.** "Though you have not seen Him, you love Him." As Christians, we pray to a God we have never seen. We read His Bible, stand in awe of His handiwork in creation, and sense His presence in worship. Though we have never beheld His countenance, we each love Him with all our heart, soul, mind, and strength.

**We Trust the Unseen Lord.** "And though you do not see Him now, (you) believe in Him." Christians do not see and believe. Rather, we believe without seeing. We are saved by grace through faith in Christ (Ephesians 2:8). We walk by faith, not by sight (2 Corinthians 5:7). Though we have not seen Jesus, we trust Him now and forever.

**We Rejoice in the Unseen Lord.** "You greatly rejoice with joy inexpressible and full of glory." Obedient Christians are the most joyful people on earth. The source of our joy is not of this world. Rather, the fountain of our joy is Christ. The elation and ecstasy we know surpasses anything this world has to offer. It is "inexpressible" indeed!

One day we will see Jesus, and then we will become as He is (1 John 3:2). "What a day that will be, when my Jesus I shall see, when I look upon His face, the One who saved me by His grace!" Until then, may we love, trust, and rejoice in our unseen God.

## AN EXCELLENT WIFE

**Proverbs 31:10** — *"An excellent wife, who can find? For her worth is far above jewels."*

My wife left town and suddenly I entered a different realm — "Mom-World." I picked up our youngest daughter from school at 3:00 p.m. I had a staff meeting at 3:30. After it was over, we went home, my daughter changed clothes, and I took her to cheernastics practice at 5:30. Our middle daughter called about that time and said, "Dad, where are you? You were supposed to pick me up at cheerleading practice at 5:30!" "Oh yeah! I'll be right there," I replied. I picked her up and took her home. When we arrived, my oldest daughter asked, "Dad, what's for supper?" I said, "Supper?" I thank the Lord that her facial expressions could not kill! I left, picked up our youngest, and brought her home. We then feasted on, you guessed it, warmed up pizza (and corndogs).

The next morning we ate breakfast at a diner. I took the youngest daughter to school, and then met the two older girls at the physician's office at 8:15 a.m. for their physical exams for cheerleading. I went to work, but that afternoon it all began again. The oldest had a Geometry tutoring session at 4:30 p.m. and a Bible study at 6:00. The middle daughter's cheerleading practice was over at 5:30, and she had a youth event at 6:30. The youngest had choir rehearsal at 5:30. I preached at our church at 7:00. When my wife finally returned, I hugged her and said, "Sweetheart, how do you do it? You must be Superwoman!" She laughingly said, "It's O.K. I'm back. You can relax now!"

Our text speaks of the inestimable value of "an excellent wife." I thank the Lord for my wife, and for every godly woman who daily serves the Lord and her family. Heavenly crowns await these precious ladies. Indeed, their worth is far above jewels!

## Delight Yourself In Abundance

**Isaiah 55:1-2** — *"Ho! Every one who thirsts, come to the waters; and you who have no money come, buy and eat. Come, buy wine and milk without money and without cost. Why do you spend money for what is not bread, and your wages for what does not satisfy? Listen carefully to Me, and eat what is good, and delight yourself in abundance."*

It is amazing to think about how much it costs to live these days. When I was young, gasoline only cost 29 cents per gallon. A new automobile was $1,999. My parents bought their first house for only $5,000. I can remember as a child having 25 cents and thinking I was rich. I could buy a Coca Cola for 10 cents, a bag of peanuts for a nickel, and have a dime left over! Financial inflation is a reality which all of us face. Costs seem to just keep going higher. Living on this planet can be expensive!

God has another kind of economy. He promises to give us food and drink "without cost." Unlike earthly food which "does not satisfy" the deepest needs of our souls, God's provisions are exactly what we need. They fulfill our primary longing, which is spiritual, not physical. Many people try to fill the void in their hearts with worldly possessions. But "things" will never meet that need. We all have a God-shaped vacuum within us. Only a personal relationship with God through His Son, Jesus Christ, can fill our hungry, thirsty hearts. When we drink from His living water and eat from His table of abundance, we are saved from our sin and satisfied forevermore. We partake of heavenly sustenance that the world knows nothing about (John 4:32).

Are you tired of feasting on worldly pleasures only to discover that you are still hungry? God alone can satisfy you with good things (Psalm 103:5). If you thirst and hunger, come to Christ! In Him you will feast and "delight yourself in abundance!"

## WE WILL GO TO THEM

**2 Samuel 12:23** — *"But now he has died; why should I fast? Can I bring him back again? I will go to him, but he will not return to me."*

As the family gathered around his bedside, Justin breathed his final breath and went to be with Jesus. For almost three years he had struggled with cancer. If he had lived just two more weeks, he would have been nine years old. He was a valiant little warrior. Though he endured tremendous pain and suffered immeasurably for many months, he *never* complained. Rather, he encouraged and touched many lives. Though his life was brief, it was full. Life is not only measured in length but also in depth. Justin packed a lot of life into a few short years. Many prayed earnestly in faith for the Lord to perform a miracle of healing for Justin. Instead, God saw fit to take him home to heaven.

King David's son was sick. For seven days after the child's birth, David prayed and fasted asking the Lord to heal him. The Lord, however, allowed the child to die. When David learned of his son's death, he arose from his place of prayer, washed himself, changed clothes, went to the place of worship, and praised Jehovah. He then sat down and ate a meal. His servants were speechless. They finally asked David why he had come out of mourning. David said that although he would never see his son again on this earth, he knew that he would see him again one day in eternity. When David died, he would go to heaven and see his boy. And what a day that would be!

Have you lost a loved one? If that person knew Jesus as Lord and Savior, he is in heaven right now. The good news is that you will see him again *if* you too know Jesus. Death is only a temporary separation for Christians. As much as we would love to see our saved loved ones, they will not come back to us. But, hallelujah, we will go to them!

## THE EXCHANGED LIFE

**Galatians 2:20** — *"I have been crucified with Christ; and it is no longer I who live, but Christ lives in me; and the life which I now live in the flesh I live by faith in the Son of God, who loved me and gave Himself up for me."*

When a person becomes a Christian, he experiences a tremendous exchange. He trades his sin for Christ's righteousness (2 Corinthians 5:21). His darkness is replaced by Jesus' glorious light (1 Peter 2:9). He is buried with Christ through a spiritual baptism into death so that he can be raised to walk with Him in newness of life (Romans 6:4). Simply put, his old ways are gone and the Lord's new ways emerge (2 Corinthians 5:17). What an amazing exchange! We give God our worst, and He gives us His best!

Paul referred to this exchanged life in our text. He said that when he became a Christian, he was "crucified with Christ." His sin was nailed to the cross and he bore it no more. At Calvary, Christ also purchased Paul's life. Thus the apostle could say, "it is no longer I who live, but Christ lives in me." Elsewhere, Paul celebrated concerning the presence of the indwelling Christ in every believer by saying, "Christ in (us), the hope of glory" (Colossians 1:27). Paul pointed out that since Christ lives within us, "the life which (we) now live in the flesh (we) live by faith in the Son of God." We walk by faith, not by sight. We live every day based on what we believe about Christ — not on what we see in this present world (2 Corinthians 5:7). The exchanged life that we receive from Christ is graciously offered to us as a gift because "(He) loved us and gave Himself up for (us)."

Christian, you stopped living when you met Christ. He now lives in you and through you. Everything you were without Him, He has forgiven. Everything you were not without Him, He has provided. Thank God today for your wonderful exchanged life.

## No Unwholesome Word

**Ephesians 4:29** — _"Let no unwholesome word proceed from your mouth, but only such a word as is good for edification according to the need of the moment, so that it will give grace to those who hear."_

When I was a child I learned a rhyme that said, "Sticks and stones may break my bones, but words can never hurt me." I have come to realize that phrase is a lie. Words _can_ and often _do_ hurt people. What we say _does_ have a remarkable impact on others. Hurtful words leave permanent impressions on people's hearts and minds. That is why God says to avoid unwholesome words at all costs, and speak words of edification.

The word "unwholesome" (Greek _sapros_) means, "decayed, rotten, evil, unstable, bad, unfit." It is the word from which we derive our word "septic," as in "septic tank." The King James Version calls it "corrupt communication." The New Living Translation renders it "foul or abusive language." Such rotten words belong literally in a garbage dump.

College and pro-football players often engage in "trash talk." They arrogantly try to intimidate their opponents with X-rated, threatening words. "Unwholesome" speech is similar to that since it is unfit to be spoken. No Spirit-filled Christian should take part in unholy "trash talk." We should ask God to baptize our speech in His grace, and teach us to speak words that are "good for edification" that build others up rather than tear them down. Husbands and wives ought to speak kindly to one another. Parents should do the same with their children. Our words ought to encourage and "give grace" to others.

If you are speaking unwholesome words unfit for a Christian, you should ask God for help. He can transform your words from being a dump of discouragement into a garden of encouragement. Today, may your _every word_ edify others and glorify Jesus!

## A RANSOM FOR ALL

**1 Timothy 2:6** — *"Who gave Himself a ransom for all, the testimony given at the proper time."*

For whom did Jesus die? That issue has been debated for centuries. Some say that He died exclusively for the elect. Others say that Jesus died for everyone, even those who die in sin and spend eternity in hell. I personally adhere to the latter view. I agree with my Evangelism Professor, Dr. Roy Fish, who says, "Frankly, it would emaciate my evangelism if I could not say to a total stranger, without a shadow of a doubt, 'Jesus died for you!'" If they are honest, those who believe that Jesus died only for the elect cannot say that. They must say, "Jesus died for specific sinners, and if you are one of them you can be saved. If not, you are hopelessly damned." Is *that* the Gospel of grace?

The fact of the matter is, no one who believes that Jesus died exclusively for the elect can point to even one verse in the Bible that explicitly says that. However, there are *many* verses, such as our text, that clearly point to the fact that Jesus died for *everyone* who has ever walked on the face of this earth. Jesus "gave Himself *a ransom for all*." To say that this verse refers to "all of the elect" is to be guilty of reading something into the text that simply is not there. God the Father "did not spare His own Son, but delivered Him over *for us all*" (Romans 8:32). He (the Father) sent Jesus "so that He (Jesus) by the grace of God might taste death *for everyone*" (Hebrews 2:9). Jesus died "not for (our sins) only, but also for those of *the whole world*" (1 John 2:2).

We can say truthfully and confidently to anyone, "Jesus died *for you*." Not everyone *will* be saved, but anyone *can* be saved. Christ's death paid the ransom for all. As a result, "whosoever will" can come to Christ and be redeemed (Revelation 22:17)!

## IN REMEMBRANCE OF ME

**1 Corinthians 11:24** — _"And when He had given thanks, He broke it and said, 'This is My body, which is for you; do this in remembrance of Me.'"_

As my family and I stood on the platform of the memorial to the U.S.S. Arizona, I wondered what it must have been like on that Sunday, December 7, 1941 at Pearl Harbor in Honolulu, Hawaii. Early that morning, hundreds of Japanese warplanes invaded the United States' naval fleet that was stationed there, killing thousands. Over 1,000 were trapped within the Arizona itself when it was bombed and sunk. That significant event ushered America into World War II. The common cry among our nation's citizens at that time was, "Remember Pearl Harbor!" Indeed, how could they forget?

Almost two thousand years earlier, Jesus sat with His disciples. Within a few hours He would be arrested, subjected to several kangaroo courts before both Jewish and Roman authorities, and later crucified. As He and His disciples celebrated the Passover meal, Jesus instituted a new ordinance that is commonly referred to as "The Lord's Supper." After He had given thanks, He took the bread, broke it, and gave it to those with Him, saying, "This is My body, which is for you; do this _in remembrance of Me._" He also took the cup, saying that its contents represented "the new covenant in (His) blood," and that they were to drink it _"in remembrance of (Him)"_ (v. 25). That ordinance is to be observed from the time of His death until He returns (v. 26). Thus, the common cry of heaven's citizens should be, "Remember the cross!" Indeed, how can _we_ forget?

A great hymn says, "When I survey the wondrous cross on which the Prince of Glory died, my richest gain I count but loss, and pour contempt on all my pride!" May your meditation be filled today with thoughts of the One who bled and died at Calvary.

## THE EVIL WORLD SYSTEM

**1 John 2:15** — *"Do not love the world nor the things in the world. If anyone loves the world, the love of the Father is not in him."*

How should we relate to the world? We know that God loves the world (John 3:16). Yet Scripture tells us not to love the world or the things in it (1 John 2:15). Is this a contradiction? Absolutely not! "World" is used in the Bible in three ways. It refers to the earth itself (1 Samuel 2:8), the people on this planet (John 3:16), and also, as in our text, to the world system that is anti-Jesus, anti-Christian, and anti-Bible. Satan controls this evil world system. Thus, Jesus called him "the ruler of this world" (John 12:31), and Paul called him "the god of this world" (2 Corinthians 4:4). Satan offered this world system to Jesus when he tempted Him in the wilderness (Luke 4:5-6).

No wonder Christians are commanded not to love the world. We are not to be conformed to its ways (Romans 12:2). We must not think like it, speak like it, or act like it. We are aliens and strangers in this world and we will never fit in here. We must live *in* the world, but we must not live *like* it. Friendship with this world is hostility toward God. If we compromise and blend in here, we are God's enemy (James 4:4).

Some denigrate Christians by saying that they are "too heavenly-minded to be any earthly good." In truth, the only people on earth who do anything that is completely good are those who *are* heavenly-minded. They are much better than those who are "so worldly-minded they are no heavenly good!" This evil world is passing away. Turn your back on it. Set your mind on things above, not on the things of this world (Colossians 3:2). Maintain a heavenly perspective, and you will enjoy this life as well as the next!

## WHEN THE ROLL IS CALLED UP YONDER

**Matthew 7:21-23** — _"Not everyone who says to Me, 'Lord, Lord,' will enter the kingdom of heaven, but he who does the will of My Father who is in heaven will enter. Many will say to Me on that day, 'Lord, Lord, did we not prophesy in Your name, and in Your name cast out demons, and in Your name perform many miracles?' And then I will declare to them, 'I never knew you; DEPART FROM ME, YOU WHO PRACTICE LAWLESSNESS.'"_

The girls and their parents waited nervously in the cool weather outside the high school gym. Cheerleading tryouts are tough on your nerves, no matter how many times you may have experienced them. Finally, after what seemed like an eternity, someone posted a list of the new squad. The parents and their daughters rushed to see it, with everyone thinking the same thing: "Is her/my name on the roll?" The reactions were predictably bittersweet. Those who made it squealed in joy and relief, while those who did not gasped or cried. The ones on the list were happy they made the cut, but also grieved for their friends who did not. It was a very difficult, awkward moment.

As we drove away, I could not help but think of our text and what Jesus said would happen at the final judgment. On that day, some people who think they will spend eternity in heaven will discover that they are actually bound for hell. There will even be people who have preached, performed exorcisms, and prayed successfully for people to be healed, whose names will not appear in God's Book of Life. On that day, Jesus will tell them, "I never knew you; depart from Me." The most important question concerning salvation is not, "Do I know Jesus?" Rather, it is, "Does Jesus know me?"

One day, God will declare His heavenly roll call. The names of those who "made it" will be "posted." The reactions will be conflicting. Some will shout with joy, while others scream in disbelief. Not everyone who says, "Lord, Lord," will enter. Will you?

## JEHOVAH-ROHI: THE LORD OUR SHEPHERD

**Psalm 23:1** — *"The LORD is my shepherd, I shall not want."*

One night in a field near Bethlehem, a shepherd watched over his father's flock. Suddenly he realized that he himself was a sheep and that the Lord was *his* Shepherd! David knew God as Jehovah-Rohi, "the Lord our Shepherd." What does that mean?

The Shepherd gives us *peace*. He makes us lie down in "green pastures" beside "still waters" where He restores our "soul" (mind, emotions). He then keeps us in perfect peace (Isaiah 26:3), even in periods of tribulation (John 16:33). The Shepherd also gives us *guidance*. The Lord eventually led David to become Israel's greatest earthly king. As we follow our Shepherd, He will also instruct and teach us in the way we should go with His eye upon us (Psalm 32:8). The Shepherd gives us *protection*. Even when we walk through "the valley of the shadow of death," He guards us. Neither Goliath, King Saul, the Philistines, nor Absalom could defeat David. The Shepherd who defended him will go before us as well to be our shield and rear guard. He will also give us *provision*. He provides us with food, clothing, and shelter. He even prepares a table before us in the presence of our enemies, causing our cups to overflow. When we seek His kingdom, He supplies all our needs. Finally, the Shepherd gives us *eternal life*. David walked in God's goodness and mercy all the days of his life, and then dwelt in His house in heaven forever after he died. God gives us abundant, eternal life as well (John 10:10; 14:1-3).

It is the joy of every Christian to say, "The Lord is *my* Shepherd." His sheep still hear His voice. He knows them and they follow Him (John 10:27). Is Jehovah-Rohi *your* Shepherd? Let Him guide, feed, and protect you, not only today, but forevermore.

## I SHALL NOT LACK PEACE

**Psalm 23:2-3a** — _"He makes me lie down in green pastures; He leads me beside quiet waters. He restores my soul."_

One benefit of knowing Jesus as your Shepherd is His gift of supernatural peace. Christians are not promised perfect circumstances, but we are promised peace in the midst of our circumstances. The Lord gave peace to David. He will give it to us as well.

**God Plans Our Peace.** "He makes me lie down." God desires for each of His children to walk in harmony with Him and with others. He is not a God of confusion, chaos, or turmoil. He gives us the same kind of peace Jesus had while He was on earth (John 14:27). Though we experience tribulations in this life, in Him we have peace (John 16:33). If we defiantly rebel and refuse to enter His rest, He will "make (us) lie down."

**God Provides Our Peace.** He provides pleasant "green pastures...quiet waters." God provides both aesthetic beauty as well as abundant bounty. "Green pastures" are beautiful to behold and bountiful in supply. Likewise, "quiet waters" are picturesque and plentiful. Even as God gave Elijah peace and supplied His needs through ravens, a widow, and an angel (1 Kings 17-19), God will supply the tranquility we need to worship and serve Him.

**God Has a Purpose for Our Peace.** "He restores my soul." Within the context of His peace, the Lord restores our mind, will, and emotions. These areas make up the soul, which is relentlessly taxed by the grueling challenges of life. God allows us to recharge and refocus for future service, and it all occurs in the setting of His "shalom."

God desires for us to abide in His peace. He has provided "green pastures" and "quiet waters" to refuel and refresh us. He should not have to force us to "lie down." We should do so willingly. Only then will His calmness completely control us in Christ.

## I SHALL NOT LACK GUIDANCE

**Psalm 23:3b** — *"He guides me in the paths of righteousness for His name's sake."*

One of the greatest blessings any Christian will ever enjoy is the opportunity to take a pilgrimage to the Holy Land. My first trip to Israel was in 1995. I had put off going there because I did not understand the significance of it. I had three degrees from Baptist universities and seminaries. What could a trip to a tiny Middle Eastern country add to that? Answer? More than you could imagine!

Before I left the United States, I told my wife that I did not want to take many pictures because I did not desire to be a preacher who shows "slides" of the Sea of Galilee, etc. But when I arrived I was so overwhelmed with the places we were visiting, I took over four hundred pictures! One reason our trip was so memorable was our guide, Arale Lahav. He knew the land and its rich heritage. Since then, he has assisted several groups from our church that have visited the Holy Land. Our people have appreciated his expertise. He is the most essential person on the pilgrimage.

When we accepted Jesus as our Savior, we began a journey that has heaven as its ultimate destination. According to our text, if the Lord is our Shepherd, we do not have to lack for guidance in life. Jesus will "guide (us) in paths of righteousness for His name's sake." When we lack wisdom, we are to ask Him (James 1:5). He will instruct us and teach us in the way we should go and guide us with His eye upon us (Psalm 32:8).

Are you trying to find your own way, or are you allowing Jesus to be your guide? He has walked the road before you. He knows the way you should go. Stop groping in the darkness. Hear Him saying to you today, "This is the way, walk in it" (Isaiah 30:21).

## I SHALL NOT LACK PROTECTION

**Psalm 23:4** — _"Even though I walk through the valley of the shadow of death, I fear no evil, for You are with me; Your rod and Your staff, they comfort me."_

As I sat in Hebrew class, I was impressed with my professor's passionate explanation of the Twenty-third Psalm. I had heard pastors use the fourth verse of this Psalm to talk about God taking care of His children when they leave this life and enter God's presence through physical death. But my teacher explained that this text also offers a promise of protection to God's people who are facing various dangers in this life.

The phrase "valley of the shadow of death" can also be translated "valley of shaded death." David, who wrote this Psalm, and other shepherds like him, would lead their flocks to find green pastures and water. They would often pass through valleys that ran between steep mountains on either side. On those mountainsides were rocks with dark, shady crevices. Within those crevices, wild animals would lurk and await the unsuspecting flocks. When they passed by, the animals would attack them in an attempt to feed on a sheep or goat. David himself talked about protecting his father's flocks from both lions and bears (1 Samuel 17:34-36). Those crevices became known as places of "shaded death" because danger and death for both man and beast often hid within their dark shadows. Yet David said that he did not fear the shadows, animals, or valleys. He knew that the Lord, His Shepherd, was capable and ready to protect him. The Lord who watched over David and his sheep also protected him throughout his life.

If you are passing through a "valley of shaded death" right now, fear not. Your Shepherd is more powerful than any enemy who stealthily hides in the shadows. Relax and pass through. With Jesus beside you, nothing in the valley should cause you to fear.

## I SHALL NOT LACK PROVISION

**Psalm 23:5** — *"You prepare a table before me in the presence of my enemies; You have anointed my head with oil, my cup overflows."*

God is a God of abundance. He knows no shortage. He has never experienced a limitation of any sort. He is able to supply every need His children will ever have. He owns the cattle on a thousand hills (Psalm 50:10). He even owns the hills! He is a loving heavenly Father who loves to share His abundance with His precious children.

David experienced diverse circumstances during his lifetime. He was the exalted, illustrious, successful King of Israel. But before that, he was a fugitive who was forced to flee into the wilderness in order to escape the wrath of Saul who served as king before him. As he roamed the mountains and plains of the Judean wilderness, David learned that he could depend on God to supply his needs. In our text, his confidence in God's provision is obvious. David said, "You prepare a table before me *in the presence of my enemies.*" Even as Saul and his armies searched relentlessly for David, God protected the future king, and also provided for him physically. The great judge and prophet, Samuel, had anointed David to be Israel's next king and the Spirit of God had come upon David mightily (1 Samuel 16:13). David acknowledged that in our text by saying, "You have anointed my head with oil." Eventually God blessed David by allowing him to follow Saul as Israel's highest leader. When David surveyed the events of his life and thought of how good God had been to him, he could only say, "My cup overflows!"

Do you have a need? Take it to the Lord in prayer. He is able to be your supply because He is a God of abundance. If Jesus is your Savior, then God is your Shepherd. He guarantees that His sheep will have ample provision. Enjoy God's abundance today.

## I SHALL NOT LACK ETERNAL LIFE

**Psalm 23:6** — _"Surely goodness and lovingkindness will follow me all the days of my life, and I will dwell in the house of the LORD forever."_

When a person becomes a Christian, he receives eternal life. Before he was saved, he was "dead in (his) trespasses and sins" (Ephesians 2:1). Jesus, the source of life (John 1:4; 14:6), changes that. Christ's eternal life is both abundant and everlasting.

**Eternal Life Is Abundant.** When David wrote our text, he emphasized the fact that the Lord, who was his Shepherd, promised to pour out upon him the dual blessings of "goodness and lovingkindness" during this life. The word "goodness" (Hebrew _tob_) literally means "a good thing, benefit, welfare, or prosperity." David was saying that God would bless his life on earth with good gifts and cause him to prosper and be successful. Christians can claim the same promise. Our heavenly Father gives us "good" and "perfect" gifts from above (James 1:17). The word "lovingkindness" (Hebrew _chesed_) refers to God's mercy and unchanging love. It is similar to the New Testament word, _agape_, which is used to describe sacrificial love. If we have eternal life, both of these, God's goodness and lovingkindness, will follow us "all the days of (our lives)."

**Eternal Life Is Everlasting.** David said that the Lord would not only bless him on earth, but also in heaven! Because the Lord was his Shepherd, David would "dwell in the house of the LORD forever." So will we if we know Jesus as Savior! He is preparing a mansion for us in His Father's house (John 14:1-3) where we will always be with Him.

If you have received eternal life, rejoice! You are no longer spiritually dead. You are alive in Christ. You have literally "passed out of death into life" (John 5:24). You can live victoriously now, and then leave this earth to live eternally with Jesus!

## To Live Is Christ

**Philippians 1:21** — *"For to me, to live is Christ and to die is gain."*

What is the most important part of your life? What do you think about, dream about, and talk about more than anything else? If you had to fill in the blank in the following statement, what would you write? "For to me, to live is _____."

The Apostle Paul filled in that blank with the word, "Christ." Jesus Christ was not just *part* of Paul's life. Rather, Jesus *was* his life! Paul told the Christians at Rome that the eternal life they had received was "in Christ Jesus our Lord" (Romans 6:23). When he wrote his letter to the believers at Colossae, Paul emphasized that every Christian, at the moment of regeneration, "died and (his) life is hidden with God in Christ" (Colossians 3:3). He went on to say that Christ "is our life" (Colossians 3:4).

All people are sinners (Romans 3:23). Sin produces separation from God (Isaiah 59:1-2), which results in spiritual death (Ezekiel 18:4; Romans 6:23). Jesus died for our sins and was raised from the dead so that He might give us His abundant, everlasting life (1 Peter 3:18). God alone is the Creator and Sustainer of life (Genesis 1:1, 27). Jesus Christ, God's only begotten Son, is the exclusive source of real spiritual life (John 1:3-4; 14:6). Those who know Him as Savior have that life, while those who do not know Him are spiritually dead (1 John 5:11-12). Believers have "passed out of death into life" (John 5:24). Lost people may think they are living, but they are actually spiritual zombies.

Are you alive? The issue is not whether your heart is beating. Rather, do you know Christ? If you do, is He your life, or is He merely a minor *part* of your life? May this be the day that you "sell out" totally to Jesus. After all, *He* is what life is all about!

## ARE YOU READY TO DIE?

**Acts 21:13** — *"Then Paul answered, 'What are you doing, weeping and breaking my heart? For I am ready not only to be bound, but even to die at Jerusalem for the name of the Lord Jesus.'"*

As the ninety-five year old pastor from Smyrna stepped into the amphitheater, the crowd became silent. Polycarp had been converted to Christ as a young child and had actually studied at the feet of the Apostle John. Now he was facing martyrdom unless he renounced his lifelong faith in Jesus. The Roman proconsul, out of respect for his age, tried to reason with the bishop. But Polycarp made it clear that he would not renounce Christ under any circumstance. He said, "For eighty-six years I have been His servant, and He has never done me wrong. How can I blaspheme my King who has saved me?" The proconsul grew angry and threatened Polycarp with death by means of being mauled by wild beasts or by being burned alive. Polycarp boldly replied, "Why do you hesitate? Do what you want!" He did die that day, and his blood, as Tertullian said, became "seed" for Christ to sow. Polycarp was ready to die because He knew and loved Jesus Christ.

A group of Christians in Caesarea were trying to dissuade Paul from traveling to Jerusalem because they feared that the Jews there would kill him. He answered them in our text. Paul let everyone know that he was ready not only to be imprisoned for Christ, but also to die for Him if necessary. He did not fear death. In fact he said, "To die is gain" (Philippians 1:21). Paul was ready to live or ready to die, whichever Jesus desired.

Are you ready to die? I am not asking if your finances are in order. I am asking if your eternal soul is in order! No one is capable of truly living unless he is prepared to die. Christian, do not fear dying. Death for you will not be a foe, but a welcomed friend.

## SEEK THE LORD

**Isaiah 55:6-7** — *"Seek the LORD while He may be found; call upon Him while He is near. Let the wicked forsake his way and the unrighteous man his thoughts; and let him return to the LORD, and He will have compassion on him, and to our God, for He will abundantly pardon."*

There is a delicate balance described in Scripture between God and man. On one hand, man is encouraged to seek God. On the other hand, the Bible teaches that God seeks after man (Luke 15:4). The Scriptural symmetry is that the Seeker desires to be sought by those He Himself is seeking! He blesses those who diligently pursue His heart.

**When Should We Seek God?** "Seek the LORD *while He may be found*; call upon Him *while He is near*." We cannot seek the Lord whenever *we* want. Rather, we are to seek Him "while He may be found" and "while He is near." He must first draw us to Himself (John 6:44; 12:32). When He woos us to Himself, then we should respond.

**How Should We Seek God?** "Let the wicked *forsake his way* and the unrighteous man *his thoughts*; and let him *return to the LORD*." We must seek the Lord with humble, repentant hearts. He will not tolerate haughtiness. We must learn to soften our hearts, bend our stubborn necks, and walk humbly with our God (Micah 6:8).

**Why Should We Seek God?** "The LORD...will *have compassion*... and...*will abundantly pardon*." When we seek Him diligently and humbly, He will allow Himself to be found by us (Jeremiah 29:13). He will "have compassion" and will "abundantly pardon" our sin. He will also restore what sin has stolen from us (Jeremiah 29:14).

Are you lost? Seek the Lord for salvation. Are you saved? Seek Him so that you can know Him more intimately. If today you hear His voice do not harden your heart (Hebrews 3:7-8). Draw near to Jesus, and He will draw near to you (James 4:8).

## BE STRONG AND COURAGEOUS

**Joshua 1:9** — _"Have I not commanded you? Be strong and courageous! Do not tremble or be dismayed, for the LORD your God is with you wherever you go."_

God is looking for strong leaders. He is seeking believers who will faithfully take up their crosses and follow Him in faith without fearing the enemy. Satan wants God's people to be weak and cowardly. God wants us to "be strong and courageous!"

**The Call to Strength and Courage.** "Have I not commanded you? Be strong and courageous!" The Lord called Joshua to lead His people into battle in the Promised Land. Though Moses was dead, God was not! His work had to continue. Likewise, God is calling us to serve Him faithfully in these difficult days. We must not disappoint Him.

**The Enemies of Strength and Courage.** "Do not tremble or be dismayed." The Lord warned Joshua about the devil's two most lethal weapons against the believer — fear ("Do not _tremble_") and discouragement ("or be _dismayed_"). These two fangs of the serpent, Satan, will paralyze us unless we fight the good fight of faith (1 Timothy 6:12).

**The Source of Strength and Courage.** "For the LORD your God is with you wherever you go." Joshua was not left to himself to "work up" the strength and courage he needed to lead God's people. God Himself would provide what was necessary. Like David, Joshua learned to "strengthen himself in the Lord" (1 Samuel 30:6). The Lord will also provide strength and courage to us if we ask Him to do so.

The world has seen enough feeble and spineless Christians. Where are the Joshua's of our day who will take the land by God's power and for His glory? He called Joshua, and He will also call and empower you with His strength and courage. You can bring glory to Jesus in these dark days before His return. What else really matters?

## REASONS FOR REJOICING

**Psalm 31:7-8** — *"I will rejoice and be glad in Your lovingkindness, because You have seen my affliction; You have known the troubles of my soul, and You have not given me over into the hand of the enemy; You have set my feet in a large place."*

As we approach the Christmas season, we recognize that we all have much for which to be grateful. Our text points out several specific reasons for rejoicing.

**God's Compassion.** "I will rejoice...in Your lovingkindness." David led and lived passionately. He also sinned passionately by committing adultery, but God forgave him when he repented. He will do the same for us, which is a valid reason for rejoicing!

**God's Identification.** "You have seen my affliction, (and) known the troubles of my soul." David rejoiced that God cared about the daily trials he experienced. Likewise, God feels our pain. He sees every tear, and knows every burden you are going through.

**God's Protection.** "You have not given me over into the hand of my enemy." David had enemies: his brothers, Goliath, King Saul, the Philistines, and his own son, Absalom, to name a few. Through it all, God protected David. God will protect us as well. If we walk by faith, He will be our Sword and Shield (Deuteronomy 33:29).

**God's Promotion.** "You have set my feet in a large place." David became Israel's greatest king. Promotion comes from God, not man. He elevates one and abases another. Humble yourself, obey Him, seek His face, and He will exalt you in due time.

Christians should rejoice (Philippians 4:4)! God's joy gives us strength (Nehemiah 8:10). We should rejoice because God forgives us, identifies with our sufferings, protects us, and promotes us though we do not deserve it. May our confession be, "This is the day the Lord has made; *I will rejoice and be glad in it* (Psalm 118:24)!"

## THE GRACE OF CHRISTMAS

**2 Corinthians 8:9** — _"For you know the grace of our Lord Jesus Christ, that though He was rich, yet for your sake He became poor, so that you through His poverty might become rich."_

Christmas is about giving, therefore, it is about grace. The greatest Bible verse of all says, "For God so loved the world, He _gave_ His only begotten Son" (John 3:16). The best gift anyone will ever receive will not be found wrapped under a Christmas tree. Instead, it is found at the foot of Calvary's cross. There we see the grace of Christmas.

**The Author of Grace.** "Though He was rich." Before He ever came to this earth, Jesus existed as God. He is God's eternal Son (Colossians 1:15-20). In Jesus "all the fullness of deity dwells in bodily form" (Colossians 2:9). Before His birth in Bethlehem, Jesus reigned on high as the King of all kings and Lord of all lords.

**The Act of Grace.** "Yet for your sake He became poor." Jesus humbled Himself by leaving His celestial glory and by coming to earth as the Father's suffering Servant (Philippians 2:5f). He was born of a virgin and confined to a baby's body. He grew and became a man. He "became poor" in His humanity while retaining His full deity.

**The Acceptance of Grace.** "So that you through His poverty might become rich." The ultimate "poverty" that Jesus experienced was on the cross. He became the atoning sacrifice required by God to provide salvation to mankind (1 Peter 2:24). In order to be saved, we must repent of sin (Acts 3:19) and receive Christ (John 1:12).

Because Jesus humbled Himself, left His riches in glory, and became poor, we can be saved. Christ's death gives us life, His obedience corrects our sinful disobedience, and His poverty makes us spiritually rich. _That_ is the awsome grace of Christmas!

## THE BABE OF BETHLEHEM

**Isaiah 9:6** — *"For a child will be born to us, a son will be given to us; and the government will rest on His shoulders; and His name will be called Wonderful Counselor, Mighty God, Eternal Father, Prince of Peace."*

When Jesus came to earth, few understood who He really was. Angels attempted to tell Mary, Joseph, and the shepherds, but they still were unable to grasp the complete meaning of God's message. People are still confused about Jesus' identity. Who is He?

**The Wonderful Counselor.** Jesus came to be our Counselor. He came to give us wisdom. He is always available to listen to us. When we are lonely, He is our Friend. When we are discouraged, He lifts us up. When we are confused, He gives us guidance.

**The Mighty God.** Jesus came to give us power. He gives us salvation and sets us free from sin. He loosens us from the bondage of fleshly desires. He shields us from Satan's attacks. He protects us from the temptations of the world. He forgives, heals, and delivers us (Psalm 103:1-5). He is the Mighty God who still works miracles today.

**The Eternal Father.** Jesus is both eternal and one with the Father (John 10:30). The fullness of deity dwells within Jesus (Colossians 2:9). He is just as divine as the Father or the Spirit. They are co-equal, co-eternal, and co-existent with one another.

**The Prince of Peace.** Jesus came to give us the kind of peace He had while He was on earth (John 14:27). In Him we have peace *with* God through salvation (Romans 5:1), and the peace *of* God as we pray (Philippians 4:6-7). His peace is absolutely perfect (Isaiah 26:3). We can sit at the feet of the Prince of Peace and enjoy utter calmness.

May this Christmas season find you more in love with Jesus Christ than ever before. Worship and adore the Babe of Bethlehem. He is God's special gift to us all.

## ACCORDING TO YOUR WORD

**Luke 1:38** — *"And Mary said, 'Behold, the bondslave of the Lord; may it be done to me according to your word.' And the angel departed from her."*

The day began as usual for the poor young peasant girl from Nazareth. Mary, the fiancée of Joseph, was busily occupied with the routine affairs of the day when abruptly a stranger appeared. His manifestation and eccentric greeting shocked her. Gabriel, one of God's highest ranking angels, informed her that she had been chosen by God to be the mother of the Jewish Messiah. The Holy Spirit would come upon her and cause her to conceive. Consequently the holy offspring would be called the Son of God. Such a deed might seem far-fetched for man, but not for Almighty God. Mary's response was one of complete surrender and obedience to God's will. She said, "Here I am, God's servant. Let His perfect will be done in my life according to your word." That response was music to Gabriel's ears. Having accomplished his mission, he departed back to heaven.

No doubt Mary soon suffered ridicule from others when they discovered she was expecting a child prior to marriage. Few, if any, in Nazareth would believe that her child came from the Holy Spirit and not Joseph. Yet, despite the scorn and shame, she willingly accepted God's will for her life. The Lord blessed her with the privilege of bearing Jesus, and also of being able to bring him up in her home. She actually had the joy of spending more time with Jesus than anyone else did while He was on earth!

God reserves His best gifts to those who surrender completely to His will. If we will lay aside our agendas and plans, and submit ourselves unreservedly to the Lord, He will bestow abundant blessings on us. It all starts with a willingness to obey Him. May we, like Mary, submissively say, "May it be done to me according to (God's) word!"

## A HOLY BELIEVER

**Matthew 1:24** — *"And Joseph awoke from his sleep and did as the angel of the Lord commanded him, and took Mary as his wife."*

When God was ready to send His Son, Jesus, to earth, He chose a man named Joseph to be Jesus' stepfather. Imagine the responsibility Joseph felt when he learned he would be the primary male mentor for the Son of God! Why did God choose Joseph?

Joseph is described as "a righteous man" (Matthew 1:19). That means he was a holy believer. He loved the Lord and sought to live a godly life. His holiness manifested itself in several specific ways. For instance, Joseph was *disciplined*. Though he and Mary were engaged, they had not come together sexually. He also "kept her a virgin until she gave birth" to Jesus (Matthew 1:25). Joseph was very *gracious*. When he first learned that Mary was pregnant, he thought that she had been unfaithful to him. Despite his heartache and disappointment, Joseph did not plan to disgrace and publicly expose Mary as an immoral person. Rather, he planned to "send her away secretly" (Matthew 1:19). The Bible also says that Joseph was a *spiritual* man who heard from God. An angel visited him in a dream and told him that the child in Mary's womb really was the Son of God. She had not been unfaithful to him. Joseph then showed that he was truly holy by being an *obedient* man. Our text says that when he awoke from his sleep, he did what God had commanded him to do. He then became a very *blessed* man. He was able to live in the same house as the Messiah and watch Him grow up to become a man.

Like Joseph, God wants us to be righteous and holy believers. We would do well to emulate the characteristics of this humble carpenter from Nazareth. God desires to use pure vessels. Be holy unto the Lord, and He will bless you abundantly. Just ask Joseph!

## MERRY CHRISTMAS!

**Luke 2:11** — _"For today in the city of David there has been born for you a Savior, who is Christ the Lord."_

Today is the day on which Christians around the world celebrate the birth of Jesus. Of course, no one knows the actual date of His birth, but it is nevertheless good to take the opportunity every year on December 25th to thank the Father for sending the Son to be the Savior of the world (1 John 4:14). Christmas is all about Jesus Christ!

**Jesus Is the Savior.** "For today in the city of David there has been born for you a Savior." Jesus' name means, "Jehovah is salvation." His primary mission on earth was "to seek and to save that which was lost" (Luke 19:10). Has Jesus saved you? If not, today you can receive the greatest Christmas present of all — eternal life in Christ!

**Jesus Is the Christ.** The word "Christ," or "Messiah," means "Anointed One." The Holy Spirit anointed Jesus at His baptism (Luke 3:21-22; Acts 10:38). Jesus said, "The Spirit of the Lord...has anointed Me to preach the gospel" (Luke 4:18). He fulfilled every Old Testament Messianic prophecy. Jesus _is_ the Jewish Christ/Messiah.

**Jesus Is Lord.** "Who is...the Lord." Jesus is King of kings and Lord of lords (Philippians 2:11; Revelation 19:16). He is the head of the Church (Colossians 1:18). He rules and reigns in heaven now at the Father's right hand (Hebrews 10:12-13). He will rule as Lord of all during His earthly Millennial Reign (Revelation 20:1-6). He will then be in control in heaven with the Father and the Spirit for all eternity (Revelation 21-22).

As you gather with family and friends, or if you are spending time alone with the Lord today, be sure to read the "Christmas story" (Luke 2:1-20) and other related texts about Jesus' birth. Focus on the true meaning of the season — Jesus. Merry _Christ_mas!

## THEY WORSHIPED HIM

**Matthew 2:11** — *"After coming into the house they saw the Child with Mary His mother; and they fell to the ground and worshiped Him."*

At Jesus' birth, a star shown brightly above His manger in Bethlehem. A group of wise men (magi) living in a foreign land east of Jerusalem (most likely Arabia) saw His star and journeyed a long distance to see Him. The men were scientists, probably astronomers. Once they arrived in Jerusalem, they conferred with Herod the Great, the Roman ruler over the Jews in Palestine. They told him that they had come to see the one who had been "born King of the Jews" (v. 2). Herod, paranoid by the thought of any rival, devised a plot to have Jesus killed. Consulting with the wise men, he learned that Jesus' star had first appeared two years earlier (vv. 7, 16). The Jewish theologians also told Herod that the Messiah was to be born in Bethlehem (vv. 4-6). Aware of the time and place of the Messiah's birth, Herod told the wise men to notify him when they found the new King.

As they left Herod, the star reappeared and led them to Bethlehem. They found Jesus, no longer in a stable, but in a "house." They fell reverently at His feet and "worshiped Him." Note: they did not worship Mary. Warned by God to avoid Herod, they returned home another way. Herod was infuriated and dispatched forces who murdered all the male children two years old and under in Bethlehem and its vicinity.

It is noteworthy that when Jesus came to earth, nature honored Him (the star), Herod persecuted Him, and the Jewish rabbis ignored Him. But these Gentile magi worshiped Him. Why? Because Jesus was, is, and always will be the glorious King of kings and Lord of lords! He is worthy of our praise, our devotion, our gifts, and our very lives. May we today, like those ancient magi, fall at Jesus' feet in humble praise and reverent adoration!

## RACHEL WEEPING FOR HER CHILDREN

**Matthew 2:18** — _"A VOICE WAS HEARD IN RAMAH, WEEP-
ING AND GREAT MOURNING, RACHEL WEEPING FOR HER
CHILDREN; AND SHE REFUSED TO BE COMFORTED,
BECAUSE THEY WERE NO MORE."_

Bethlehem has been an important city in biblical history
for many centuries. It was the city where Ruth and Boaz met
and married. It was the city where David grew up. Years
earlier, Rachel, Jacob's wife, died there while giving birth to
her son, Benjamin. Later, Bethlehem witnessed a tragedy
involving the deaths of children. Once again it became a place
of severe sorrow. Two years after Jesus' birth, King Herod
"sent and slew all the male children who were in Bethlehem
and all its vicinity, from two years old and under" (v. 16).
Bethlehem and its entire vicinity mourned in shock and
disbelief.

Matthew tells us in our text that this despicable act of
barbarism fulfilled a prophecy from Jeremiah 31:15. The
historical context of that Old Testament verse was when
Jeremiah warned the Lord's people in Jerusalem and its
environs that He was sending the Babylonian army to invade
their land in order to punish them for their sins of idolatry.
The Babylonians would slay not only the adults, but also their
children. There would be uncontrollable weeping and
unbearable misery in the hearts of the survivors. Jeremiah's
book, _Lamentations_, describes the horrific results of that brutal
invasion.

Centuries later, another madman, Adolph Hitler, extermi-
nated six million Jews in Nazi death camps. One million of
them were children. Today in Jerusalem, there is a memorial
honoring those children who died. Outside its gates are the
words of our text.

Satan and evil men have always hated the Jews, especially
their children. But there was one Jewish Child born in
Bethlehem whom they could not kill — Jesus!

## FREE INDEED

**John 8:36** — *"So if the Son makes you free, you will be free indeed."*

Many people in our world live in social and political slavery. Communism still has a death grip on millions of citizens on this planet. They are persecuted if they seek to worship God in any way not sanctioned by their despotic governments. They are forced to go underground in order to worship the Lord Jesus Christ. Many times if they are caught in Christian worship, they are arrested, mistreated, imprisoned, and even executed.

While totalitarian regimes continue to oppress countless numbers of people in our day, there are others living in democratic societies that are likewise in bondage. Though they enjoy social freedom, they are enslaved spiritually. "Everyone who commits sin is the slave of sin" (John 8:34). The Bible clearly teaches, "All have sinned" (Romans 3:23). Therefore, everyone is a slave of sin until he meets Christ in salvation. Christ forgives us and sets us free from bondage to become the disciples God wants us to be.

One of my favorite songs says, "So long I searched for life's meaning, enslaved by the world and my greed; then the door to my prison was opened by love, the ransom was paid, I was freed! I'm free from the fear of tomorrow; I'm free from the guilt of my past! I've traded my shackles for a glorious song; I'm free, praise the Lord, free at last!" I love that song because Christ has saved me and set me free. He has also continued to liberate me from sinful strongholds as I have walked with Him through the years.

It is wonderful to know that we do not have to live in spiritual oppression. Christ, and the truth of His Word, will set us totally free (John 8:31-32). Jesus can deliver you from whatever bondage enslaves you. Call on Him today. He will make you free indeed!

## FINISH WHAT YOU START

**2 Corinthians 8:11** — _"But now finish doing it also, so that just as there was the readiness to desire it, so there may be also the completion of it by your ability."_

If I heard it once, I heard it hundreds of times from my parents when I was growing up: "Finish what you start; don't quit in the middle of a job." As a result, I have never quit in mid-stream on anything. Whether it was playing football, writing papers for seminary, or preparing sermons to preach, I have always felt the need to finish every task.

Paul was not a quitter either. He completed the assignments God gave to him. He knew how to enlist and train others to work with him to accomplish goals. He rallied the support of many churches to take up a monetary offering for the financially beleaguered Christians in Jerusalem. A year before he wrote our text, the Christians at Corinth had begun the process of participating in that offering with several other churches. However, due to problems within their fellowship, the Corinthians had placed the offering on the back burner and had not fulfilled their promise to give. In our text, Paul told them that they should "finish doing it," and they should begin "now!" He reminded them of their "readiness to desire" to participate in the offering earlier. He encouraged them to rekindle that same enthusiasm for the stalled project "so there (might) be also the completion of it." They were to give "by (their) ability." In other words, he told them to finish what they started. They were to start where they were, do what they could, and use what they had. They needed to stop sitting and looking at each other, and finish the job!

Anyone can start a project, but it takes a disciplined Christian to finish one. "The end of a matter is better than its beginning" (Ecclesiastes 7:8). Do not consider quitting. Fight the good fight and complete the course (2 Timothy 4:7). _Finish what you start!_

## WORTHY TO BE PRAISED

**Psalm 18:3** — *"I call upon the LORD, who is worthy to be praised, and I am saved from my enemies."*

One of the greatest privileges of the Christian life is to offer praise and thanksgiving to God. We praise Him for who He is, and thank Him for all that He has done. He is great and glorious, majestic and holy, exalted and eternal, high and lifted up. He is gracious, kind, and abundant in provision. He alone is worthy of our praise!

**The Object of Our Praise.** "The *LORD*...is worthy to be praised." David did not offer praise to Baal or any other Canaanite god or idol. Rather, he worshiped the Lord (Jehovah) exclusively. David had already referred to the Lord as his "strength, rock, fortress, deliverer, God, refuge, shield, and stronghold" (vv. 1-2). David's "Lord" is the God and Father of every believer in Jesus, and is the object of our praise as well.

**The Outcry of Our Praise.** "I *call* upon the LORD." The word "call" can also be translated, "cry out; cry for help; utter a loud sound." David was praying a passionate prayer. His cry to God was out of desperation. It was not quiet and reserved, but earsplitting and urgent. Sometimes we need to call upon God fervently at full volume.

**The Outcome of Our Praise.** "I am *saved from my enemies.*" Like any true child of God, David had enemies. The Philistines, as well as wicked King Saul, were always seeking to kill him. But God prevented that from happening because David called to Him in perpetual, passionate praise. God delivers and defends those who exalt Him.

Praise is both worship and warfare. When we cry out to God in adoration, He blesses us with protection from our enemies. Focus on Jesus today, not your opponents. He is *your* rock, fortress, deliverer, shield, and stronghold. He is worthy of your praise!

## FACING A NEW YEAR

**Philippians 3:13-14** — *"Brethren, I do not regard myself as having laid hold of it yet; but one thing I do: forgetting what lies behind and reaching forward to what lies ahead, I press on toward the goal for the prize of the upward call of God in Christ Jesus."*

December 31st is my birthday. My father once told me (jokingly I hope) that the only money I ever saved him was when he was able to count me as a full tax deduction for all of 1957! The end of the year is an ideal time for every Christian to do three things:

**We Should Forget the Past.** "Forgetting what lies behind." We should *look* at the past and *learn* from the past, but we must not *live* in the past. Now is the time to repent of past sins, confess and forsake them, and receive Christ's forgiveness. You cannot relive a single day. Give your past to Jesus, and let Him heal you of those hurts.

**We Should Face the Future.** "Reaching forward to what lies ahead." While we cannot change the past, we can do something about the future. The coming year can be a fresh beginning for you. God has a perfect plan for you (Romans 12:2). Set godly goals and devise a realistic plan to achieve them this year for His glory.

**We Should Focus on the Lord.** "I press on toward the goal for the prize of the upward call of God in Christ Jesus." Like Paul, our priority must be Jesus. We must seek first His kingdom and righteousness in the coming year, spending time with Him every day in worship, prayer, and Bible study. If we honor Him, He will bless us!

What will the New Year bring? One thing is sure, it will be better if you will forget the past, face the future, and focus on the Lord. Walk with Jesus in the coming year. Place your sin-stained hand of faith into His nail-scarred hand of grace, and you will see how wonderful a year can be. May His blessings be upon you and yours!

*"Your words were found and I ate them, And Your words became for me a joy and the delight of my heart; for I have been called by Your name, O LORD God of hosts."*

(Jeremiah 15:16)

# Index

### New Testament

~~~~~~~~~~~~~~~~~~~~~~~~~~~~~~~~~~~~

~~~~~~~~~~~~~~~~~~~~~~~~~~~~~~~~~~~~~~~~~~

# How To Become A Christian

## 1. Realize God's Love for You.

*"For God so loved the world, that He gave His only begotten Son, that whoever believes in Him shall not perish, but have eternal life"* (John 3:16).

*"In this is love, not that we loved God, but that He loved us and sent His Son to be the propitiation for our sins"* (1 John 4:10).

## 2. Recognize Your Sin Before God.

*"For there is no distinction; for all have sinned and fall short of the glory of God"* (Romans 3:22b-23).

*"For the wages of sin is death, but the free gift of God is eternal life in Christ Jesus our Lord"* (Romans 6:23).

## 3. Rejoice That God Desires to Save You.

*"'As I live,' declares the Lord GOD, 'I take no pleasure in the death of the wicked, but rather that the wicked turn from his way and live. Turn back, turn back from your evil ways! Why then will you die, O house of Israel?'"* (Ezekiel 33:11).

*"This is good and acceptable in the sight of God our Savior, who desires all men to be saved and to come to the knowledge of the truth"* (1 Timothy 2:3-4).

## 4. Remember What Jesus Did for You on the Cross.

*"But God demonstrates His own love toward us, in that while we were yet sinners, Christ died for us"* (Romans 5:8).

*"For Christ also died for sins once for all, the just for the unjust, so that He might bring us to God, having been put to death in the flesh, but made alive in the spirit"* (1 Peter 3:18).

- continued next page

## 5. Repent of Your Sin.

*"Therefore repent and return, so that your sins may be wiped away, in order that times of refreshing may come from the presence of the Lord"* (Acts 3:19).

*"The Lord is not slow about His promise, as some count slowness, but is patient toward you, not wishing for any to perish but for all to come to repentance"* (2 Peter 3:9).

## 6. Receive Jesus as Your Savior by Faith.

*"Jesus came into Galilee, preaching the gospel of God, and saying, 'The time is fulfilled, and the kingdom of God is at hand; repent and believe in the gospel'"* (Mark 1:14-15).

*"But as many as received Him, to them He gave the right to become children of God, even to those who believe in His name"* (John 1:12).

## Would you receive Christ as your Savior now?

If so, pray a prayer like this:

"Lord Jesus, thank you that you love me. I know I am a sinner. I believe that you died on the cross to forgive my sin. I repent of my sin and surrender my life completely to You. I ask You to save me right now, Lord Jesus. Come into my life. Wash me with Your blood. Fill me with Your Spirit and make me whole. Write my name in Your eternal Book of Life. Help me to live for You for the rest of my life on earth, and then take me to heaven when I die. Amen."

~~~~~~~~~~~~~~~~~~~~~~~~~~~~~~~~~~~~~~~~~~~~~

# Additional Copies

You may order additional copies of *MORNING MANNA* by calling *Bellevue Christian Bookstore* at Bellevue Baptist Church, 2000 Appling Road, Cordova, Tennessee 38016:

**901.347.5670**

You may also purchase books over the Internet. Please visit us online at:

**www.bellevue.org/SteveGaines**